BLESSING AMERICA FIRST

BLESSING AMERICA FIRST

RELIGION, POPULISM,
AND FOREIGN POLICY IN THE
TRUMP ADMINISTRATION

DAVID T. BUCKLEY

Columbia University Press
New York

Columbia University Press
Publishers Since 1893
New York   Chichester, West Sussex
cup.columbia.edu
Copyright © 2024 Columbia University Press

Library of Congress Cataloging-in-Publication Data
Names: Buckley, David T., author.
Title: Blessing America first : religion, populism, and foreign policy in the Trump
administration / David T. Buckley.
Description: New York : Columbia University Press, [2024] |
Includes bibliographical references and index.
Identifiers: LCCN 2024009372 (print) | LCCN 2024009373 (ebook) |
ISBN 9780231207546 (hardback) | ISBN 9780231207553 (trade paperback) |
ISBN 9780231557016 (ebook)
Subjects: LCSH: Christian conservatism—United States—History—21st century. |
United States—Foreign relations—2017–2021. | Christianity and politics—United
States—History—21st century. | Populism—United States—History—21st century.
| Trump, Donald, 1946–
Classification: LCC BR115.C66 B84 2024 (print) | LCC BR115.C66 (ebook) | DDC
327.73009/0512—dc23/eng/20240409
LC record available at https://lccn.loc.gov/2024009372
LC ebook record available at https://lccn.loc.gov/2024009373

Cover design: Milenda Nan Ok Lee
Cover images: Shutterstock

TO JESS

CONTENTS

ACKNOWLEDGMENTS

My deepest thanks to those who tolerated the multiple life disruptions that went along with this book's creation. My parents, James and Christine Buckley, were incredibly supportive of the logistics involved in making daily family life work during the fellowship year that grounds this project. During that year, my eldest daughter Sarah and son Xavier were too young to know exactly why I suddenly had to wear a suit to work, but they certainly knew that their preschool patterns and sleeping arrangements had changed without prior approval. The person most impacted, personally and professionally, was Jessica Belue Buckley, my partner in many moving trucks over the years. Since our return to Louisville, she has been a font of wisdom and patience as I wrestled with what I actually wanted to say in this book, including during a pandemic that dramatically reshaped our family life. *Blessing America First* is dedicated to her for a simple reason: it would not exist without her love. With any luck, this is my last project that will involve a turkey coming through her windshield.

This book's origin story lies in a year working as an academic fellow in the Office of Religion and Global Affairs (RGA) at the State Department. The community of staff in RGA provided an extraordinary (and extraordinarily patient) set of colleagues during my time working in government. This book is not intended to speak for that group, but I do hope that my respect for their service comes through in its pages. A specific note of thanks goes to Shaun Casey, who was open to the idea of a wandering academic taking up space in his suite. I have benefited from Shaun's counsel since my first days working in Washington, D.C., and am very grateful for the chance to have taken part in what he and his team built at State. At various points, Liora Danan, Claire Sneed, and Amy Lillis had to supervise my efforts, in addition to the more important parts of their jobs. Nida Ansari, Evan Berry, Rebecca Linder Blachly, Jerome Copulsky, Laterica Curtis, Priscilla Flores, Ira Forman, Usra Ghazi, Michael Hamburger, Qamar-Ul Huda, Holly Robertson Huffnagle, Mariam Kaldas, Helene Kessler, Rachel Leslie, Christina Li, Peter Mandaville, Matt Nosanchuk, Maryum Saifee, Albar Sheikh, Arsalan Suleman, Toiyriah Turner, Jennifer Wistrand, and Shaarik Zafar provided varying combinations of professional guidance and good spirits. May the precepts of Coffee Club Platinum outlive us all. Numerous colleagues beyond RGA similarly shaped that year.

The fellowship term at the State Department would not have been possible without the generous support of the Council on Foreign Relations' International Affairs Fellowship (IAF) program. Thanks to Janine Hill and Victoria Alekhine for their support in planning and carrying out the fellowship year. Thanks, as well, to colleagues in the Dean's Office of the College of Arts and Sciences at the University of Louisville who supported my temporary leave from the university for the IAF. The College of Arts and Sciences provided financial support to *Blessing America First* via its Research and Creative Activities grant program. I am continually grateful to hold the Paul Weber Endowed Chair of Politics, Science & Religion, which provided resources and research time to see this project through.

Several academic colleagues provided guidance and encouragement as I went through the extended process of figuring out how to turn my experience at RGA into a book that would be more than the memoir of an unimportant government temp. That especially includes Jeremy Menchik and Tim Longman, whose Institute on Culture, Religion & World Affairs at Boston University provided the first, very preliminary, opportunity for me to test out aspects of the book's eventual argument. Subsequent workshops, thanks to Peter Ochs at the University of Virginia's Initiative on Religion, Politics, and Conflict, and Mohammad Tabaar and Annelle Sheline at Rice University's Baker Institute for Public Policy and Boniuk Institute for Religious Tolerance, provided further chances for critical engagement. Conversations with Tom Banchoff, José Casanova, Shaun Casey, Michael Kessler, and Katherine Marshall at Georgetown University's Berkley Center for Religion, Peace, and World Affairs were essential in distilling *Blessing America First*'s unique contribution. Various other friends and colleagues provided informal advice and formal research responses along the way, including Gregorio Bettiza, Ruth Braunstein, Steven Brooke, E.J. Dionne, Michael Driessen, Ron Hassner, Peter Henne, Dennis Hoover, Jason Klocek, Damon Mayrl, and Dan Philpott. Colleagues in the Department of Political Science at the University of Louisville encouraged me to pursue the initial fellowship and push through with this book, particularly Chuck Ziegler, Rodger Payne, and Jasmine Farrier. *Blessing America First* features survey data collected through a collaborative research project at the University of Louisville headed by the indefatigable Adam Enders, along with colleagues Dewey Clayton, Jason Gainous, Tricia Gray, Melissa Merry, Laura Moyer, and Rodger Payne.

The editorial team at Columbia University Press was both supportive and flexible during a very challenging professional period. The initial proposal related to this project went to Caelyn Cobb in the fall of 2019, with an estimate (on my part) that a full manuscript could exist by late 2020. The real world had something to say about that timeline. Caelyn, Monique Laban, Emily Simon, Kathryn Jorge, and the team were very patient with my attempt(s) to estimate how the pandemic's impact on our home life would affect actual delivery. I thank the two manuscript reviewers for comments that substantively improved various aspects of the final product. Thanks, as well, to Anna Kelly at the University of Louisville for editorial support in finalizing the manuscript.

BLESSING AMERICA FIRST

INTRODUCTION

Seeking Divine Intervention

An outside observer may have thought that the U.S. State Department needed some divine intervention during the first year of the Trump administration. Even before the Senate confirmed Rex Tillerson as secretary of state in February 2017, approximately one thousand department employees signed an internal "dissent channel" message, registering their disagreement with the administration's Executive Order 13769, "Protecting the Nation from Foreign Terrorist Entry into the United States," commonly referred to as the "Muslim Ban."[1] Within months, Trump's administration instituted a hiring freeze, proposed 30 percent departmental budget cuts, and lagged far behind other recent administrations in making senior political appointments. By the end of Trump's term, the State Department experienced the second-largest percentage decline in its workforce of all executive agencies,[2] and the largest such decline in its senior executive service, the top ranks of career government employees.[3] State faced a hiring freeze for sixteen months of Trump's term, resulting in declines in both Foreign Service Officers and career civil servants working in the department.[4] Headline writers competed with one another to describe Tillerson as "The Worst Secretary of State in Living Memory"[5] or as presiding over the "Unraveling of the State Department."[6] Reports indicated long, aimless lunches and furniture cluttering the hallways.

Yet, amid this bureaucratic turmoil, the new administration appeared to actively promote the place of religion in U.S. foreign policy—even, at times, through formal governmental channels. Domestically, President Trump was elected with the support of roughly four-in-five white, evangelical voters, and members of the campaign's "Evangelical Advisory Board" trumpeted their direct access to the White House. Enthusiasm extended to certain quarters of Jewish America, with a speaker at a gathering of the Zionist Organization of America stating that Trump's election was "divinely directed."[7] Senior White House foreign policy advisors like Steve Bannon, Michael Flynn, and Sebastian Gorka publicly expressed views that seemed to foretell a Huntingtonian "clash of civilizations." While he served in Congress, CIA Director (and eventual secretary of state) Mike Pompeo sponsored legislation aimed at designating the Muslim Brotherhood a foreign terrorist organization (FTO). *The Atlantic*'s David Graham dubbed President Trump's initial journey abroad, to Saudi Arabia (where he delivered a much-anticipated address on Islam and U.S. foreign policy), Israel, the Palestinian Territories, and the Vatican, an "excellent Abrahamic adventure."[8] The State Department may have withered on the whole, but Trump nominated an ambassador-at-large for International Religious Freedom fairly promptly, and his State Department eventually launched splashy initiatives like the "Ministerial to Advance Religious Freedom."

Why did an administration, supposedly allergic to the State Department's bureaucratic capacity, seem to be so actively involved in religion and diplomacy, including, at times, leveraging the official bureaucracy to its ends?

BLESSING AMERICA FIRST: POPULISM AND PREEXISTING CONDITIONS

Blessing America First sets out to resolve this apparent contradiction. Were Trump and his administration anti-institutional bomb throwers, intent on degrading expertise and ignoring bureaucracy to govern via Twitter? Or were they a new generation of ideological Christian soldiers, assertively deploying governmental capacity on the part of aggrieved constituents? In short, this book argues that each contains a kernel of truth. Explaining the seeming contradiction requires attention to the *domestic* politics of Trumpism, in particular to its populism, which shaped both the substance of foreign policy goals and the processes in the bureaucracy through which the administration pursued those goals.

As Daniel Drezner observed in the opening year of the administration, "Most political analyses of populists focus on how they govern domestically, but we can extrapolate from these observations to project how they will act at the international level."[9] To summarize, I argue that two distinct dimensions of populism are necessary to make sense of changes to the substance and process of religion in U.S. foreign policy during the Trump administration. First, populists may instrumentalize religion to draw identity boundaries around "the people," with implications for *substantive* foreign policy decisions.[10] Additionally, a second dimension of populism, largely overlooked to date in scholarship on populism and religion, is essential to understanding changes in the *process* of religion in the foreign policy bureaucracy during the Trump administration: populism's personalist structure.[11] Emphasizing only Christian Nationalist identity overstates the ideological consistency of populism, while highlighting only hostility to formal government bureaucracy underpredicts the extent to which populists may, at times, leverage institutionalized state power in governance.

This intersection of identity and personalism came with nuanced implications for the diverse array of offices in the State Department and the U.S. Agency for International Development (USAID) tasked with integrating religion into American statecraft. An essential step in making sense of religion in Trump administration foreign policy is to document variation *within* the governmental bureaucracy in the effect of Trump's governance. As Gregorio Bettiza has thoroughly documented, a "regime complex" of multiple offices and individuals tasked with integrating religion into U.S. foreign policy emerged over roughly the last three decades.[12] The Secretary's Office of Religion and Global Affairs (RGA), where I served as an academic fellow and senior advisor from 2016–2017, existed in parallel to offices like the Office of International Religious Freedom (IRF) at the State Department, as well as the Office of Faith-Based and Neighborhood Partnerships at USAID.[13] Trump's populism shaped all of these offices, but the effects were far from uniform. At times, IRF-related initiatives seemed to become high holy days on the Trump administration's foreign policy calendar. RGA, in contrast, looked more like the empty boxes and disassembled office dividers that reporters noted in State Department hallways in mid-2017. And religion-related work at USAID became a site of true confrontation between Trump officials and career bureaucrats when they were perceived to constrain populist prerogatives.

The Trump administration's incorporation of religion and foreign policy into its populist governance begs a subsequent question: why did it largely succeed? This question structures the second half of the book. There, I explain the limited operation of three potential sources of institutional stability during the Trump administration. Building on recent insights from the comparative study of religion and democracy, as well as scholarship on the fragility of democratic political institutions, I argue that preexisting conditions among (1) career bureaucrats, (2) non-executive branch political institutions, and (3) public opinion combined to make religion and the foreign policy bureaucracy (perhaps) uniquely subject to populist change, at limited cost to the populist. The intersection of religion and U.S. foreign policy became an underappreciated venue of what scholars have termed "the crisis of liberal democracy" in the United States.[14] It is ironic that this research area, termed "the missing dimension of statecraft" over a quarter century ago, is now an ideal venue to observe broad institutional challenges to American democracy.[15]

RESEARCH DESIGN AND MANUSCRIPT STRUCTURE

Blessing America First toggles between foundational theories of populism and qualitative evidence from the Trump administration's term in office to develop observable mechanisms through which populism's distinct dimensions might alter religion's role in U.S. foreign policy. It then draws on a blend of qualitative and quantitative evidence to analyze the relative weakness of several potential constraints on populist change. I endeavor to meet George and Bennett's standard: "While this strategy relies on induction, it is analytical, theory-driven induction."[16] The "repertoire of causal mechanisms" that this approach generates accounts for variation in populist effects across distinct portions of the U.S. diplomatic bureaucracy.[17]

Empirically, my analysis draws heavily, though not exclusively, on my first-hand experience in the State Department's Secretary's Office of Religion and Global Affairs (RGA) from August 2016–August 2017. I arrived at RGA as an academic fellow, largely ignorant of the importance of org charts, and non-conversant in the jumble of acronyms that structures day-to-day life in the bureaucracy. RGA was a fairly new office, as described in detail later, although by the summer of 2016 it had roughly thirty staff members and a full workload. My own portfolio was meant to focus on issues tied to democracy and governance, a set of "functional" responsibilities that cut across the regional structure of the department. After several months, I was (just about) capable of navigating the building without getting lost and keeping up in conversations heavy on three-letter abbreviations. Then, on November 8, 2016, a new and unexpected kind of adjustment began: the election of Donald Trump to the presidency. The transitional period, and then the initial six months of the new administration, provided a unique, working-level view of changes at the intersection of religion and U.S. foreign policy.

While that focused time period, in one particular office, provides a significant amount of empirical material behind this project, I have worked to provide a broader account grounded in social scientific research related to religion and populism, rather than a memoir or autoethnography. My goal is to leverage personal observation as one tool for documenting outcomes, tracing causal processes, and linking change observed firsthand to broadly relevant trends in the study of religion, democracy, and populism. Experiences in the RGA office coexist with relevant, unclassified documents, executive orders, legal filings, press conference transcripts, public opinion analyses, and social science theory about religion and populism. In part, this reflects my own training as a comparative political scientist with an interest in theory testing and an approach to data collection that is eclectic and somewhat suspicious with generalizing from personal experience. It also reflects the fact that a comprehensive, first-person account of RGA's growth is better told by the senior officials most closely tied to the office's founding (a story that has, helpfully, been written).[18] My hope is that the tools of a working-level academic fellow might create an account that contributes, in substance and scope, what it lacks in flashy anecdotes of high diplomacy.

Blessing America First's analysis also extends beyond my time in RGA, reflecting my conviction that the first six months of a new administration in a single, fairly high-profile bureaucratic office could, in fact, drive misleading conclusions if taken to represent the treatment of religion across the bureaucracy as a whole throughout the years of the Trump administration. While the depth of my experience is naturally richest in considering RGA's fate in the initial months of the new administration (likely possessing the highest measurement validity, to use some jargon from the social sciences), evidence from other offices at State and USAID is essential to developing a more complete picture of changes under populist governance. I do not presume to speak for career staff in those offices (or in RGA for that matter) but believe that integrating their histories is essential in documenting the nuanced effects of Trump's populism on religion in the bureaucracy.

The book moves forward in four main empirical parts. In chapter 1, I theorize the role of religion and foreign policy in populist governance, while chapter 2 contrasts this with a close look at religion's role as a tool of statecraft during a period of pre-populist equilibrium, primarily in the Office of Religion and Global Affairs (RGA). Chapters 3 and 4 document areas of change during the Trump transition, tying these effects to two distinct dimensions of populism: its thin ideology and its personalist structure. I then explore why several preexisting conditions generally facilitated populist change, rather than constraining it: norms and interests among career staff (chapter 5); relatively flexible institutional conditions, particularly related to religion-state relations and foreign policy (chapter 6); and polarization in public opinion on questions of religion and foreign policy that incentivized bids for change from both populist leadership and its religious acolytes (chapter 7). The concluding section then assesses implications of this populist turn in religion and U.S. foreign policy, first by exploring evidence of unexpected international cooperation (chapter 8) and then, on a preliminary basis, probing the legacies of populism after Trump's electoral defeat in 2020 (conclusion).

In an attempt to avoid a wall of dense theoretical text early on, chapter 1 gives a condensed overview of the different components of the book's

theoretical framework, essentially providing theoretical snapshots relevant to later chapters. Subsequent chapters then (frequently) open by
expanding on that theoretical snapshot, before presenting their empirical analysis in full.

IMPLICATIONS OF BLESSING AMERICA FIRST

While the empirical material in *Blessing America First* is largely focused
on changes in U.S. foreign policy, the implications of this tumultuous
period resonate more broadly in the study of the comparative influence
of religion on public policy and the impact of religious dynamics on international relations. In comparative politics, significant recent scholarship
has highlighted the subtle ways in which religious elites utilize "institutional access" to generate significant policy impact, while running the risk
of depleting religious "moral authority" in service to partisan politics.[19]
The Trump administration suggests a slightly more nuanced interplay
between access and authority. It may be true, as the manuscript later
demonstrates, that religious elites generate blowback by serving populist masters. However, they may simultaneously strengthen their
authority among core supporters, generating polarization rather than
uniform declines in moral authority. Both populists and those giving
them religious blessing may have short-term interests well met by such
arrangements.

In looking at religion in international relations, this study highlights
the nuanced, domestic mechanisms through which religion can shape foreign policy processes and, ultimately, the policies that states pursue on
the international stage. While analysts are right to highlight the civilizational rhetoric spoken by many Trump administration advisors, religion
was also deeply implicated in the *process* of Trump's foreign policy, including its avoidance of constraint from national security professionals, preference for personal ties, public displays of loyalty, and its theatrical style.[20]
This opens new avenues for tracing religion's importance to foreign policy, both in the United States and abroad.

The book is titled *Blessing America First* to reflect the dual nature
of populism's impact on religion and foreign policy during the Trump

administration. On one level, Trump and his appointees used foreign policy decisions as opportunities to lend moral motive to the identity boundaries represented by the "America First" slogan, linking their conception of "the people" to a sacred mission. On another front, blessing America First reflects populism's personalism, as the act of *blessing* America First is more suited to religious loyalists than the bureaucratized institutions typically central to foreign policy. I now turn to fleshing out this theoretical foundation, linking foreign policy change to populism's combination of identity boundaries and personalist governance.

PART I

RELIGION AND FOREIGN POLICY

Statecraft and Populist Governance

❖

1

WHAT DOES POPULISM HAVE TO DO
WITH RELIGION AND FOREIGN POLICY?

This chapter steps back temporarily from the theatrics of the Trump administration to offer a theoretical account linking religion, populism, and foreign policy. It has now been a quarter century since analysts termed religion "the missing dimension of statecraft."[1] In the interim, policymakers have engaged in a variety of efforts to alter this state of affairs, and scholars have devoted a significant amount of time to integrating religion into the mainstream of political science and international studies. In the richest empirical treatment of the topic of religion and U.S. foreign policy, Gregorio Bettiza documented what he termed a "regime complex" of religion across the foreign policy bureaucracy, with special attention to the State Department and United States Agency for International Development (USAID).[2] Religion seems to be as present as ever in the foreign policy bureaucracy, through political appointees, congressionally mandated offices, and global diplomatic monitoring.

At the same time, the 2016 election of Donald Trump brought tremendous instability to America's political institutions, perhaps most dramatically those very agencies tied to the foreign policy process. Distinguished scholars of the presidency and American political institutions referred to America's "institutions under siege," with particular attention paid to Trump's attacks, in rhetoric and bureaucratic process, on alleged "deep state" opposition to his legitimate election.[3] Amid these attacks, it was plausible that the regime complex of religion and foreign policy would be pressed into service to new ends, or simply wither away, replaced by diplomacy via Twitter.

After presenting a brief review of recent scholarship, this chapter moves to its primary goal: presenting the case that the changes to religion in U.S. foreign policy during the Trump administration were more subtle than other accounts predict because of the intersection of the *populist* nature of Trump's leadership with conditions, largely predating his election, that reduced constraints on his governance. In both substance and process, religion shifted from an implement of what Bettiza calls "postsecular statecraft" to a tool for rallying religious support to the populist movement, what this volume terms "blessing America First." Certain offices faced attacks, some flourished, while others largely faded away, but all did so in response to the nature of populism, a domestic political logic often overlooked in studies of religion and international relations. Subsequent chapters expand on this theoretical foundation and present more focused empirical evidence.

Blessing America First met two constitutive needs of populism: providing substance to a "thin" ideology of "the people," and deploying a personalistic structure of rule. Religion in the *substance* of foreign policy provided an opportunity for constructing the populist, ideological boundaries between "the people" and excluded outgroups. The *structure* of religion in the foreign policy bureaucracy was reshaped to reflect populism's preference for personal ties and rejection of institutional constraint. The intersection of the two dimensions of populism explains why the Trump administration's governance record did not perfectly match either more rigid ideological prediction: the comprehensive mobilization of bureaucratic resources to serve Christian interests, or the consistent dismantling of all aspects of the federal bureaucracy, including those dealing with religion. Instead, religion in foreign policy became a flexible tool of securing populist domestic power.

Next, the chapter considers preexisting conditions of American democracy that explain why the regime complex in religion and foreign policy proved relatively easy terrain for populist change. Religious foreign policy was an especially inviting arena of populist governance for the Trump administration because of several domestic conditions that predated Trump's election, and have outlasted his term: cultures that channeled dissent among career officials, the flexibility of American secular and national security institutions, and polarization over religion and foreign policy in American public opinion. These essentially domestic-level variables are easily overlooked by theories that tend to focus on international-level variation in explaining foreign policy processes.

BEYOND THE "MISSING DIMENSION"

Religion may have been a "missing dimension" of statecraft in the post-Cold War period, but it has attracted significant attention from scholars and practitioners of U.S. foreign policy in subsequent decades.[4] Social scientists have set out frameworks for integrating religion into foreign policy analysis and international relations theory, analyzing the interplay between religious actors and state interests.[5] Several volumes have focused on the foreign policy impact of particular religious traditions such as Roman Catholicism[6] and evangelicalism,[7] or more specific topics such as the ideological underpinnings of Christian support for Israel.[8] Especially after the 9/11 terrorist attacks, special attention has fallen on the role of Islam in foreign policy, both in the United States and abroad.[9]

I briefly synthesize four strands within this scholarship. Each offers valuable insight and will feature in the later analysis of Trump administration foreign policy. However, each is ultimately limited in conceptualizing recent variation and explaining its roots, largely because the populist nature of the Trump administration has received limited attention in the study of religion and foreign policy.

CIVILIZATIONAL CONFLICT

No single argument regarding religion's influence on international relations in general, and U.S. foreign policy in particular, has had a broader and more contentious impact than Samuel Huntington's work on civilizational clash. At the Cold War's end, the search for a new logic of international order drew Huntington to hypothesize clashes between civilizational blocs largely, although not entirely, defined in religious terms. Islam, Orthodox Christianity, and Confucianism would all play a role in balancing against the West, and countries would be drawn into international conflict via "kin-country syndrome," whereby "Muslim" states in particular would rally to the defense of coreligionists.[10] Civilizational theory generated a small industry of academic and policy analysis, and was generally cast aside for a time as underspecified, essentialist, and empirically unsustainable.[11] However, the rise of the Trump administration led to something of a renaissance, with scholars and policymakers arguing that this "tainted worldview" provides new assistance in understanding trends in foreign policy, particularly related to Islam.[12]

The initial weaknesses of Huntington's theory remain. However, recent analysts are right that civilizational rhetoric is regularly heard on the global stage again, and thus could be important in understanding ongoing patterns of variation. This acknowledgment comes with two important qualifications. First, civilizational theory itself offers limited guidance for why such rhetoric emerged at this particular point in time in U.S. foreign policy. For this, analysis needs to turn to the nature of essentially domestic political changes in the current period of instability. Second, civilizational theory overpredicts ideological constraint. It offers limited guidance on the internal bureaucratic processes that institutionalize religion's place in agencies like the State Department and USAID, which were not all leveraged equally to serve the administration's priorities.

THE CRITICAL TURN IN RELIGION
AND U.S. FOREIGN POLICY

A second group of scholars could be grouped together as offering genealogical critiques of religion in the foreign policy process. Many voice particular concerns about U.S.-backed efforts to promote international religious freedom, and the implication of religious freedom promotion in longer histories of exclusion and state power.[13] In a related vein, an array of scholars has highlighted the problematic ways in which foreign policy in the United States (and Europe) has become preoccupied with perceived security threats from actors claiming to represent Islam, and broader ambiguities of power in the relationship between Islam and secularism in the West.[14] This scholarship serves as a powerful reminder that Islam's fraught place in U.S. foreign policy did not begin with the Trump administration's populism.

These scholars rightly spotlight the power dynamics that shape religion and the foreign policy bureaucracy. No scholar can deploy concepts like religious freedom or secularism naively in the wake of this research. However, *Blessing America First* steps beyond this scholarship based on two wagers. First, there is significant value in attention to variation within the foreign policy bureaucracy. Religious freedom's genealogists struggle to differentiate variation within the bureaucracy, particularly between the promotion of religious freedom and other mechanisms of religion and diplomacy.[15] Second, these studies provide ambivalent guidance over whether something *new* was actually going on in religion and U.S. foreign policy in the Trump era. If religion in foreign policy is a constant source of domination or control, there is limited guidance in making sense of tumultuous changes in the recent policy environment.

BUREAUCRATIC COMPLEXITY AND POSTSECULARISM

If critical approaches to the study of religion in foreign policy have tended to elide internal variation within the foreign policy bureaucracy, other scholars have begun to turn their attention to grappling with the fact that religion in the foreign policy bureaucracy extends well beyond religious freedom. American practitioners have published numerous volumes on the place of religion in the practice of diplomacy.[16] In recent research, Bettiza traces the multidimensional development of a "regime complex" of religion in U.S. foreign policy across multiple governmental agencies in a "postsecular world."[17] Analysts of the European scene have noted trends in religion and the conduct of EU foreign policy, at times developing in direct dialog with American diplomatic initiatives.[18] These studies are an essential foundation for tracing the roots of the institutional equilibrium that in many ways culminated in the closing years of the Obama administration.

However, for understandable reasons, this research only begins to come to terms with the unique variation brought by Trump administration foreign policy, and how an "America First" foreign policy may reshape the bureaucracy. A key contention of *Blessing America First* is that recent variation in the United States, and related dynamics in a range of global cases, are neither idiosyncratic outliers nor "standard" foreign policy practice, consistent with earlier conservative periods of bureaucratization. Rather, they are the unique result of the populist nature of those wielding executive power. The populist logic of power maintenance is especially challenging to make sense of under the rubric of bureaucratic complexity because it, at times, explicitly undermines bureaucratic structures, while at other times leveraging them to its ends. Furthermore, much of its "action" takes place *outside* of those formal structures, either via personalistic exchanges or populist initiatives unmediated by bureaucracy.

RELIGION AND SOFT POWER

A final productive turn in the study of religion and the foreign policy process has pushed scholars to think more clearly about the mechanisms through which religion might exercise influence. A significant body of scholarship has drawn on the concept of "soft power" in international relations literature to explain why religious ideas and actors, who often lack the direct coercive capacity or material resources so prominent in analysis of international relations, might exercise influence. As scholars have argued for several decades, soft power seeks to shape behavior, not through coercion or financial incentives, but rather "new power resources" such as "attraction to shared values" that persuade via logics of appropriateness.[19] This turn to soft power was particularly helpful because, as Jeffrey Haynes puts it, "although many authors attest to the significance of religion in international relations . . . there is less agreement on *how* religion affects foreign policy."[20] A range of ongoing research mobilizes the concept of religious soft power to make sense of statecraft from Saudi Arabia to Russia to India.[21]

Soft power puts welcome attention on the material implications of distinct forms of what Bettiza calls "sacred capital."[22] There are two particular ways, however, in which analysis of soft power seems to leave recent variation unaddressed. First, how does the domestic nature of political regimes systematically impact the role of soft power? Limited attention to this question may be, in part, because of soft power's origins in international relations, where blackboxing the state brings certain advantages of parsimony. However, there are also costs, as more systematic attention to domestic political variation may help to clarify how religion interfaces with soft power differently within a given case, across time. To borrow from Mohammad Tabaar's analysis of Iran, religion may operate primarily as a tool of contestation among domestic "factions" within the regime, rather than as a unified source of state ideology.[23] Second, soft power's emphasis on attraction and persuasion at times presumes the sincerity of certain leaders, while underestimating the importance of religion even for thoroughly unpersuaded leaders. Haynes's ideal-typical path of soft power influence, for example, seems to rest on "[religious elites] influencing foreign policy by encouraging policy makers to incorporate religious beliefs, norms and values into foreign policy."[24] But what if religion, rather than grounds for conversion in the hands of non-state elites, is instead a tool of control wielded not for grand strategy, but personalistic survival?

WHAT IS NEEDED? INTEGRATING POPULISM INTO THE STUDY OF RELIGION AND FOREIGN POLICY

In distinct ways, civilizational, critical, postsecular, and soft power accounts of religion and U.S. foreign policy make important, but incomplete, contributions to understanding the nature and origins of recent variation. My central theoretical claim is that any account of religion and Trump administration foreign policy must be more attuned to the basically *domestic* conditions that explain seeming inconsistencies in recent variation. This follows on Jocelyn Cesari's advice to spotlight "the mutual influence of domestic and international politics."[25] To borrow again from Tabaar's analysis of Islam and Iranian foreign policy, "Religion is a ubiquitous, and yet mercurial feature . . . elites have constructed and used religious narratives for political purposes, and changed these narratives in the process."[26]

In the context of making sense of religion and Trump administration foreign policy, this entails, first and foremost, grappling with the populist nature of Trumpism, and the unique ways that populism's political logic shaped religion in the substance and structure of foreign policy. In contrast to the regime complex designed to "manage and marshal the power of faith globally in pursuit of America's interests and values abroad," religion in the foreign policy bureaucracy transformed into an implement of populist power maintenance.[27]

Engaging recent scholarship on populism and religion helps to clarify the unusual pattern of variation observed in the Trump administration, with some positions eliminated entirely, others weakened in "incremental fashion," but still others growing in visibility and resources.[28] Populism is a contested, multidimensional concept in political science, and, as Angelos Chryssogelos helpfully notes, "Different conceptualizations of populism have different implications about the role of populism in policy outcomes."[29] In particular, two dimensions that distinguish populist politics come with observable implications for the foreign policy bureaucracy. First, populism rests on a "thin ideology" that distinguishes "the people" from undesirable out-groups. Foreign policy and religion provide opportunities for populists to engage in the construction of these ideological boundaries. Second, populists adopt a personalistic strategic logic that rejects institutional constraint. This personalism comes with implications for religion's place in the foreign policy bureaucracy.

LINKING POPULISM TO RELIGION AND FOREIGN POLICY

The populist nature of President Trump's leadership sheds unique light on recent shifts in religion and the foreign policy bureaucracy. In sum, Trump's populism accounts for a dramatic, but easily confused, variation *away* from the bureaucratization of religion as a "tool of statecraft," and toward populism's core political logic: a tool of identity-based boundaries and personalistic control. This reflects the "shifty" nature of populism itself, with its "pragmatic and opportunistic" strategic choices serving only the interests of the personalistic leader.[30]

While not a new concept, populism has received a burst of recent attention in comparative politics. Many contemporary scholars of populism, particularly right-wing varieties in Europe, define the concept primarily as a "thin-centered" political ideology advocating rule that expresses the "general will," "pit[ting] a virtuous and homogenous people against a set of elites and dangerous 'others' who are together depicted as depriving (or attempting to deprive) the sovereign people of their rights, values, prosperity, identity and voice."[31] Others advocate a more "political-strategic approach" that defines populism as a structure of rule characterized by a "personalistic leader . . . exercising power based on direct, unmediated uninstitutionalized support from large numbers of mostly unorganized followers."[32] Populism can emerge in both left- and right-wing variants, making it "practically impossible to define" along a traditional left-right ideological axis.[33] Instead, it is "notorious for its twists and turns, driven by the opportunistic efforts of personalistic leaders to concentrate power."[34] Scholars of foreign policy formation have begun to account for populism's rise, particularly noting the implications of populist ideology for distinct patterns of foreign policy decision-making.[35]

Religion initially remained peripheral to comparative studies of populism.[36] This may be because, as Andrew Arato and Jean Cohen put it, populism's deification of the people was "tantamount to idolatry."[37] The fact that contemporary right-wing populism has surged in Europe, one of the most secularized regions in the world,[38] implies to some an inverse relationship between religiosity and populism.[39] Whatever the cause, recent scholarship has begun to revise this oversight, documenting the role of religion in populist movements, whether in Europe[40] or in broader comparative perspective.[41] Yet, while this recent scholarship has helpfully placed religion onto the agenda of the study of populism, much work remains, in particular specifying how populism's political logic shifts after a populist leader actually achieves political power.[42] I draw on this recent scholarship to set out distinct mechanisms through which religion may intersect with populist approaches to governance, and how these mechanisms may have implications for the content and process of foreign policy.

Both *ideological* and *political-strategic* approaches to populism generate distinct, observable expectations about populism's impact on religion and foreign policy. First, for the ideological approach, religion may help fill in the "thin" bounds between "the people" and out-groups. This need to preserve the people while inveighing against outsiders could come with implications for the substance of foreign policy decision-making, and privilege bureaucratic offices helpful in that process. Second, the political-strategic approach raises the possibility that populism's effect may be as much on the *process* as outcomes of foreign policy, as personalistic politics rejects bureaucratic constraint while empowering actors directly tied to the populist leader. The following discussion of each mechanism is rooted in theories of religion and populism, with brief comparative evidence illustrating its broader operation. Each then moves to implications specific to the study of the foreign policy process.

RELIGION AND POPULISM'S THIN IDEOLOGY

Ideological approaches to populism tend to emphasize the need for populists to construct identity boundaries both horizontally, uniting "the people" while excluding out-groups, and vertically, criticizing unaccountable elites who thwart the people's legitimate sovereignty.[43] Once in power, such thin ideological appeals may transition from campaign rhetoric into governance outcomes. Populists may be especially well-equipped to integrate religion into this process because of the "thin-centered" nature of their ideological commitments. Unlike some left-wing political parties, for instance, there are no particular ideological barriers to populists delivering policy payoffs to potential religious allies. Foreign policy provides an opportunity for pursuing the inclusionary and exclusionary aspects of this ideological approach. Populism's effect here is primarily observable via the *content* of foreign policy decision-making.

The role of religion in contributing to identity boundaries has received significant recent attention from scholars of populism. As Nadia Marzouki and Duncan McDonnell put it, "Populists express strong moral judgements . . . portraying society in Manichean terms as divided in a good 'us' and a bad (even 'evil') 'them.' In defining both of these categories, religious identities often play an important role."[44] In this pathway, religion functions as an identity type rather than a set of credal beliefs. Rogers Brubaker calls populist use of religion "strikingly contradictory . . . its identitarian Christianity is devoid of religious content."[45] On similar grounds, Tobias Cremer terms this populist move "a Godless crusade."[46] Olivier Roy similarly argues that religion is "a purely nominal marker of identity, without any positive content."[47] As Zoltán Ádám and András Bozóki conceptualize the Fidesz party in Hungary, "The 'national Christian' political identity . . . has played an instrumental role, but conveyed no substantial religious content."[48] It bears noting that populist boundary construction may rest on substantive theological commitments, beyond simple religious identity. For instance, the Philippines's populist Rodrigo Duterte has enjoyed backing from certain Christian ministers who lend theological blessing to his violent "penal populist" approach to anti-drug policy.[49]

The content of populist foreign policy provides one significant opportunity to offer content to "thin" in-group boundaries. Scholars have noted the role of "Christian nationalism" in driving support for President Trump,[50] and such Christian identity claims may provide opportunities for international partnership.[51] It may be most intuitive that foreign policy issues tied to forms of social conservatism, for example treaties related to gender, sexuality, and reproduction, would be especially useful in constructing shared religious identity.[52] However, a broader net of foreign policy issues could become salient in promoting shared identity, from security policy and prisoner release efforts, to foreign assistance and humanitarian policy, to efforts to combat human trafficking. Shared identity stretching across borders could encourage alliance formation, reduce threat perception, or impact the likelihood of costly collective action during moments of crisis. While such international effects are plausible, the real driver of this in-group boundary construction is the fundamentally domestic need of the populist to build ties to an unmediated political constituency.

If religious identity could play a role in binding an in-group, thin ideology has an exclusionary face as well. Religious identity among contemporary populist movements contributes to out-group exclusion, notably with both anti-Semitic and Islamophobic implications in many Western cases. Populism's anti-elitism could also drive rhetorical attacks on clerical elites, especially where those elites are closely linked to establishment politics. Left-wing populists in Latin America have, at times, demonstrated this mechanism. For instance, Hugo Chávez declared critics in the Catholic hierarchy "liars," "perverts," and "Neanderthals," while similar rhetoric emerges among current right-wing populists in Europe.[53]

Mechanisms of exclusionary policy influence are, in many ways, the inverse of the inclusionary dimension of identity: increased threat perception and diminished incentives for collective action across identity boundaries. Exclusion of out-groups should, of course, be observable in populist rhetoric, but once in power, it should also emerge in exclusion-ary policy decisions. It may seem risky to allow the domestic political logic of populism to influence hard-power foreign policy decisions, but such calculation is in keeping with the short-term personal power maintenance that is the first priority of a populist leader.

This raises a final point about populism's ideological boundaries: ulti-mately, they serve populist leaders, rather than constraining them. Thicker accounts of religious ideology in nationalism or foreign policy could high-light the ability of ideology to impose significant material costs on policy makers, perhaps even mandating "conversion abroad" to religious forms seen as more welcoming to state interests.[54] Cesari's "processual" analy-sis of "God's people," for instance, is more diffuse than the centralized project of populist identity construction.[55] The logic of populist ideology flexibly serves the interests of government, rather those than of state or nation. As Kurt Weyland puts it, populist ideology is "a façade . . . driven by the opportunistic efforts of personalistic leaders to concentrate power and stay in office."[56]

RELIGION AND POPULISM'S PERSONALISTIC STRUCTURE

While populism may be defined as a thin ideology, it can also be analyzed in "political-strategic" terms. In this view, populism is not different because of its normative content, but instead a structure of rule "through which a personalistic leader seeks or exercises government power based on direct, unmediated, uninstitutionalized support from large numbers of mostly unorganized followers."[57] The key characteristics of this dimen-sion of populism are, thus, its intense concentration on the personal lead-ership of a key individual, and that individual's rejection of constraint from existing institutional checks. While not prominent in existing scholarship on religion and populism, this strategic approach has impli-cations for religion and foreign policy. Its emphasis on "the clear predom-inance of a powerful leader" empowers those with personal ties to the populist leader, rather than traditional intermediaries in parties or civil society. Once in power, this could entail official or informal designation of religious allies as foreign policy emissaries. It could, in some contexts, include direct funding of religious activities of loyalists, or, indirectly, support for religious charitable activities of domestic allies via state development assistance.[58]

Beyond privileging personalism, a political-strategic approach emphasizes the rejection of institutionalized constraints on executive power once a populist comes into office. Populism's skepticism of elitism could undercut much of the formal bureaucratization of religion documented in recent scholarship.[59] Career bureaucrats or process-oriented checks on executive discretion have been a particularly tempting target for such attacks. The populist is "constantly on the lookout for enemies" working against the will of the people, and bureaucratic constraints have regularly fit this description.[60] Populists may deploy religious loyalists to provide moral justification for such anti-institutional behavior. European populists have spent decades building their popular appeal by criticizing the "democratic deficit" in institutions of the European Union. Stirring up the threat posed from a supposed "deep state" in the United States, particularly centered on the foreign policy bureaucracy, has "been elevated to the status of public enemy number one" in Trump administration rhetoric.[61] As Skowronek, Dearborn, and King put it, "In Trump's America, the Deep State came to stand for cadres of administrators operating throughout the executive branch who put their own interests and ideology ahead of the preferences of the nation's 'chief' executive."[62]

Populism's personalist structure resonates with other scholarship emphasizing populism's performative "style" or emphasis on charismatic leadership.[63] It was partially this unique style, including in the conduct of foreign policy, that caused Daniel Drezner to label Trump the "toddler in chief."[64] Certain religious leaders may share a populist style that facilitates personalistic ties. Foreign policymaking provides ample opportunities for actions consistent with this personalistic style. The slow grind of diplomacy fades in importance when compared to the glare of bright lights at grand summits and theatrical confrontations.

To be clear, a political-strategic approach to populism does *not* imply an ideological hostility to all use of institutionalized state power. Instead, populists reject *constraint* on their individual discretion, especially potential institutional checks in bodies like courts, political parties, or career bureaucracies. Populists may leverage the bureaucracy to their ends where costs are low, and constraint limited.

TABLE 1.1 Religion, Populism, and Foreign Policy: Dimensions of Influence

	Dimension of Populism	Potential Links to Religion	Potential Indicators in Foreign Policy
Populism as Thin Ideology	Populist thin ideology constructs an in-group, "the people."	Affinity between religious identity and boundaries of the populist in-group.	Rhetorical identity construction in foreign policy addresses. Prioritization of policy goals of religious majority.
	Populist excludes out-groups, particularly elites, and threats to "the people."	Religious minorities or critics among those excluded.	Foreign policy threat assessments targeting out-groups. Foreign policy as an avenue for confronting domestic religious critics.
Populism and Personalistic Governance	Populist privileging of personal loyalists.	Populist delivery of material inducements such as: political appointments or state funding.	Patterns of political appointments. Undermining formal offices or processes attempting to constrain populist initiatives.
	Populist rejection of constraint from existing formal institutions.	Religious endorsement of populist anti-institutional activities.	Populist style in foreign policy speeches and convenings.

Populism is a slippery concept. Distinguishing ideological and strategic approaches to populism helps to clarify distinct implications of populism for religion and foreign policy. Table 1.1 summarizes the distinct, observable implications of these two dimensions in religion and U.S. foreign policy. This explains why the variation that populists bring to religion and foreign policy is so maddeningly complex. It is not a matter of "more" or "less" religious influence, or of a consistent, religiously grounded foreign policy ideology guiding grand strategy. It is, rather, a self-serving repertoire of power maintenance, leveraging the complex intersections

between religion and foreign affairs to serve populism's only fixed preference: the populist's personal political survival.

PRECONDITIONS ENCOURAGING
BLESSING AMERICA FIRST

If the rise of a populist movement is the proximate cause of variation under
the Trump administration, this leaves a broader question unresolved: why
did religion's place in U.S. foreign policy, which grew over a period of
decades within a highly professionalized bureaucracy, undergo such rapid
change? *Blessing America First* turns to three factors that can be thought
of as preexisting conditions of the domestic American political landscape
that account for why Trump's populist approach proved so impactful.
First, the culture and structure of the professional civil and Foreign Service channeled checks from within the bureaucracy, limiting overt
resistance. Second, the flexible institutional nature of the American
religion-state relationship, and foreign policy decision-making, reduced
opportunities for constraint on executive action from other branches of
the federal government. Third, polarization over religion and foreign policy in public opinion created domestic incentives for Trump's foreign
policy moves and religious loyalists advocating them. As chapters 5
through 7 will show, each of these factors did, in limited ways, contribute
to institutional stability during the Trump administration. But none could
fully check populist changes in religion and the substance or process of
U.S. foreign policy.

Presidents come and go, causing some to speculate, perhaps wishfully,
that the current global populist outburst would fade away in time, leaving limited lasting impact on the international system and American
foreign policy. While this is certainly possible, there are several well-
established features of the American foreign policy process, and of religion's role in American politics, that have facilitated this pattern of change
and are unlikely to fade with a single presidential transition. As William
Howell and Terry Moe argue, a failure to understand these preexisting
conditions could make Trump's 2020 electoral defeat "little more than an
exercise in denial, offering temporary relief from the recent populist

turmoil but leaving the causes of that turmoil unaddressed and the potential for continued democratic backsliding firmly in place."[65]

FAITH IN THE DEEP STATE? BUREAUCRATIC CULTURE AND INTERESTS

A first preexisting condition that ultimately struggled to constrain populist changes to religion and foreign policy has remained largely off the radar for scholars of religion and politics: features of bureaucratic politics.

Bureaucratic politics has a distinguished history in the study of foreign policy, from the Miles Law aphorism that "where you stand depends on where you sit," to detailed tracing of bureaucratic responses to key events like the Cuban Missile Crisis.[66] The bureaucratic politics canon is internally diverse, with some accounts emphasizing the rational interests of bureaucratic turf and others more focused on the influence of ideas or individual agency in the bureaucracy.[67] Both rationalist and cultural accounts help to make sense of why religion in the U.S. foreign policy bureaucracy was so susceptible to the changes posed in the Trump administration. As Robert Mickey et al. put it, "those pinning their hopes on push-back from the bureaucracy are likely to be disappointed."[68]

In rationalist terms, engrained features of the foreign policy process, and religion-related offices in particular, made any effective bureaucratic resistance costly and challenging to coordinate. The first is the nature of staffing within the State Department, especially the regular global rotations that constitute the careers of Foreign Service Officers, and the increasing reliance on contractors who lack the employment stability of career foreign and civil servants. Second, more specific to offices tied to religion, an office's location within the organizational chart impacts its response during a period of populist challenge. David Lewis highlights the importance of political appointments in explaining whether a portion of the bureaucracy is vulnerable to shifting political winds.[69] Many religion-related offices or initiatives have relied heavily on appointees or discretionary executive action, increasing their susceptibility to populist challenge. Furthermore, religion-related foreign policy offices generally resemble what Drezner terms "embedded agencies," whose greatest resource for survival is their ability to persuade other bureaucrats of their merit.[70] This may open a bureaucratic door for post-populist resto-ration, but is of little use when the greatest threat to an office comes, not from within the bureaucracy, but from external political forces.

Organizational culture shaped responses to populism as well, in two ways. First, strong internal norms among career staff did motivate resis-tance to some populist transgressions. This is very much in keeping with the expectation from Drezner's work on "missionary institutions" (no pun intended) that emphasizes their success at inculcating strong internal val-ues among staff.[71] Such strong, internal organizational culture should facilitate some bureaucratic checks if populists violate established norms, whether those norms relate to bureaucratic process or more substantive questions of religion and foreign policy. However, another aspect of orga-nizational culture is likely to constrain bureaucratic response: norms about the appropriate means of registering dissent, and if need be, logics that could drive individuals out of government service entirely. This inter-section of strong internal culture with dedication to *certain process* of resistance makes career bureaucrats significantly constrained in respond-ing to a determined populist in office.

SALVATION IN INSTITUTIONS? A FLEXIBLE "WALL" AND EXECUTIVE FOREIGN POLICY DOMINANCE

Populist instrumentalization of religion in the foreign policy process lies, in part, with the institutional conditions that confront a populist leader. While populists share a political logic of personalistic rule that encourages extra-institutional behavior, they still must confront poten-tial institutional constraints, especially in a democracy characterized by the separation of powers. Indeed, it is because the American consti-tutional system is "unusually rigid" and remains "firm and stable" that Weyland sees limited prospects for a populist threat to American democracy.[72] While this characterization may apply to aspects of American institutions, quite the opposite is true in the two areas most related to blessing America First: the American religion-state relation-ship and the foreign policy process itself. Instability within the suppos-edly solid "wall of separation" has intersected with minimal institu-tional constraint on executive influence over foreign policy to make religion and foreign policy one of the *least* constrained areas for populist manipulation.

The importance of institutional context in explaining religious politics has become one of the most fertile areas of research in religion and politics. It has been nearly two decades since the late Alfred Stepan observed that, in spite of frequent normative assumptions to the contrary, there is no requirement that religion and state be rigidly separated in order for a country to fit conventional definitions of democracy.[73] Scholars of American institutions have repeatedly demonstrated the flexibility within a supposedly "secular" state. Legal scholars trace debates between separationists and accommodationists, while scholars of a more critical bent question the plausibility of guaranteed constitutional religious freedom.[74] With Supreme Court cases regularly decided by the slimmest majorities, American legal secularism is far from "rigid" and "stable." As Elizabeth Shakman Hurd and Winnifred Sullivan point out, First Amendment guarantees are even *less* rigid in the realm of foreign policy, where courts are loathe to constrain executive action.[75] This resonates with recent analysis of the risks of American democratic backsliding, arguing that "the ambiguities of the U.S. Constitution leave considerable room for executive abuse on various fronts."[76] While some of the Trump administration's variation in the realm of religion and foreign policy has drawn dissent and even legal challenge, the flexible, executive-dominated nature of political institutions in this policy sphere ultimately facilitated the Trump administration's strategy.

Populists, with their general preference for personalized executive power, should find constraints on their actions particularly limited in policy spheres where potential institutional checks in the legislature or judiciary are weaker. Where legislatures can exercise effective power of the purse, or courts can vet executive orders for constitutionality, populists should face higher internal costs in governance, including attempts to alter the place of religion in foreign policy. Populists are likely to resist such constraint, and examples abound of populist executives stripping intransigent courts or legislatures of their authorities in places like Turkey and Venezuela. There is particular reason to doubt the effect of such constraint in the study of U.S. foreign policy. Scholars have long noted the weakness of other branches in constraining executive dominance in foreign policy decision-making.[77] This, combined with the inherent flexibility of the U.S.

religion-state relationship, helps to account for the limited checks on the Trump administration's populist recasting of religion and foreign policy.

POPULISTS IN THE PEWS: PUBLIC POLARIZATION
AND RELIGIOUS FOREIGN POLICY CHANGE

Finally, populism arrived in the foreign policy bureaucracy after several decades of polarization in American public opinion over religion and politics that limited direct popular pushback on Trump and his allies. It is true, as Weyland and Raúl Madrid observe, that Trump was not nearly as popular as other populists who "achieved commanding popular support," like the Philippines's Rodrigo Duterte and some in Latin America.[78] Indeed, many of Trump's populist forays into religious foreign policy provoked ferocious public protest and may have contributed to his eventual defeat at the ballot box. This could have, in theory, also constrained religious elites from actively blessing America First, if it risked running afoul of views in their pews, potentially undercutting their moral authority.

However, in the United States, polarization minimized these costs, and indeed provided an opportunity to utilize religion and foreign policy to buttress Trump's core support and the core popularity of his religious endorsers. Scholars of religion and American politics have noted the strengthening relationship between religiosity and conservative voting for white Americans.[79] Wide partisan gaps also exist over questions like the status of Islam in the United States, the legal separation of religion and state, and the links between Christianity and American nationalism.[80] International relations scholars have shown that elements of "Moral Foundations Theory" from social psychology correspond "strongly and systematically to foreign policy attitudes."[81] Public opinion scholarship in religion and American politics has found similar ties between religion and American exceptionalism, as well as preemptive use of military force.[82] Aspects of American evangelicalism have been shown to increase support for Israel,[83] as well as skepticism of international diplomacy to address climate change.[84]

This growing polarization over questions relevant to religion and U.S. foreign policy meant that a populist leader would face little public

TABLE 1.2 Preexisting Conditions, Populist Change,
and Potential for Foreign Policy Constraint

	Potential Mechanism of Constraint	Limitation on Constraint	Likely Outcome of Constraint
Career Staff	Agency from career staff (Foreign Service Officers, career civil servants, contractors) constrains populism by engaging in internal resistance.	Obstacles to collective action among career staff (i.e., rotations in postings). Bureaucratic culture of nonpartisan service and procedural dissent.	Internal dissents of low salience to populist leaders. Preserve bureaucratic function in areas beyond populist interest.
Institutional Structure	Existing institutional checks, primarily from judicial and legislative branches, constrain populism by ruling against changes or serving oversight functions.	Flexibility of American religion-state relationship. Executive dominance in foreign policy.	Observable constraint only where legal precedent is most clear-cut or Congressional mandates explicit.
Public Opinion	Public opinion constrains populism, threatening to punish an executive who bucks consensus or undermines the authority of religious loyalists.	Strong partisan polarization over religion and foreign policy. Religious incentives from core audience to bless America First.	Short-term empowering of populist and religious loyalists. Polarized public opinion may facilitate institutional restoration if populist departs office.

pushback from core supporters for running afoul of the relatively bipartisan bureaucratization of religion that predated Trump's election. Civil society actors, what Hurd terms "expert religion," were closely involved in that bureaucratization of religion over the past quarter century, and some took action to try to stabilize institutions throughout Trump's time in office.[85] But these voices were generally outside of the core actors loyal to the Trump campaign. Those new actors reflected polarization that has built in the last quarter century and faced little pressure from their own constituencies to insulate the bureaucracy from populist change.

Table 1.2 summarizes potential constraints on populist governance, as well as the features of the American landscape working against the effectiveness of these constraints. In sum, while the Trump administration had a unique populist logic that guided its restructuring of religion in U.S. foreign policy, this logic did not operate on a blank slate. Well-established features of the American political landscape facilitated efforts to bless America First. Bureaucratic culture, institutional flexibility, and popular polarization created a welcoming set of opportunities, encouraging the success of the populist strategies set out earlier.

RELIGION, POPULISM, AND INTERNATIONAL EFFECTS

To this point, this argument has focused on the nature of religion and the domestic foreign policy bureaucracy under populist governance. This raises important questions regarding the international influence of the Trump administration's form of religious populism. Following "second image" approaches to international relations, the domestic characteristics of populist governance come with implications for international ties.[86] This may be particularly important at a time when scholars of international relations are questioning the end of American hegemony and alternative sources of international order.[87] Existing research provides some guidance, drawing from analysis of the populist difference in foreign policy.[88]

The role of religion in drawing identity boundaries, for instance, could facilitate coordinated behavior among states with similar conceptions of in-group belonging, while driving confrontation with states aligned with out-groups. Policy priorities rooted in this conception of identity may lead populists to pursue substantive foreign policy alignment to satisfy domestic partners. The political-strategic approach to populism may privilege personalistic ties in foreign relations and empower personalistic allies of the populist leader to freelance in diplomacy. The populist style may facilitate ties to similarly charismatic, performance-oriented global leaders, and draw domestic religious leaders blessing America First into surprising international-religious partnerships.

Understanding the impact of the Trump administration on religion and U.S. foreign policy requires attention to the populist nature of the Trump presidency. Different definitions of populism suggest distinct mechanisms through which populism would alter the substance and process of foreign policy. In contrast to the bureaucratization of religion as an implement of statecraft in the post-Cold War period, populism utilizes religion in foreign policy as a tool of identity construction and personalist governance, with wide implications for the bureaucracy. While the Trump administration was, in some ways, a unique phenomenon, several persistent conditions of the American political landscape encouraged this variation and are unlikely to have ended with a governmental transition. This makes it all the more important to understand the nature of the change currently facing religion in the foreign policy bureaucracy, and the mixed effect of efforts to insulate bureaucracy from populist challenge. Before documenting this populist difference, I turn to establishing a bureaucratic baseline from mid-2016.

2

THE BLOB GETS RELIGION

RGA and the Prepopulist Equilibrium

I n September 2016, the Secretary's Office of Religion and Global Affairs (RGA) at the U.S. State Department convened a capstone Religion and Diplomacy Conference (RaDCon) to highlight the office's growth. Special Representative for Religion and Global Affairs Shaun Casey opened the multiday gathering by confidently stating, "The question we're pursuing is not why, or if, but *how* the State Department should be engaging religious actors and assessing religious dynamics."[1] The event included White House Chief of Staff Denis McDonough and numerous high-ranking career State Department officials. To borrow from Obama National Security Council (NSC) aide Ben Rhodes, it seemed like the latest indicator that the foreign policy "blob" was getting religion.

Although attendees had no way of knowing it at the time, that conference may well have been a high-water mark for one part of Gregorio Bettiza's "regime complex" of religion in the U.S. foreign policy bureaucracy. It happened to coincide with my first month as an academic fellow in the RGA office, attempting to navigate the literal and metaphorical maze of State Department bureaucracy.

In this chapter, I offer an overview of the workings of one component of Bettiza's regime complex, the RGA office, at or near the height of its capacity. Over its three years in existence, RGA developed a nuanced approach to its work, essentially blending *internal* work building the capacity of American diplomats with more *external* efforts engaging with religious partners on matters of mutual concern. The job, at times, involved *assessment* of religion's impact on a given policy area, and at other times *engagements* to pursue policy goals. This work took place in Foggy Bottom, as well as in conjunction with diplomatic posts in a wide variety of global regions and functional policy areas. It involved several high-level political appointees, but also a spectrum of career staff and subject matter experts. As the 2016 election approached, the office faced obvious questions about its long-term future, but also had a record of achievement that made Casey's confident remarks seem fairly uncontroversial.

I document RGA's work during this time period as a kind of baseline against which to measure the variation that came later through the Trump administration's populism.[2] Within this book's broader research design, this baseline helps to establish the relative absence of the features of populism (thin ideology and personalism) in the religion foreign policy bureaucracy before the arrival of the Trump administration. Publications from high-ranking political officials, notably Casey's writings on RGA's development, offer a more thorough firsthand account of RGA's origins and highest-level workings.[3] Work like Bettiza's has given a systematic look at the regime complex across the foreign policy bureaucracy (including areas like the Office of International Religious Freedom and the faith-based office at the United States Agency for International Development) at approximately this time. The goal here is not to replicate that work, but rather to offer a working-level view that sets the stage for tracing the variation analyzed in chapters 3 and 4.

The chapter moves forward in three parts. First, I summarize the structure and origins of the RGA office, providing fine-grained detail tracing the two core dimensions of the office's work: assessing religion's impact on U.S. foreign policy interests, and guiding diplomatic engagements in response to those assessments. Second, I illustrate how these two dimensions played out in practice with examples from my own portfolio, which focused on issues of governance and democracy. The chapter then closes with two forward-looking sections: how did the office's operations in mid-2016 relate to the theoretical dimensions of populism set out in chapter 1? And what open questions about the office's structure and function remained unresolved in late 2016, before election day?

RGA'S STRUCTURE AND APPROACH

By fall 2016, the RGA office had been in existence for roughly three years, and established its role as a complement to the array of religion-related offices that Bettiza characterizes as a regime complex tasked with integrating religion into U.S. diplomacy.[4] Following Bettiza, it is helpful to think of RGA as one of four bureaucratic channels related to religion and the U.S. foreign policy bureaucracy.[5] The Office of International Religious Freedom (IRF), along with the ambassador-at-large for International Religious Freedom, draws on the IRF Act of 1998, and subsequent legislation, to monitor and promote religious freedom around the world. At the United States Agency for International Development (USAID), an office then known as the Center for Faith-Based and Community Initiatives (FBCI), primarily coordinated with religious nonprofits partnering with the U.S. government to implement development programs around the world. And various offices, including the Bureau of Counterterrorism and Countering Violent Extremism, the Global Engagement Center, and others, focused on responding to terrorist threats, which at times involved assessment and engagement related to religion. While RGA worked regularly with officials in these offices, and they feature in later analysis of Trump's populism, they were distinct in late 2016, with different locations in the bureaucracy and substantive mandates.

Secretary of State John Kerry publicly launched the office that would become known as RGA in August 2013. This was the end of an extended process of consultation and planning involving diplomats, religious leaders, and interested parties in civil society about the need for the State Department to develop bureaucratic capacity related to religion. In 2010, the Obama administration launched an initiative to document preexisting levels of engagement with religious leaders in embassies and consulates around the world. By October 2012, the Religion and Foreign Policy Working Group of the Secretary's Strategic Dialogue with Civil Society issued a white paper summarizing the need for "a national capacity" to improve State Department engagement with religion. The Working Group recommended "an institutionalized mechanism through which the State Department and religious communities worldwide might better communicate and potentially collaborate, and that will improve understanding of religious dynamics relevant to foreign policy."[6] This combination of an analytic capacity with an outreach mission would become a theme for RGA's activities. The Working Group contributed to the Obama administration National Security Council's U.S. Strategy on Religious Leader and Faith Community Engagement, which aimed to "focus engagement [with religious leaders] on key policy objectives, promote best practices, and spur greater department and agency coordination."[7]

To meet this goal, Secretary Kerry launched an office in summer 2013 that would eventually become known as RGA. This office was initially called the State Department Office of Faith-Based Community Initiatives, reflecting its creation under the general set of executive orders permitting the establishment of faith-based centers within various executive branch agencies.[8] While many of these centers reflected the priority of the George W. Bush administration's "faith-based initiative" on facilitating social service partnerships involving religious charities, the State Department office would have a distinct mandate. Kerry's remarks at the launch noted a "clear" and "compelling" mission: "engage more closely with faith communities around the world, with the belief that we need to partner with them to solve global challenges."[9] Dr. Shaun Casey, announced that day as the inaugural office head, struck a common theme in the office's work: a desire for a middle ground between "some who were claiming that religion poisons everything, [and] others saying that religion would save and solve everything."[10] In practice, this would mean blending an analytic function to understand religion's role in foreign policy interests with an engagement mission to strengthen ties to relevant faith-based partners.

From its founding, RGA was charged with a more diverse policy portfolio than other, more focused, portions of the bureaucracy that dealt with religion. In his August 2013 remarks, Secretary Kerry mentioned issues that might be commonly thought of as "religious" in nature, such as "sectarian strife," but also highlighted global climate change, health care provision, and migration. Casey's subsequent remarks that day similarly mentioned countering violent extremism, but also human rights promotion and efforts to advance international development. The U.S. Strategy on Religious Leader and Faith Community Engagement reflected this balance, with explicit reference to the need for religious engagement in three policy spheres: "sustainable development and humanitarian assistance," "pluralism and human rights, including the protection of religious free-dom," and "prevent, mitigate and resolve violence conflict and contribute to local and regional stability and security."[11] In short, RGA's policy remit was meant to be broad and flexible, open to assessing and engaging religion in diplomacy in a wide range of geographic and functional policy areas, beyond relatively focused areas like IRF promotion and counter-terrorism work.

By fall 2016, this founding mission had grown into an office with significant capacity, both in terms of size and bureaucratic real estate. RGA was located within the relatively small bureau of offices reporting directly to the secretary of state (the "S Bureau"), placing it in close physical proximity to the Policy Planning Staff and the secretary's suite of offices on the State Department's 7th Floor. At that point, it also included several political appointees with briefs broadly related to religious engagement. Casey served as the special representative for RGA, and the suite also housed Special Representative to Muslim Communities (SRMC) Shaarik Zafar; Special Envoy to Monitor and Combat Antisemitism (SEAS) Ira Forman; and Acting Special Envoy to the Organization of Islamic Cooperation (SEOIC) Arsalan Suleman. These appointees had their own distinct mandates. For instance, congressional legislation grounded the SEAS position. However, by late 2016 all were gathered under the RGA umbrella by virtue of their focus on engaging with religious communities and assessing the impact of religion on U.S. foreign policy interests.

Beyond this high-level leadership, the RGA office consisted of an additional two dozen staff in various capacities, marking a rapid scaling up in a brief period. In general, working-level staff were grouped together into two teams that reflected the overall organization of the State Department: regional focus or functional expertise. Regional assignments followed the major world regions of the State Department's Political Affairs bureaus (African Politics, East Asian and Pacific Affairs, Near Eastern Affairs, South and Central Asian Affairs, and Western Hemisphere Affairs), reflecting the core need for RGA to interact with the diplomatic guts of the State Department housed in those regional bureaus. Functional assignments related to more thematic policy portfolios, including environmental negotiations, conflict prevention, and refugee policy. Functional bureaus frequently tackled policy portfolios of key importance to religious communities. Working-level staff reflected a blend of Foreign Service

Officers, career civil servants, contractors, and several academic advisors serving as temporary fellows in the department.

This last pathway marked my entry to RGA. As a comparative political scientist with expertise in the relationship between religion and democracy, I joined RGA to develop a functional portfolio focused on issues of democracy and governance. My research background was especially focused on topics tied to religion and elections and constitutional law which, as discussed later, fit comfortably within RGA's mandate, given the extensive involvement of State Department and USAID officials in election planning around the world. The portfolio grew over time, as a focus on governance raised diverse policy issues including combatting corruption and even wildlife trafficking. Given the common misconception that professors are adequate teachers, I also became closely involved with RGA's training modules for fellow diplomats, as well as developing office materials related to research guidance for assessing religion's impact on the policy environment.

From its founding, RGA balanced a three-part mission, across regional and functional portfolios. RGA would "advise the Secretary on policy matters as they relate to religion," "support posts and bureaus in assessing religious dynamics and engaging religious actors," and "serve as a first point of entry for those seeking to engage the State Department on matters of religion and global affairs."[12] Two themes stand out in each of these areas: assessment of religion's role and engagement with religious actors. Whether advising Secretary Kerry or career staff in a consulate far from Washington, D.C., RGA staff first worked to assess or analyze religion's actual role in a given sphere of foreign policy, and then conduct or advise on religious engagement involving American diplomats.

The September 2016 Religion and Diplomacy Conference (RaDCon) reflected this structure and the diverse set of policy spheres linked to RGA's work. There was discussion of religion and violence, but topics stretched widely, from environmental diplomacy to refugee resettlement, gender to public health, combatting anti-Semitism and Islamophobia to engaging young religious leaders. In a panel on religion and conflict, for instance, one presentation focused on the need for a clear understanding of what "lived religion" means in practice in a conflict zone, while another pointed to the engagement track record of mediation by religious elites in the Central African Republic.

RaDCon made clear that by September 2016, RGA was much more than the broom in a closet that founders joked about in the office's early days. While I learned the difference between a regional and functional bureau, as well as the semisacred policies regulating coffee in the office, colleagues convened diplomatic engagements, interfaced with embassies and consulates, and participated in consultations around the world. The general election was approximately two months away, and our attention was on diplomatic challenges facing the country on farther shores, as well as institutionalizing RGA's work for whatever leadership would come after Secretary Kerry's term concluded.

"RIGHT-SIZING" AND RELIGIOUS DIPLOMACY: THE IMPORTANCE OF ASSESSMENT

The first dimension of RGA's work focused on rigorous, nuanced assessment of religion's impact on U.S. foreign policy interests. After a few years on the job, RGA staff knew that before American diplomats could respond to religion in their work, they needed a significantly improved capacity to assess what role, if any, religion played in their particular area of regional or functional responsibility. Casey regularly trotted out an observation from the ethicist Fr. Bryan Hehir to make this point: "U.S. policymakers need to learn as much as possible about religion, and incorporate that knowledge into their strategies . . . this work is akin to brain surgery—a necessary task, but fatal if not done well."[13] Assessment could stray in several ways, whether over or understating religion's importance. On the one hand, certain policy challenges regularly linked to religion, such as terrorism, may be more adequately addressed by attention to "nonreligious" factors like poor governance or social exclusion. At the same time, "religion is relevant to many foreign policy priorities, not just those with an explicitly religious dimension or those conventionally viewed as connected to religion."[14] RGA staff would often refer to this as "rightsizing" religion's role, and worked by late 2016 to institutionalize this analytic approach.[15]

In late 2016, RGA's mix of permanent staff, political appointees, and academic fellows took steps to institutionalize the approach to assessment that they had developed over the previous years. Staff with research and analytic training took leading roles in systematizing this work. It was not an accident that Casey noted the total number of graduate degrees among the RGA staff in his 2016 remarks opening the Religion and Diplomacy Conference, citing "a vast reservoir of global experience in interpreting religion in local and regional contexts," along with the partnership of outside researchers and academics who advised the office in its approach.[16]

In this section, I sketch out some of the assessment principles that guided RGA's work, beginning at a more abstract level and drawing especially on an important, unclassified document, "Religion and Diplomacy: A Practical Handbook," that RGA staff generated over the course of 2016. I also consider how the framework from the Handbook played out in various assessment trainings developed by RGA staff. On the whole, after three years, RGA had developed an assessment approach that prized localized analysis of religion's contingent political impact, while in the process attempting to guide diplomats away from prior mistakes in religious assessment. However, this framework's nuance presented challenges in implementation that remained somewhat unresolved as the Obama administration moved into its last months in office.

If the assessment principles of the Handbook had a subtitle, it could have read: Religion: Probably not what you think! Religion's importance to American diplomacy should *not* be confined to "those typically tied to religion in the United States," such as countering violent extremism or Middle East peace negotiations.[17] Religion in international affairs is *not* inherently a good or bad thing for U.S. national interests. Religion does *not* only consist of abstract beliefs codified in holy texts. Islam is *not* unique in its political impacts. And religious leaders are *not* only (as it was sometimes put only tongue half in cheek) old guys with beards and hats. In the "Core Considerations" section of the Handbook, RGA sets out an approach to assessing religious impacts on international affairs that explicitly challenges each of these assumptions. "In short, *religion does not always look the way one expects it to, appear in the places one expects, or behave how one expects.*"[18] This essentially negative framing of RGA's mission reflected the office's determination to avoid diplomatic malpractice in the realm of religion.

With those trip wires in mind, the Handbook moves on to set out several "dimensions of religious dynamics assessment" that diplomats could consider before developing an engagement plan. Throughout, these assessment dimensions stress contextual knowledge and disaggregating the abstract concept of religion in local contexts. Assessment might start with demographics but should also include attention to "religious institutions and their organizational structures," which could include schools, health centers, media networks, or sectors of the economy tied to religious communities. RGA leadership advised careful attention to what scholars of religion have termed "lived religion,"[19] the diffuse process through religion is "subject to continual reinterpretation" in "the daily lives of rank and file members."[20] Assessment should be attentive to the importance of "less visible and/or marginalized voices" in impacting the public role of religion. In particular, RGA advised awareness of the fact that formal religious leadership may obscure the importance of often-marginalized voices, especially among women, youth, or marginalized communities in shaping public religion. And RGA advised awareness of the reality that the American religion-state relationship is unusual on the global scale, neither necessary nor sufficient for robust democracy or human rights. As the Handbook summarizes, "[Posts should] take into consideration the significant variation in relationships between religion, state and society around the world."[21]

Because assessment is not intended as an isolated research exercise, the Handbook's strategy then moves to "connecting U.S. policy priorities" with the religious dynamics identified above. This could "focus on a specific policy challenge" or else "identify points of intersection with integrated country strategies," the country-specific documents that guide diplomacy in the field.[22] RGA sets out a process of "crosswalking" policy objectives in a given context to the assessment of religion, as a way to set the stage for an effective post response to any overlap between objectives and religious landscape.

RGA staff also spent significant time developing internal training materials designed to apply the fairly abstract general assessment approach to more concrete policy scenarios. Training is a priority of advocates for institutionalizing religion in the foreign policy bureaucracy, and so RGA joined a landscape with significant attention already placed on the Office of International Religious Freedom. IRF training received a particular boost with Congress's 2016 passage of the Frank R. Wolf IRF Act, which "require[s] the Director of the George P. Shultz National Foreign Affairs Training Center to conduct training on religious freedom for all Foreign

Service Officers and all outgoing deputy chiefs of mission and ambassadors."[23] In the interim of filling that mandate, IRF shared space with RGA, and other elements of the State Department religion bureaucracy, in the Religion and Foreign Policy training course offered through the Foreign Service Institute. RGA also developed an internal training course to be offered on an ad hoc basis, tailored to the needs of particular bureaus and offices, whether an interested regional bureau like African Affairs or a functional training focused on an area like anti-corruption. Training may lack the glamor of international diplomatic outreach, but it plays a meaningful role in building the capacities of American diplomats to integrate religious engagement in their own work.

These trainings challenged diplomats to apply the assessment principals described earlier in hypothetical scenarios. As a first step, staff facilitated a brainstorming session in which training participants were encouraged to list examples of: 1) U.S. policy interests that might have something to do with religion and 2) religious leaders or actors who policymakers might need to know as part of their work. While conversations were varied, responses tended to highlight security issues and formal religious authorities. RGA staff then moved to presenting a hypothetical, but true to life, scenario related to a tense election in a fragile democracy. Without further context, participants were asked to read the scenario carefully, and "find the religion." Scenarios were constructed to contain some obvious references to formal religious institutions, as well as more subtle references to the role of gender in impeding voter registration and postcolonial dynamics that may impact the authority of certain religious leaders. RGA staff adapted these trainings for scenarios involving anti-corruption campaigns, environmental advocacy, and electoral violence prevention. Finally, participants received information about U.S. foreign policy interests in the country, via an adapted Integrated Country Strategy, which they then linked to the diverse religious dynamics embedded in the scenario description.

By late 2016, RGA staff had begun to institutionalize an approach to assessing religious dynamics that attempted to combine a nuanced, contextualized understanding of religion with a diverse spectrum of U.S. foreign policy interests that went well beyond the "usual suspects" like terrorism. In summative documents like "Religion and Diplomacy: A Practical Handbook," RGA staff set out general principles designed to guide engagement in diverse settings, and a flexible approach to training demonstrated the portability of the approach in diverse settings.

THE PRACTICE OF RELIGIOUS DIPLOMACY:
TURNING TO RELIGIOUS ENGAGEMENT

After drafting one of my first substantive memos in RGA, I submitted it to a more seasoned colleague for feedback. It was primarily a work of assessment, although I did my academic best to discuss what I viewed as its practical implications for U.S. diplomats. The colleague read the (very concise) four pages (in fourteen-point font) carefully, smiled, and said something along the lines of, "This is great, really interesting stuff. But remember, you have to tell them how to do their jobs differently. That's why they read." It was a fair response, and also a reminder that RGA's emphasis on assessment was only a means to an end. Ultimately, the goal of an assessment framework was to generate guidance for both RGA staff, and colleagues throughout the State Department, on how to respond to the concrete work of diplomacy, whether at the level of the Secretary Kerry and senior principals or more junior career staff.

After its extended section on assessment, the Handbook moves on to guidance on "engaging religious actors." RGA advised that at embassies and consulates, engaging with local religious contacts should be a part of "routine diplomatic work," conducted in advance of a crisis or specific embassy priority in order to "gain a more nuanced understanding of dynamics within the country context."[24] The Handbook offers various "models of engagement." This could involve "engaging religious actors and organizations in high-level diplomatic initiatives," such as the common role for clerical elites in postconflict, transitional justice initiatives like South Africa's Truth and Reconciliation Commission, or peace missions like those carried out in the Central Africa Republic by the country's Interfaith Peace Platform.[25] These sorts of elite-focused engagements could be appropriate at times.

However, the Handbook also presents examples of engagement drawing on distinct understandings of religion and leadership. Religious engagement could rely on more grassroots contact with religious organizations embedded in local communities. For instance, disaster response might benefit from engagement through rural religious schools or clinics. Here, the assessment principle that "religious organizations" often mean far more than simple houses of worship comes with practical diplomatic implications. Beyond infrastructure, religious traditions may offer "new narratives about policy and values" that resonate beyond conventional discourse from the U.S. government or other international organizations, such as regarding public health guidance related to disease outbreaks like Ebola and Zika. "Due to their special status and role in society, religious leaders and organizations are sometimes able to say and do things that other civil society and political groups cannot."[26] The Handbook sets out various examples of existing engagements that can serve the needs of diverse diplomats working at different levels of American embassies and consulates.

RGA's advising on engagement regularly sought to challenge assumptions about religious relevance or avoid potential diplomatic missteps that could have unintended consequences. Some of this advice is basic, culturally sensitive diplomacy, such as local religious etiquette and protocol— from the use of honorifics to appropriate conduct in meetings. Similarly, there is advice that "questions about the legality of particular programs and activities [under the Constitution's Establishment Clause] should be directed to the appropriate Office of the Legal Adviser office."[27] The Handbook advises understanding "unique [religious] perspectives, frames and worldviews" that religious communities may bring to a subject, such as diverse religious motives for involvement in environmental politics.

Cautionary engagement advice went beyond this in some substantial ways. Throughout the Handbook, RGA encourages diplomatic awareness that relevant "religious" authorities quite often stretch beyond the official hierarchy of religious institutions or organizations. The Handbook advises "proactive outreach to women religious influencers, as well as youth, and others who represent a diversity of religious practice and perspectives" to ensure a comprehensive approach to securing U.S. interests.[28] While "your first point of contact in the sphere of religion will likely be the head of religious orders, councils of religiously-affiliated NGOs," a more comprehensive engagement strategy "will provide a richer and perhaps more accurate understanding of local dynamics."

Similarly, RGA advised diplomats to consider carefully how "perceptions of U.S. engagement" could impact their religious contacts. Certain religious actors might enjoy cultivating their image as partners of the U.S. government, while others might be entirely unwilling to engage in such partnership in public. Religious actors with ties to American religious leaders should not be assumed, as such, to be more or less useful in securing U.S. national interests. The Handbook openly acknowledges that "sensitive topics," especially related to gender and sexuality could, at times, place religious leaders in positions of social conservatism, "responsible for safeguarding particular prevailing conceptions of public morality."[29] Instead of avoiding these subjects or attempting to convert local leaders to views held in U.S. policy statements, the Handbook advises "constructive conversation, even if the upshot of such engagement is simply to allow differences of perspective to emerge and serve as the basis for ongoing dialogue."[30]

In these ways and others, RGA's advice attempted to demonstrate an awareness that religious engagement could raise unintended consequences and, at times, even alter the nature of the local religious communities in question. Concerns over precisely this potential were a major and important charge of work from Elizabeth Shakman Hurd and others, writing in the early days of RGA's existence about the power exercised in "governed religion." RGA staff were aware of Hurd's warning that "government-sponsored religious outreach requires that the government decide which groups count as 'religious' and to discriminate among vying sects and denominations, privileging some at the expense of others."[31] In another, more specific, passage, Hurd contends that a particular project "seems to have favored established, institutionalized religions and their adult male leaders."[32] Bettiza, in a distinct, but related, vein writes that the increasing presence of religion in U.S. diplomacy could lead to religion itself "be[ing] potentially transformed along American understandings and practices of faith."[33] The Handbook's approach does not eliminate this risk. However, it demonstrates that RGA leadership was, at the very least, aware of the need to interrogate the nature and effects of engagement strategies in the field and institutionalize guidance that pointed to a distinct model.

Did this approach to religious engagement amount to "instrumentalizing" religion on behalf of the U.S. government? While not directly addressed in the Religion & Diplomacy Handbook, RGA staff developed an answer that blended the realities of diplomatic work with respect for the agency of religious actors. Engagement and outreach efforts undertaken by the State Department were, by their very nature, always designed to serve and advance U.S. foreign policy goals and priorities. That statement would be true whether engagement involved religious leaders, business executives, or partners in a government's security sector. With that said, where areas of mutual concern exist, there is clearly room for such engagement with a wide variety of local actors, including religious groups. As discussed later in more depth, RGA did caution that certain engagements could be perceived as undercutting the moral authority of local religious leaders, and thus problematic and counterproductive.

As with RGA's approach to assessment, the engagement strategies laid out in the Handbook, and associated trainings, were designed to promote multifaceted engagement with religious actors, to challenge conventional assumptions about who constituted relevant partners for religious engagement, and to consider carefully potential pitfalls of religious engagement on behalf of the U.S. government. In scenarios ranging from mapping out an economic development initiative to planning for environmental disaster mitigation, RGA attempted to build capacity for religious engagement across regions and functional areas.

ASSESSMENT AND ENGAGEMENT IN PRACTICE: A GOVERNANCE PORTFOLIO

By late 2016, the assessment principles and engagement strategies summarized in the Handbook were becoming a matter not just of abstract analysis and internal training, but external diplomatic response. Several examples, drawn from the early months of work on my governance portfolio, help to illustrate how these principles played out in two concrete areas of policy: anti-corruption efforts and, in an area never on the religion and politics shortlist, diplomacy to counter wildlife trafficking. While other streams of work within RGA were just as active, a set of functional policy issues tied to governance became among the clearest cases to illustrate the potential of RGA's approach to make a unique contribution to diplomatic work.

Religion's potential role in anti-corruption diplomacy was among the most fully developed illustrations of the RGA model before I arrived in summer 2016. A specialized stream of work, related to integrating religion into U.S. anti-corruption diplomacy, received its own panel at RaDCon, and with good reason, as it illustrated both the assessment and engagement potential of the RGA model in a policy sphere not often linked, in American minds anyway, to religious dynamics. In the Kerry State Department, anti-corruption work took on a prominent role involving various regional and functional bureaus, including International Narcotics and Law Enforcement Affairs (INL) and Economic and Business Affairs (EB). Corruption is linked to a host of outcomes that run counter to U.S. interests, from undercutting human development to encouraging political instability and violence. The technocratic or law enforcement side of anti-corruption work was well-established, but how might religion fit into the process of promoting this priority in U.S. foreign policy?

RGA worked with diplomats in Nigeria to answer this question. Corruption was a major challenge in Nigerian politics, with the country faring poorly on various comparative measures of corruption such as Transparency International's Corruption Perceptions Index.[34] In 2015, Muhammadu Buhari raced to victory in the Nigerian presidential election after a campaign in which he focused significant attention on corruption allegations during Goodluck Jonathan's previous administration. The confluence of domestic political conditions with U.S. interests clearly presented a diplomatic opening. How could religious engagement play a part in that response?

As a first step, RGA staff worked with partners in diplomatic posts on the ground to assess the potential impact of religion on corruption-related issues in Nigeria. On the one hand, many prominent Muslim and Christian clergy spoke regularly about the threat that corruption posed to the country, and the diverse religious motives that could drive anti-corruption campaigns. Consultations with subject matter experts and initial assessment research highlighted individuals, congregational networks, and communications infrastructure involved in this area. There was no shortage of moral resources advocating probity in the use of government funds. Both local and national religious networks understood the impact of corruption on broader normative goals in the country, especially promoting human development and peace.

Assessment revealed more nuanced dimensions of the issue, as well. Certain clergy in the country were, themselves, subject to allegations of corruption. In one tragic example, corrupt building practices allegedly contributed to the very high-profile collapse of a church in the country that killed over one hundred worshipers.[35] At the same time, some alleged that corruption investigations were leveraged selectively to target clergy from particular traditions or denominations, raising the possibility that anti-corruption campaigns could inadvertently stoke sectarian tensions in the short term. On a broader, societal level, even sympathetic clergy may have reservations about total transparency in disclosing congregational donors, and diffuse social expectations related to mutual aid within communities may, at times, justify behavior perceived as corruption by some advocates.[36] Any response would clearly require nuance to avoid unintended consequences.

After a period of assessment, RGA staff worked with diplomats on a multi-stage engagement process in which an interfaith Religious Leaders Anti-Corruption Committee (RLAC) gathered in Lagos to develop an anti-corruption charter, grounding policy engagement in their distinct religious traditions.[37] That initial meeting led to the development, by committee members, of an action plan to be implemented in partnership with one of Nigeria's leading anti-corruption organizations in civil society, known as BudgIT.[38] The religious leader group worked with BudgIT officials to develop an online platform known as Report Yourself, designed to encourage localized citizen corruption monitoring.[39] This initiative spread to distinct portions of the country under local leadership, and continued over time with a related web portal launch as recently as January 2022.[40]

The Nigeria-based anti-corruption work was, in a way, a proof of concept, and not without obstacles. Relationships between religious actors and civil society leaders in the anti-corruption space were not as strong before the engagement as they were in other development sectors like public health. Anti-corruption work raised the specter of inadvertently stoking inter or intrareligious tensions. As with any engagement relying on religious leadership, the voluntary nature of participation meant that implementation was, at times, uneven. Finally, further monitoring and evaluation was needed to test the pragmatic effectiveness of these programs.[41] Without minimizing any of these concerns, in the blending of assessment and engagement to pursue a priority of shared importance to the U.S. and local religious leaders, anti-corruption work provided one illustration of the viability of the RGA approach in relation to governance policy.

In my first weeks in the office, RGA staff began to develop a strategic plan to not only build on the Nigerian work with other potential anti-corruption engagements in the field, but also to expand governance work into an area far outside of my own expertise: countering wildlife trafficking (CWT).

CWT work, while probably not on the short list of U.S. foreign policy interests that one would instinctively tie to religion, turned out to be a fairly natural fit for RGA's approach. One reason for this was the issue's functional location at the intersection of two State Department bureaus where its work had proven productive: those dealing with law enforcement (via the anti-corruption work) and environmental affairs (via previous engagements primarily related to the Paris Climate Agreement). Through personal relationships and demonstrated expertise, career staff in these bureaus had come to understand the potential for religious assessment and engagement to impact their work, which provided a bureaucratic opportunity for the policy entrepreneurs in RGA to build a new area of governance-related engagement.

CWT became a foreign policy priority for the U.S. government, not only because of the intrinsic interest in environmental protection, but also because of the close ties between wildlife trafficking and a host of negative foreign policy outcomes, from drug trafficking, to extrajudicial violence, and even terrorism.[42] It is a transnational challenge, and one facing policy makers and advocates, in distinct forms, on every continent of the globe. Work stretches across multiple federal agencies, including the U.S. Fish and Wildlife Service, USAID, the Department of Justice, different portions of the intelligence community, military commands, and bureaus at the State Department. Diplomatic efforts respond to countries that are sources, transit points, and eventual destinations for trafficked wildlife, with attention paid to supply and demand. Programmatic funding related to CWT is not on the scale of some foreign policy priorities, but in 2020 the issue did receive nearly $120 million in U.S. government financial support.[43]

By October 2016, initial consultations both within and outside of the State Department began to assess the diverse pathways through which religion might factor into CWT diplomacy. In ways that resonated with anti-corruption efforts, CWT advocates were already aware of several high-profile efforts from clergy to leverage religious rituals and beliefs in favor of practices that protected wildlife. Muslim authorities in Indonesia had issued a 2014 fatwa against wildlife trafficking, and the country's expansive religious education networks had then become engaged in trainings in partnership with international NGOs to build teacher capacity to engage on the issue. An interfaith group of leaders came together in Kenya in 2012, in partnership with the World Wildlife Fund and the Alliance of Religion and Conservation, for an ivory burn to emphasize that "halting the illegal wildlife trade is a moral issue."[44] Religious networks in various parts of the world engaged in this work, not only as a matter of responsible care for animal species, but also because of the ways in which wildlife trafficking contributed to local criminality, underdevelopment, and even the finance of terrorist networks.

As with much of RGA's work, it also became apparent that distinct forms of religious practices and beliefs, at times, played a less than helpful role in CWT work. This was probably most obvious in some cases where beliefs tied to religion or spiritual practices directly fueled demand for trafficked goods, whether in the case of traditional Chinese medicine and the trade in pangolin scales, or the use of smuggled ivory in various forms of religious iconography, from Buddhist temples in Sri Lanka to Christian sculptures in the Philippines.[45] In initial consultations, both governmental leaders and advocates in civil society raised the difficulty of responding to such dynamics, for fear of alienating local religious leaders and their followers.

After these forays into assessment, RGA convened a first-of-its-kind engagement of government officials across regional and functional bureaus, civil society experts, journalists, and religious leaders concerned about the issue, to discuss existing practices and opportunities for further work. Roughly three dozen experts gathered, in person and virtually, to share best practices and discuss potential next steps for integrating religious communities into CWT work across regions. The consultation highlighted the potential for religious traditions to adapt practices that might be inadvertently pressuring vulnerable species, for instance the partnership between Panthera and South Africa's Shembe Church to transition to the use of synthetic leopard pelts in ceremonial practice, rather than furs from vulnerable species.[46] As was common in

RGA's work, "religion" took on importance not only through beliefs or ritual practices, but also the concrete infrastructure of religious networks, especially in areas beyond the reach of many advocacy organizations. Religious networks in border areas around the Central African Republic, for instance, developed a radio monitoring network through preexisting local peace councils to track the activities of poachers and smugglers, to both minimize violence associated with trafficking and protect animal populations.[47]

While the bulk of the planning for this initial workshop took place in fall 2016, the actual convening happened in early December. The presidential transition did not particularly feature in the day's conversations, other than remarks from State Department leadership that CWT was traditionally an issue of bipartisan concern. RGA, along with colleagues on the wildlife trafficking staff of relevant functional bureaus, spent mid-December distilling the workshop's discussions into policy guidance, and discussing how this initial D.C.-based step might set the stage for subsequent, field-based engagements to put the model into practice.

In sum, by late 2016, issues tied to governance were among the most prominent examples of the ability of RGA's combination of assessment and engagement to generate a unique contribution to U.S. diplomatic efforts. While a political transition certainly loomed, issues like anticorruption work and countering wildlife trafficking were not, traditionally, particularly partisan in nature, and RGA staff had every reason to expect continued work both in D.C. and abroad in these areas. Moreover, staff had begun to take steps to build a subsequent work portfolio related to an additional significant area of American governance diplomacy: strengthening electoral institutions abroad.

RGA AND THE DIMENSIONS OF POPULISM

In addition to describing RGA's peak functioning in mid-2016, this chapter serves an important role in this book's broader research design: establishing a baseline for comparison to changes that came in light of the Trump administration's populism. As chapter 1 points out, scholars of populism highlight both its thin ideology and uniquely personalist political strategy. To what extent did the various offices associated with religion in the foreign policy bureaucracy, especially RGA, demonstrate these twin dimensions of populism in mid-2016?

Populism's thin ideology rests on construction of an in-group, "the people," and the exclusion of out-groups, frequently threatening outsiders and elites conspiring against the general will. There is little indication of narrow in-group construction in RGA's founding documents and policy speeches. The U.S. Strategy on Religious Leader and Faith Community Engagement, which guided RGA's work, explicitly called for diplomacy to be "inclusive of a wide range of religious and non-religious actors."[48] In her remarks at RGA's launch, Melissa Rogers, head of the Obama White House's Office of Faith-Based and Neighborhood Partnerships, insisted that "Our engagement with religious and other civil society leaders should strive to promote pluralism and respect for the human rights of all people, including members of minority or marginalized groups . . . Increasing our engagement with a diverse spectrum of religious as well as secular communities will help us to underscore the universality of these crucial rights."[49]

The exclusionary aspect of populist boundary construction was similarly absent. Documents like the "Religion and Diplomacy: A Practical Handbook" took pains to emphasize that RGA's work was not uniquely intended to account for Islam's influence over politics, and that Islam itself represents no more of a challenge to U.S. values and interests than any other religious tradition. Other typical targets for populist exclusion, such as corporate interests, refugees, or petty criminals are similarly absent from RGA documents and remarks. It is hard to imagine an initiative of Secretary Kerry as embodying anti-elitism. RGA assessment consistently drew on experts at elite universities, and Shaun Casey, RGA's founding director, regularly boasted of the advanced academic credentials of his staff. If anything, RGA's approach could have been subject to charges of elitism, in spite of the office's attempts to advocate for analyzing "lived religion" in diplomatic tradecraft.

Beyond thin ideology, populism involves a personalist strategic logic, where a leader exercises power directly and rejects external constraint. To reinforce this unmediated structure of rule, the populist mobilizes a unique style involving charismatic appeals and an emphasis on crisis and emergency. While certain elements of personalism are structurally engrained in the American foreign policy process, RGA, on the whole, represented an approach much closer to Hurd's "expert religion" than the personal discretion implied in populism.[50] It is true that RGA's existence owed, to an extent, to the life experiences of Secretary of State John Kerry, and that the office was under the leadership of multiple political appointees, each of whom had biographical connections to the administration that they served. Those appointees regularly pointed to their personal access to Kerry and other departmental leadership as an indicator of the office's importance. As argued in more depth in chapter 6, the general discretion to executive power over foreign policy may have made these offices especially susceptible to populist personalism once Trump came into office.

However, in several ways, this falls short of the indicators of personalism that scholars of populism analyze. First, it misses out on the active populist rejection of any constraint on discretionary decision-making. By my arrival in late 2016, RGA staff had become quite familiar with the State Department's Office of the Legal Adviser, in an effort to ensure that efforts to "assess religious dynamics" and "engage religious actors" remained appropriately constrained by the U.S. Constitution's Establishment and Free Exercise Clauses. While a minority of experts within prominent advisory groups like the Chicago Council on Global Affairs' Task Force on Religion and the Making of U.S. Foreign Policy had argued that the Establishment Clause simply ought not restrict religious engagement abroad,[51] RGA took a voluntarily self-limiting approach, acknowledging the existence of such restrictions, and emphasizing forms of engagement that avoided the strongest Establishment Clause concerns. The Obama administration's decision to appoint a widely respected legal scholar, Melissa Rogers, with a history of careful work related to permissible religion-state partnerships, to head up its faith-based office hammers home this point.

Second, RGA staff and appointees were well aware that their office had an unusual number of political appointees, and discussed, both in private and in public, a likely future in which appointees yielded to career staff. One goal of such a change: to reduce the potential perception of religion-related diplomacy as reflecting personal whims of a given administration. On stylistic grounds, RGA initiatives were more likely to involve closed-door information exchange than bombastic public events featuring high-level appointees and large crowds.

In sum, in mid-2016, RGA faced some uncertainty, but one thing was fairly clearcut: it showed little trace of either the ideological or structural features of populism. If anything, whether in diplomatic engagements that spotlighted European anti-Semitism and Islamophobia, or in a structure that privileged academic expertise and under-the-radar engagement, it was precisely the type of office that may have attracted populist suspicion.

THE ORDINARY UNCERTAINTY OF FALL 2016

This chapter has described the RGA office as a project that began to crystallize in the summer of 2016. Building from very little existing infrastructure, RGA leadership had structured an office of roughly thirty staff, blending career officials, political appointees, and wandering academic experts. RGA leadership seemed correct to predict that "the question we're pursuing is not why, or if, but *how* the State Department should be engaging religious actors and assessing religious dynamics."[52] With that said, there were remaining questions, after three years of existence, that loomed about the future of the RGA model in the face of the transition to any new presidential administration. Two were essentially questions of bureaucratic design: RGA's long-term location within the State Department's organizational chart and the balance between political appointees and career officials within the office. A final question touched on the relationship between RGA and other offices tasked with religion and diplomacy at State.

Probably the most obvious question about RGA's future related to its location within the arcane, but important, org chart of the State Department. For its first several years in existence, RGA was located within the secretary's bureau of offices (or "S Bureau"), which granted the office close proximity to key decision-makers on the State Department's 7th Floor. This signaled to outside partners that RGA represented a priority for the Kerry State Department and provided RGA leadership and staff easier access to key political appointees and the Policy Planning Staff. However, a new secretary, post-election, would likely bring distinct priorities to the S Bureau, so a move for RGA after its incubation phase was always likely.

Former RGA Senior Advisor Peter Mandaville argued that such a shift would not only be likely, but in many ways desirable for RGA's long-term viability. He contended that "much of State's permanent bureaucracy regards [offices like RGA] as non-essential, 'boutique' functions or as the pet projects of whoever happens to be secretary at any given time. These offices often find themselves having to work very hard to attract attention, resources, and buy-in from the core bureaucracy."[53]

Both internal staff and those outside of government floated various pragmatic futures for the RGA enterprise. Some essentially prized continuity, arguing that the benefits of S Bureau affiliation outweighed potential costs. Mandaville advocated a move into the highest levels of another bureau, then known as the Undersecretariat of Civilian Security and Global Affairs, which directed diplomacy in many of the functional areas where RGA had most successfully demonstrated its value. On this model, RGA would move closer to offices responsible for issues like conflict stabilization, trafficking in persons, and refugee resettlement. Others agreed that a shift into the guts of the bureaucracy could be helpful, but instead argued for embedding staffers with religious engagement responsibilities within the department's regional bureaus. These regional bureaus represent the lion's share of diplomatic personnel, in Washington, D.C. and in posts around the world, so the goal of devolving responsibility for engagement within those bureaus was to put RGA's work closer to the diplomatic front line. While these debates had real stakes, all shared a belief that RGA's approach to assessment and engagement had shown value across three years and would continue in some form.

A related, but distinct, set of questions centered on the balance between political appointees and career staff in conducting the work of religious engagement. Much like RGA's initial location within the S Bureau, the decision to place multiple political appointees within RGA, including its leadership under the special representative for RGA, was initially intended to signal the importance of RGA's work to State Department leadership, and to, therefore, empower that leadership with access to the resources and symbolic support of high-profile department leaders. This prominence of political leadership would then facilitate ties outside of the department, such as the White House's faith-based office and even, ultimately, the inclusion of senior officials like Chief of Staff Denis McDonough in RGA's Religion and Diplomacy Conference in late 2016.

With that said, extensive political leadership could come with costs as well. Like the office's location in the S Bureau, being top-heavy with political appointees risked isolating RGA from the career staff of the department, as well as opening it up to diminished continuity of leadership over time and, even in a smooth transition, the delays often associated with vetting and appointing the thousands of political positions in a new administration.

Here, choices essentially revolved around two decision points: how many of the four leadership roles to maintain within RGA and how many of those roles ought to be filled with political appointees. In terms of the four roles within RGA, several had distinct missions. The SEOIC related to a multilateral, intergovernmental organization, which Mandaville argued should fall under the remit of the department's Bureau of International Organization Affairs. The SRMC represented an initiative of Hillary Clinton's State Department, and while broadly related to religious engagement, was unique in its focus on a particular religious community (rather than world region or functional area). And the SEAS was charged with assessment and engagement, to be sure, but also human rights advocacy that may have been more similar to work done by State's Bureau of Democracy, Human Rights, and Labor.

RGA leadership raised a related question. The office was founded under the leadership of a political appointee, Shaun Casey, who maintained a long-standing relationship with Secretary Kerry. RGA's growth reflected the political priority that the Obama White House put on professionalizing faith-based centers in executive branch agencies. However, should political leadership be the default setting for effective religious engagement? Casey himself argued that career leadership, rather than a political appointee, would make sense after a founding period "to resist any pressure to transform the office into a partisan shop."[54] This, written after the 2017 election, could perhaps be perceived as an election-influenced statement. But the arguments did not only come from appointees. As Mandaville agreed, "having a career diplomat running the show would help to emphasize the idea that RGA's approach is first and foremost utilitarian" while perhaps "overcome[ing] some of the skepticism within the State Department about whether the religious engagement function actually adds value to the diplomatic mission." In late 2016, it remained to be seen what the future would hold for RGA's directorship. One near certainty was that some career staffer would take on an "acting" role as special representative, in keeping with precedent during presidential transitions across a range of offices.

A final set of questions centered on the relationship between RGA and the other portions of Bettiza's regime complex dealing with religion in the State Department, particularly offices associated with international religious freedom (IRF) and counterterrorism (CT)/countering violent extremism (CVE). Both of those other bureaucratic streams were intimately tied to religion in their work, and yet each operated independently, by design, from RGA's broader engagement and assessment mandate.[55] Some argued that RGA and IRF should be combined, although it remained unclear which political appointees would ultimately be in charge of the hybrid office. Former IRF staffer Judd Birdsall argued, instead, that RGA and IRF represented "distinct yet overlapping" approaches, which could be "coordinated but not combined."[56] There was no single, political violence office to subsume RGA within, but there was certainly the possibility of restricting RGA's broader engagement agenda to a narrower focus on questions of terrorism and extremism. RGA staff repeatedly emphasized that, in their assessment, religion was rarely either the only or primary driver for violent extremism, and that earlier dichotomies between "moderate" and "extremist" Islam were analytically problematic and generated self-defeating policy responses. Notwithstanding efforts to advance these arguments both internally and in public outlets, there was a real risk in late 2016 that, whatever the election's result, it would become more difficult to maintain RGA's distinction from IRF and CVE in a new administration.

Without underestimating these areas of uncertainty, RGA staff were in the thick of their work in fall 2016, less concerned with the future of the office post-election than with securing approval for travel to post for a religious conflict assessment or exploring the possibility of partnering with a new functional bureau to examine opportunities for religious engagement in their work. My notes from the last, pre-election RGA all-staff meeting only reference the election obliquely, noting that State Department officials had been designated to liaise with whichever incoming landing team in the post-election transition. Other takeaways involved checking with colleagues in IRF on a future engagement proposal and updates from the African Affairs Bureau meeting on upcoming initiatives tied to governance and elections. In what reads now like a piece of foreshadowing, I noted that I should be sure to order a recently released academic volume on the intersection of religion and populist politics.

PART II

THE POPULIST DIFFERENCE

3

"THE FAITH OF THE ADMINISTRATION"

Populist Ideology, Religion, and Foreign Policy

On February 27, 2018, a reporter asked White House Press Secretary Sarah Huckabee Sanders about the administration's plans for governmental institutions related to religion, including foreign policy offices like the Office of Religion and Global Affairs (RGA). "The President's two immediate predecessors did a lot to build and expand the faith-based programs within the White House and throughout the executive branch of government . . . It has been said that this President has not followed through on that . . . Your reaction?"[1] Sanders's response perfectly captured the changes that one year in office had brought to religion in the Trump administration, including the foreign policy bureaucracy: "Look, I don't think an office is what determines the faith of the administration . . . I think we probably have, actually, more people, front and center, speaking openly about their faith."[2]

I now move from documenting a relative equilibrium point in late 2016 to assessing the impact of the Trump administration's populism on the process, rhetoric, and substance of religion and U.S. foreign policy. The reporter's question above invoked Gregorio Bettiza's "postsecular regime complex."[3] Sanders helpfully points out that the reporter is not quite asking the right question. What is important is the amorphous "faith of the administration," and an informal set of personal relationships tied to the person of the president. The administration might choose to "build on that foundation" of existing bureaucratic offices, but that should not be the only place where change is measured. Religion in foreign policy-related settings would shift from an implement of postsecular statecraft to a tool of populist governance.

In the next two chapters, I document the observable consequences of the Trump administration's populism on the public rhetoric, bureaucratic offices, and policy outcomes tied to religion and U.S. foreign policy. In sum, I argue that it is unhelpful to ask whether the Trump administration made foreign policy "more" or "less" religious. Instead, understanding Trump-era variation requires accounting for the administration's populism. Religion in foreign policy was a central, but underanalyzed, avenue for pursuing the dual dimensions of populist political strategy summarized in chapter 1: defining identity boundaries and developing a personalistic structure of power. Parts of the bureaucracy thrived while others withered, but all were subject to the same logic of populist governance.

As chapter 1 explored in general terms, the comparative study of populism has generated a significant recent body of scholarship, particularly focused on recent growth of right-wing populist parties in Europe.[4] Distinct definitions of populism coexist in this scholarship, with some highlighting populism's "thin ideology" focused on protecting "the people,"[5] and others arguing for a "political-strategic approach" to populism that focuses on "personalistic" governance based on "direct, uninstitutionalized support" from followers.[6] While religion was often peripheral to initial studies of populism, there has been a newfound appreciation that populists may "hijack religion" in various ways to suit their interests.[7] This scholarship largely emphasizes one understanding of populism, focused on a thin ideology where religion plays a part in defining identity boundaries between in-groups and out-groups. Other scholars, adopting a more political-strategic approach, emphasize the structure of populist governance, where personalist ties predominate, and loyalists reject constraint from existing political institutions. Each of these dimensions of populism comes with observable implications for religion in U.S. foreign policy, but in distinct ways.

This chapter takes up the first of those dimensions: the impact of populism's thin ideology on the rhetoric and substance of religion and Trump administration foreign policy. Identity construction was in part rhetorical, so official remarks and policy framing provide relevant evidence of its operation. However, this chapter demonstrates that this rhetoric was not merely cheap talk, but also motivated concrete change in policy, diplomatic engagement, and even funding decisions related to religion and foreign policy.

The institutional equilibrium discussed earlier in the book conceived of religion as a tool of statecraft, whether that term was viewed approvingly, critically, or simply empirically. In contrast, religion in Trump administration foreign policy served populism's overwhelming focus on the personalistic power of the leader to represent a chosen people.

POPULISM'S THIN IDEOLOGY AND FOREIGN POLICY

Populists come to power promising to embody "the people" and vindicate them in the face of threats to their sovereignty. As Margaret Canovan summarizes, "Their *raison d'être* is an appeal to 'the people' against that people's supposed representatives."[8] This understanding of populism is ideological, to an extent, but a peculiar type of thin ideology that lacks the comprehensive nature of more programmatic political theories like socialism or liberalism.[9] As such, populists may draw flexibly on "contextually hospitable 'full' ideologies" in campaigns and governance.[10] While populists may draw their ideological boundaries in varied ways, they share a "distinct pattern" in which a polity is divided "into two opposed and antagonistic groups" with "normative and moral legitimacy" resting only on the people, and, via them, the populist leader.[11] This majoritarianism binds loyalists directly to the populist leader, while simultaneously excluding potential rivals. Twin dimensions of populism as thin ideology stand out: defining the people as a homogenous group, and excluding "outsiders," both "elites" in political and economic leadership, and "dangerous others" threatening the people's sovereignty and voice.[12]

First, at the core of studying populism as ideology is the in-group definition of the people, which Jan-Werner Müller identifies as providing the "particular moralistic imagination" of populists.[13] The people are characterized by purity and innocence, and the populist promises to vindicate their moral claim to sovereignty. "The people" is "a construction," not naturally existing, but its artificial nature does not undercut its power to generate "a shared identity between different groups."[14] This fusion of majoritarian politics with morality helps to explain why "nobody has the right to bypass the popular will," even if this involves violations of liberal rights guarantees.[15] The people may be defined in a variety of ways; recent populists have drawn on ethnic, linguistic, racial, religious, and class-based understandings of political membership. The compatibility of such diverse definitions of the people may explain why populists routinely turn to more comprehensive ideologies to complement their populist appeals, whether defining the people in class terms in Latin American cases or in terms of religious identity in places like India.

Second, an ideology focused on empowering the people also rests on multiple levels of exclusion. Populists enter into confrontation with the most direct constraint on popular sovereignty: established political elites. Elites must be identified as distinct from the people, but also "denigrated" as "antagonists of the people . . . condemning them for the identities and interests they represent."[16] As Cas Mudde and Cristóbal Kaltwasser put it, this distinction is "essentially moral," not merely about material interests.[17] Canovan argues that this rejection of elites attacks them "not only as established power-holders, but also elite values," thus drawing populists into conflict, not only with political elites, but also their allies in media and society more broadly.[18] Because of populism's contextual character, the targets of its anti-elitism vary in practice. Donald Trump and his allies railed against the "deep state" that they characterized as "disloyal and undemocratic."[19] Recent European populists have attacked institutions of the European Union, along with more particular targets like Hungarian President Viktor Orbán's obsession with George Soros. In the Philippines, Rodrigo Duterte attacked international human rights bodies threatening to investigate human rights violations associated with his drug war. However defined, identifying this hostile elite is central to thin ideological accounts of populism's rise.

As an additional component of exclusion, populism's thin ideology emphasizes threats to the virtuous people from communities of "others" who supposedly reject the people's identity and sovereignty. At its core, Müller describes populism as "antipluralist" with this exclusion in mind: "any remainder can be dismissed as immoral and not properly a part of the people at all."[20] Such others may be internal or external to national borders, but are united by "identity, behavior or beliefs [that] preclude them from being considered part of the natural community formed by the people."[21] The presence of such others is central to the populist need to construct a "heroic mission" to "combat dangerous adversaries."[22] These others promise "invasion, infiltration, contagion, conspiracy, replacement and impending irreversible crisis" in populist ideology.[23] In cases of right-wing populism across Europe, Muslim communities, particularly refugees tied to flight from the Syrian civil war, have exemplified this threat. Migration figured in Trump's populist rise as well, with Central American immigrants providing Trump with what William Howell and Terry Moe identify as "precisely the kind of foreign threat that every strongman conjures up to incite populist anger."[24] Duterte has constructed drug users as his own threatening out-group, while populists in Poland have targeted sexual minorities, among others.[25]

These features of populism as thin ideology come with numerous observable implications for the rhetoric and substance of foreign policy. Populism's need to define an in-group of the people in thin ideological terms resonates with a significant body of "second image" international relations research on how essentially domestic variables,[26] frequently attached to ideology of political parties, may drive variation in foreign policy behavior.[27] Much of this literature rested on a left-right partisan distinction in liberal democracies, but other work has pushed the study of domestic ideology into a more diverse set of countries, for instance Peter Henne's examination of regime legitimacy tied to the representation of political Islam.[28] Thorsten Wojczewski emphasizes that populist foreign policy does not simply tap into essentialized political communities, but "construct[s] a collective identity of 'the people' by linking together different (unmet) social demands."[29] Even before consideration of religion, the Trump administration's in-group boundaries came with clear implications for the substance of foreign policy. Most obviously, Trump and his officials consistently justified protectionist trade policy, whether stepping away from international agreements like NAFTA or imposing tariffs on additional categories of goods, as "making sure *our* companies and jobs stay in *our* [emphasis added] country."[30]

Anti-elite exclusion, which is "inherent in populism but need not be present in nationalism," comes with distinct foreign policy implications. This may be closest to the surface in contexts of strong regional

integration. For instance, European right-wing populists regularly deni-
grate the European Union for failing to protect the sovereignty of the
people and being in thrall to unaccountable elites. As Bertjan Verbeek
and Andrej Zaslove note, because populist ideology is thin, it may at
times defend unique forms of international integration. For example,
some Latin American populists attempt to use regionalism to oppose
neoliberalism.[31] However, such efforts would still be anti-elite in nature,
in the Latin American case rejecting the dominance of elite-driven,
U.S.-controlled transnational capitalism. Corina Lacatus shows how
anti-elite rhetoric suffused the style of Trump communication via social
media regarding foreign policy decisions tied to economics, alliances,
and migration.[32]

The additional dimension of populism's exclusion, its fixation on
threatening others, comes with similar implications for the foreign policy process. If populists construct out-groups as existential dangers to the
people, and those groups stretch across borders, the impacts on foreign
policy become readily apparent. This brings the study of populism into
conversation with longer-standing international relations debates about
threat perception and foreign policy, particularly scholarship that attempts
to integrate constructivist ideas about identity and norms into the study
of threat.[33] In Europe, this has meant right-wing populist parties that
"close ranks against multiculturalism at home and alien threats from
abroad."[34] Analysts have noted the "search for enemies" in Trump administration foreign policy, especially in the realm of counterterrorism,
which I discuss in more depth later, as it relates to religion's place in Trump
foreign policy.[35] Inflated threat perception from immigrant communities
was also a regular feature of Trump campaign rhetoric and his later governing strategy at the border.

In sum, populism's ideology is thin, but features a recurrent combination of inclusion and exclusion: advocacy for the people and rejection of
both elites and threatening outsiders. Table 3.1 summarizes these patterns,
their observable implication in foreign policy, and likely evidence tied to
religion. It is important to note that the thinness of populist ideology
means that it is characterized by "openness" and "contestability," rather
than providing rigorous constraint on the populist.[36] While the populist
leader depicts identity boundaries as enduring, this is a "façade," masking
"the essence of populism, which revolves around top-down leadership."[37]

TABLE 3.1 Thin Ideology, Foreign Policy, and Religion

	Dimension of Thin Ideology	Foreign Policy Observable Implications	Illustration Tied to Religion
Inclusion: Define In-Group	Define "the people" to generate shared identity and justify populist leadership claims.	Rhetoric of identity construction in foreign policy contexts. Policy goals aligned with interests of "the people."	IRF framing of the United States as nation of believers. Expansion of Mexico City policy.
Exclusion: Elites and Outside Threats	Identify elites responsible for limitations on "the people," justifying populist rejection. Identify out-groups responsible for threats to "the people," justifying populist heroic mission.	Threat assessments reflecting out-group targets. Rhetoric justifying security responses to preserve "the people." Political appointments tied to out-group exclusion.	Travel restrictions and refugee limits impacting Muslim-majority countries. Targeted sanctions on leftist governments responsible for religious freedom violations.

As such, we should expect religion's role in populist boundary construction to be inconsistent and flexible, in response to the political needs of the populist, rather than rigidly bound by ideological dictates.

RELIGION, "THE PEOPLE," AND TRUMP FOREIGN POLICY

Turning more directly to religion, if Walter Russell Mead is correct that Trumpism represents the latest version of Jacksonian populism in U.S. foreign policy, what did religion have to do with defining the people?[38] In short, foreign policy presented multiple opportunities to reinforce a role for religion in defining the populist community, although as is often the case, the criterion for membership shifted to meet populist needs. On the one hand, at the "Values Voters Summit" in 2019, Trump would define America to conservative supporters as an inclusive "nation of faith," distinguished because, "We don't worship government, we worship god."[39] On this standard, only secularists seem to fall outside of the political community, a contrast to some Northern European populists that Rogers Brubaker analyzes.[40] Later in the same address, however, the role of Christianity as first among equals in the political community stands out, whether in claims that "America was built by families and pilgrims," or that "[pastors] are the ones we want to hear from."[41] This flexibility occurred regularly in Trump's rhetorical in-group construction, and became observable in his administration's foreign policy decision-making.

This seeming contradiction is quite consistent with the fickle nature of populist ideology. Christianity was not necessary for membership in the political community, although it seemed to occupy privileged status. Many scholars, especially those who focus on the domestic scene, have argued that Trumpism reflected a "fusion" of Christianity and U.S. nationalism that scholars have come to term "Christian nationalism."[42] Without denying the importance of white Christianity to Trump's domestic support, this offers a too rigid account of religious identity boundaries and Trump foreign policy. Trump and his allies regularly maintained creative flexibility about the extent to which a "nation of believers" could also incorporate those of other religious traditions, most commonly Judaism but also, perhaps, religions beyond the Judeo-Christian tradition.[43] This flexibility illustrates the thinness of populist ideology, able to bend in response to the populist's whims in distinct settings.

Rhetoric constructing America as a nation of Christians and/or believers appeared regularly in foreign policy contexts. Trump, for instance, defined America as a nation of believers in 2018 remarks to an international audience at the National Prayer Breakfast, and Vice President Pence used a speech at the State Department's 2018 Ministerial to Advance Religious Freedom to similarly define America as "a nation of faith."[44] Secretary of State Mike Pompeo adopted explicitly civilizational framing in linking the United States to "fundamental moorings of the Judeo-Christian tradition . . . the foundational ideas that have made this civilization, this country here, so unique and so special."[45] Certain White House advisors went even further, with Steve Bannon, for example, remarking in a 2014 address to a Catholic group that "the Judeo-Christian West is in a crisis," which could only be addressed by "bind[ing] together and really form[ing] what I feel is an aspect of the church militant."[46] Again, while this rhetoric was often generic in its defense of "religion," the veil occasionally slipped, as in 2020 when Trump remarked at the National Prayer Breakfast: "We are going to protect *our* [emphasis added] religions. We are going to protect Christianity."[47]

While conservative Christians certainly represented many of the individuals and groups most directly incorporated by such rhetoric, membership in Trump's conception of the people was not consistently exclusive to Christians. This was most apparent in his warm relations with certain members of the American Jewish community, and in particular, his regular references to the fact that "the Jewish faith is a cherished part of our family," via his daughter and son-in-law.[48] When denouncing anti-Semitic violence, Trump clearly constructed America's Jews as part of the political community: "With one heart, America weeps for the lives lost." Of course, ever the personalist, Trump noted the "Trump yarmulke" of an attendee at one Hanukkah reception approvingly. Islam took on a much more contentious place in the definition of the American people, at times formally excluded, while at others uncomfortably acknowledged. When Trump reinstated the White House Ramadan iftar in 2018, he spent significantly more time discussing foreign diplomatic representatives in the room than he did members of the Muslim American community.[49]

The malleable entry of religion into populist in-group construction showed through in what an *Atlantic* reporter termed the "excellent Abrahamic adventure" referenced in this book's introduction: President Trump's first international trip as president, to Saudi Arabia. The public centerpiece of that trip was a summit meeting of heads of state from what President Trump called "Muslim nations" to launch an "Islamic Center for Countering Extremism."[50] In some ways, the initiative was unremarkable. The United States has funded other international centers to counter radicalization and has long had close relations with Saudi Arabia. But Trump's remarks were suffused with language reinforcing religion's role in defining the American people. Trump defined his goal as "a hopeful future that does honor to God," and calls for "celebrat[ing] tolerance and mutual respect once again" among "Christians, Muslims and Jews."

At the same time, consistent with the ambiguity over the extent to which the people truly includes all faiths, in a speech to "the Islamic World," Trump never mentions Muslims as members of the American political community.

This intentional ambiguity about the inclusivity of religion in defining the populist in-group not only appeared in populist rhetoric, but also the substance of several prominent policy decisions, including the relocation of the U.S. Embassy in Israel from Tel Aviv to Jerusalem. While the decision was of obvious importance to the Jewish-American community, rhetoric about the move touched on a broader project of identity construction, including its ambiguous pluralism. Some prominent Jewish-American associations like the Anti-Defamation League enthusiastically endorsed the decision, while public opinion among American Jews was more mixed, with several liberal Jewish-American organizations expressing nuanced responses, frequently focused on the long-term desirability of a two-state solution.[51] Trump's remarks announcing the move adopted the general Abrahamic framing seen in the Saudi Arabia address, referring to Jerusalem as "the heart of three great religions" and praising Israel as "a country where Jews, Muslims, and Christians, and people of all faiths are free to live and worship."[52]

But there was reason to doubt the truly inclusive nature of these appeals. At the embassy's dedication ceremony itself, the administration featured remarks not only from politicians and diplomats, but American pastors with a history of contentious comments about Judaism (as well as other religious minorities)—Pastors John Hagee and Robert Jeffress. Jeffress, an early Trump loyalist, claimed in 2010 that Mormonism, Islam, and Judaism "lead people to an eternity of separation from God in hell," a claim that seems to be in some tension with the idea of shared membership in the populist in-group.[53] Later, Trump remarked at a campaign rally that he made the decision "for the evangelicals," who were "more excited by that than Jewish people," a claim he later repeated in an interview with Mike Huckabee.[54] As always, what remains fixed about populist ideology is that it must involve enthusiastic loyalty to the person of the populist leader.

This rhetorical construction of the religious people moved from speeches to policy most clearly in a series of socially conservative foreign policy steps related to gender and sexuality. These steps came with direct implications for the portions of the religious bureaucracy involved in development partnerships related to religious interests. Social conservatives occupied prominent spots in the Trump administration delegation to the United Nations' Commission on the Status of Women, where references to "sexual and reproductive health" in draft resolutions were struck on several occasions after reservations from American diplomats.[55] The Trump administration expanded the Mexico City Policy, applying it not only to the relatively limited foreign assistance funding focused on family planning, but to all public health foreign assistance.[56] This, in practice, could impact some of the largest sectors of foreign assistance tied to faith-based organizations, including the billions in spending related to the PEPFAR program to combat HIV/AIDS outside of the United States. Trump appointees at USAID and the CDC expressed a desire to increase the share of U.S. public health assistance that was targeted directly to local religious institutions, including announcing $100 million in additional faith-based funding via PEPFAR.[57] Tensions extended into diverse corners of foreign assistance, with Acting USAID Administrator John Barsa writing a sharp letter to UN Secretary General Antonio Guterres expressing outrage that the UN's Global Humanitarian Response Plan to COVID-19 "cynically plac[es] the provision of 'sexual and reproductive health services' on the same level of importance as food-insecurity, essential health care, malnutrition, shelter and sanitation."[58] In each of these instances, conservative Christian status as first among equals in the populist community translated into policy influence and even bureaucratized funding processes.

Promotion of international religious freedom (IRF) also clearly showed the populist priority on identity construction. Existing bureaucratic raw material proved useful at reinforcing boundary construction, and elements of the religion regime complex received extensive attention from populist officials. In an administration marked by vacant political appointments across the diplomatic establishment, Ambassador-at-Large for International Religious Freedom Sam Brownback was initially nominated at a comparatively brisk speed, in summer 2017. At a time when Secretary of State Tillerson eliminated several specialized portfolios related to religion and foreign policy, the IRF office retained its special advisor for religious minorities in the Near East and South/Central Asia. In May 2017, Vice President Pence attended Franklin Graham's World

Summit in Defense of Persecuted Christians. There were hiccups, notably Brownback's contentious nomination languishing for months in the Senate before confirmation. But from the early months of the administration, attention to religious freedom outpaced other aspects of religion in the bureaucracy.

The pace of these initiatives accelerated with the transition to Secretary of State Pompeo, who launched multiple diplomatic forays focused on IRF promotion. Chief among these was the "Ministerial to Advance Religious Freedom," a high-level diplomatic meeting held in 2018 and 2019 in and around the State Department's Foggy Bottom headquarters and slated for expansion to regional IRF conferences before the outbreak of COVID-19. IRF-related diplomacy touched on sensitive U.S. strategic relationships, such as the release of imprisoned pastor Andrew Brunson in Turkey. It arose in the deteriorating U.S.-China relationship, with IRF-related "Global Magnitsky" human rights sanctions applied to Chinese entities implicated in the country's repression of Uyghur Muslims.[59] Attention to IRF extended to the National Security Council, where staffing responsibilities for the issue grew in novel ways.[60] IRF promotion motivated the launch of an International Religious Freedom Alliance, a U.S.-backed coalition of several dozen countries "predicated on the idea more must be done to protect members of religious minority groups and combat discrimination and persecution based on religion or belief."[61] The June 2020 Executive Order (EO) 13926, "Advancing International Religious Freedom," consolidated many of these trends, instructing State Department and USAID officials to "prioritize IRF in the planning and implementation of U.S. foreign policy and in foreign assistance programs," expand the provision of IRF training, and consider economic tools including sanctions in IRF promotion.[62]

Critics have observed, with some justification, that Trump administration IRF initiatives were inconsistently applied and impossible to square with the administration's broader record of demonizing Muslim communities.[63] Others have argued that Trump administration IRF initiatives seem "prioritized . . . according to Judeo-Christian values."[64] These observations are entirely consistent with the source of populist attention to IRF in the foreign policy bureaucracy: in-group construction simultaneously defending Christianity and all of "the faithful."

This priority is shown repeatedly in rhetoric related to IRF from key administration officials. In remarks to the IRF Ministerial in 2019, Secretary Pompeo referred to religious freedom as "deeply embedded in the American character," and IRF promotion as a "distinctly American responsibility" when releasing the 2018 IRF report.[65] Vice President Pence similarly asserted, "America is a nation of faith," at the 2018 IRF Ministerial, before (tellingly) closing with a call for "Faith in our President."[66] USAID Administrator Mark Green claimed religious freedom as "an essential part of our national self-identity," and "one of America's greatest gifts to human civilization."[67] IRF Ambassador Brownback referred to it as "a backbone, a fundamental issue for us." The special status of Christianity in the populist in-group also stood out in these remarks. Addressing IRF at an event at the United Nations, President Trump made it clear that these initiatives were about defining an in-group with special status, based on his personal discretion: "We can now listen to the people that we want to listen to." And again, in remarks to the conservative Values Voter Summit, Trump "pledg[ed] our support to Christian communities everywhere suffering under the brutal heel of oppression and violence."[68]

In this ambiguous inclusion, IRF advocacy resembled an additional area where religion and foreign policy contributed to defining in-group boundaries: Pompeo's Commission on Unalienable Rights. The Commission is described in more detail in chapter 4, because its structure and workings provide evidence of the personalistic dimension of populism in action. However, its mission and content were also linked to the construction of an idealized, morally pure people represented by the Trump administration. In discussing the Commission's works, Pompeo stated his goal as "return[ing] America's understanding of human rights . . . back to the fundamental moorings of the Judeo-Christian tradition on which this country was founded . . . the foundational ideas that have made this civilization, this country here, so unique."[69] In his remarks at the launch of the Commission's report, Pompeo continued in this vein, insisting that core rights were "a deeply Biblical idea," and that "America is fundamentally good." This was consistent with Pompeo's remarks in Cairo in 2019 asserting "America's innate goodness" in dealing with Middle Eastern countries.[70]

RELIGION AND POPULIST EXCLUSION:
DEFINING THREATENING OUTSIDERS

Populism's thin ideology centers on distinctions that the populist draws between the people and excluded out-groups.[71] This division binds loyalists directly to the populist leader, while excluding potential rivals of diverse stripes. Leading scholars of populism highlight that this exclusion takes place along both an anti-elite axis as well as, particularly for right-wing populists like Trump, the exclusion of "threatening others . . . whose identity, behavior, or beliefs preclude them from being considered part of the natural community formed by the people."[72] If the Trump administration instrumentalized religion in foreign policy to define the people, religion also featured centrally in rhetoric and policy substance related to out-group exclusion.

Populists ground exclusion in elevated threat from groups seeking to challenge the legitimate sovereignty of the people. In the case of the Trump administration and foreign policy, this was most evident in threats, domestic and foreign, supposedly posed by Muslims.[73] This religiously-inflected identity cleavage featured heavily on the 2016 campaign trail, and indeed in Trump's earliest political forays into "birther" conspiracies about President Barack Obama. His grim 2017 inaugural address resolved to "unite the civilized world against radical Islamic terrorism."[74] The religious nature of the people grounded exclusions beyond Islam as well, with Trump pledging protection against "the horrors of communism and socialism" to evangelical supporters at the 2019 Values Voters Summit.[75] Identifying a similar set of domestic enemies, Attorney General Bob Barr decried "militant secularists" for their "unremitting assault on religion," in remarks at the University of Notre Dame in 2019.[76] The people faced existential threats explicitly couched in religious terms, whether from the forces of radical Islamic terrorism or godless secularism. While Trump administration exclusion in foreign policy was not limited to Islam and secular elites, it was most readily observable there, across diverse portions of the religion and foreign policy regime complex.

In the administration's early months, officials reinforcing this definition of threats to the people assumed various foreign policy positions in the White House, from the (short-lived) term of National Security Advisor Michael Flynn to more vaguely defined advisory roles for officials like

Steve Bannon and Sebastian Gorka. Each of these officials had clearly expressed views consistent with predicting civilizational clash, particularly between the West and Islam. As Bannon remarked in his 2014 address, "We are in an outright war against jihadist Islamic fascism."[77] This framing of the populist project crept into the rhetoric and policy documents of those at the heights of the Trump administration foreign policy apparatus. The State Department's head of Policy Planning remarked that America's strategic approach to China should be grounded in a recognition that this represents "a fight with a really different civilization," and "the first time that we will have a great power competitor that is not Caucasian."[78]

Identity-based exclusion translated into several substantive changes in religion and U.S. foreign policy. This was most evident in the earliest months of the Trump administration in official rhetoric and policy outcomes tied to three intertwined foreign policy initiatives: redefinition of counterterrorism policy, various executive orders that came to be known as "Muslim Bans," and President Trump's spring 2017 "Abrahamic" mission to Saudi Arabia, Israel, the Palestinian Territories, and the Vatican.

Populist rhetoric of religious exclusion altered framing of U.S. counterterrorism policy. The Trump administration's counterterrorism policy was consistently couched in religious terms from the campaign trail through its early months in office. In February 2017, multiple sources confirmed that administration officials proposed changing the broadly framed "Countering Violent Extremism" (CVE) agenda as "Countering Islamic Extremism" or "Countering Radical Islamic Extremism."[79] In the same time period, administration officials drafted orders aimed at designating the Muslim Brotherhood as a Foreign Terrorist Organization (FTO), a step which could have had broad impacts on Muslim entities in the United States and abroad due to the Muslim Brotherhood's diffuse organization.[80] Even cabinet officials seen as relative moderates engaged in this framing, with Secretary-Designate Tillerson devoting a portion of his opening confirmation-hearing statement before the Senate Foreign Relations Committee to the urgency of "thwarting radical Islam," not only in military confrontation with ISIS but also "win[ning] the war of ideas" within Islam itself.[81]

As the Trump administration drafted its National Security Strategy (NSS) later in 2017, the Policy Planning Office at the State Department put forward a memo advising that the United States engage in "ideological competition" to advance an "Islamic Reformation" particularly centered on instrumentalizing "women and youth."[82] While this inflammatory proposal did not make it to the final NSS, the administration's 2018 National Strategy for Counterterrorism is rife with references to the "twisted ideology" that roots "radical Islamist terrorist groups," and the need for the United States to "combat violent extremist ideologies" by "demonstrate[ing] that their claims are false."[83] This obsession even influenced relatively pro forma diplomatic interactions related to religion. The White House, for instance, issued a 2017 message on Ramadan that focused primarily on "defeat[ing] terrorists and their perverted ideology," rather than customary holiday greetings.[84]

High-level policy statements like the National Strategy for Counterterrorism set the stage for more tangible policy initiatives. Among the most visible examples of the populist bid to define identity cleavage driving actual policy change is the set of executive orders grouped together as a "Muslim Ban." As with rhetorical attacks on "Islamic extremism," this began on the campaign trail, with Trump's 2015 call at a campaign rally for "a total and complete shutdown of Muslims entering the United States."[85] Shortly after Inauguration Day, draft executive orders began circulating that contained various forms of restrictions on foreign access to the United States, particularly from Muslim-majority countries. In its original January 2017 form, Executive Order 13769 explicitly argued that "the United States cannot and should not admit . . . those who would place violent ideologies over American law," while also excluding advocates of "honor killings" and "persecution of those who practice religions different from their own." Earlier drafts promised "uniform screening standards" that would identify such individuals.[86] For a period, the initial EO halted the U.S. Refugee Admissions Program entirely, and then reopened resettlement while again largely excluding Muslims by "prioritize[ing] refugee claims made by individuals on the basis of religious-based persecution, provided that the religion of the individual is a minority religion in the individual's country of nationality." The visa and refugee restrictions, along with the exceptions to those general rules, made it crystal clear that these orders rested on an understanding of the boundaries of the American political community deeply tied to religiosity, and particularly skeptical of Muslim inclusion. Responses to these "Muslim Bans," from courts and career officials, receive additional attention later in the book. At this stage, they serve as a clear indicator that religion and foreign policy served as a tool of populist out-group exclusion.

The role of Islam and populist exclusion showed through again in the 2017 Saudi Arabia address noted earlier. First, throughout the speech, Trump made efforts to construct an idea of "the Muslim world" outside of the West, and Saudi Arabia's place at the center of it.[87] This external Muslim world is why Trump "[is] not here to lecture—to tell other people how to live, what to do, or who to be."[88] "America will not seek to impose our way of life on others," but rather provide security assistance for "Muslim nations [to] take the lead" in policing the internal boundaries of "the Islamic World."

Second, the speech is rife with exclusionary denunciations of vaguely defined terrorist threats, very much in keeping with the broader exclusionary approach to Islam in Trump administration security policy. Terrorist groups need to be "driven out . . . like the plague" from "your communities . . . your holy land." "Death cults" must be excluded, not only from military action, but also from "your houses of worship" and madrassa networks. These are "brutal merchants of death who falsely invoke God's name," representing a "vile creed" spilling "streams of innocent blood soaked into the ancient ground." "This is a battle between good and evil," Trump continued, which allows "no coexistence." To those who would disagree, the populist not only promises a kinetic military response, but also that "your soul will be condemned." Commenting on the souls of opponents may seem outside the ambit of traditional foreign policy but is quite consistent with the cosmic stakes of populist exclusion.

Populism's exclusionary dimension further showed through in IRF-related appointments, rhetoric, and partners. USAID International Religious Freedom Advisor Mark Kevin Lloyd, "made anti-Muslim statements on social media, calling Islam a 'barbaric cult,' " prompting calls from both the House and Senate to investigate his hiring.[89] The IRF Ministerial garnered praise from noted Islamophobes like Frank Gaffney, and the IRF Alliance attracted support from populist countries committed to visions of international order centered on exclusive civilizational clash, notably Hungary and Poland. Beyond Islam, IRF featured heavily in exclusionary framing of several global leftist governments. Trump administration confrontations with governments in Cuba, Nicaragua, and Venezuela were justified in terms of the threats that the government in each case posed to religious freedom.[90] At the 2018 Ministerial to Advance Religious Freedom, to give one example, Vice President Pence lambasted Nicaragua's Ortega government for being "virtually at war" with the Catholic Church.[91] Similar dynamics regularly featured in Trump administration rhetoric and policy related to its confrontation with China. Ambassador-at-Large for IRF Brownback most notably delivered extensive remarks in Hong Kong in 2019 in which he accused the Chinese government of being "at war with faith . . . a war they will not win."[92]

RELIGION, FOREIGN POLICY, AND DOMESTIC EXCLUSION

Populism's thin ideology serves goals that are ultimately domestic in nature: securing the power of the populist politician. This explains why the international exclusion documented so far in this chapter so often bled into an essentially *domestic* process of solidifying the boundaries between the people and outsiders. Boundary construction was not a coherent, binding foreign policy doctrine, but one dimension of a flexible process meant primarily to serve the populist's needs.

This basically domestic logic is evident in the surprising, regular appearance of domestic political attacks in the context of Trump administration remarks related to the promotion of *international* religious freedom. President Trump, in remarks at a 2019 UN convening on IRF, attacked "people in power preach[ing] diversity while silencing, shunning or censoring the faithful" as incapable of "true tolerance."[93] Pompeo remarked on several occasions related to IRF promotion that his own personal faith "might sound unusual to a lot of folks inside the Beltway."[94] He similarly began his remarks to the right-wing Values Voters Summit in September 2018 by claiming, "There were some folks who didn't want me to come here today,"[95] and in 2019 remarks to the American Association of Christian Counselors, "some people in the media will break out the pitchforks when they hear that I ask God for direction in my work."[96] Rather than domestic politics stopping at the water's edge, populism demands a constant focus on defining the people and its enemies, with foreign policy serving that domestic logic.

A similar blending of foreign policy and domestic exclusion took center stage when Secretary Pompeo launched the report of his Commission on Unalienable Rights. As stated above, Pompeo charged this commission, in theory, with making a broad assessment of the status of human rights promotion around the world. A remarkable feature of this speech from a sitting secretary of state, in theory focused on the international promotion of human rights, was its systematic focus on exclusion of domestic targets of the Trump administration's populist ire. Pompeo attacked "leading voices [who] promulgate hatred of our founding principles," moments before equating the *New York Times* to the Chinese Communist Party. He targeted "human rights advocacy groups [that] have traded proud principles for partisan politics," followed by "multilateral human rights bodies . . . doing the bidding of dictators" and "international courts [that] have largely abandoned unalienable rights."[97] In journalists, international organizations, and civil society organizations, Pompeo identified several of the most common targets for populist exclusion.

A final example of a threats to the religious people blending domestic and international exclusion emerged in Trump administration initiatives related to combatting anti-Semitism. The special envoy to monitor and combat antisemitism (SEAS) was one of few religious appointees at the State Department to receive a Trump administration nominee, even if it was only after significant delay. The Trump administration's Executive Order 13899, "Combating Anti-Semitism," issued in December 2019, particularly threatened American higher education institutions as supposed sources of threat.[98] The nature of this threat was tied to campus support for the Boycott, Divestment, and Sanctions (BDS) movement, and based on that order, Secretary of State Mike Pompeo pledged, in the waning days of the Trump administration, to "immediately take steps to identify organizations that engage in hateful BDS conduct and withdraw U.S. government support for such groups."[99] Although of unclear impact, Pompeo's consideration of applying such anti-Semitic designations to major human rights NGOs like Amnesty International and Human Rights Watch underscores the fact that practical effect of the exclusionary dimension of religious populism extends beyond Muslims.

POPULIST IDEOLOGY, INTERNATIONAL
RELATIONS, AND RELIGION

This story about variation in U.S. foreign policy rests on analysis of the populism's thin ideology during the Trump administration. It highlights a nuanced pattern of change, and traces that to well-documented exclusionary and inclusionary elements of that ideology. As I point out in chapter 1, much of the existing research on religion and the U.S. foreign policy bureaucracy is rooted in diverse branches of international relations theory that generally pay less attention to variation in the nature of the domestic political regime, or stress more conventional sources of variation like partisanship. To close this chapter, I briefly consider how these claims about the nature of the Trump administration interacted with theorizing in some of these international relations theoretical traditions.

On first glance, civilizational theory may seem to be comfortably supported by the variation laid out in this chapter. There is no doubt that civilizational rhetoric is a component of Trump's populist definition of the people and distinction from out-groups, particularly Muslims. Trump appointees, in public and private settings, made civilizational arguments, and there is evidence that rhetoric of civilizational identity has actually corresponded to foreign policy change. The strongest evidence of this is executive orders restricting access of certain Muslims to the United States. Civilizational theory's interplay with aspects of populism clearly merits significant attention when explaining recent foreign policy variation. And civilizational theory has a similar ambiguity over its religious inclusiveness, at once defined in non-Christian terms (usually as "the West") while privileging the influence of Christianity within that sphere.

While civilizational theory is consistent with the foreign policy approaches of several senior Trump administration officials, the variation in this chapter suggests several needed amendments. First, the causal pathway through which civilizational rhetoric operates is clearly tied to the *domestic* political interests of the incumbent, what Jeffrey Haynes calls the "glocalization" of civilizational conflict.[100] Domestic politics was involved in Samuel Huntington's civilizational framework, but his primary focus was the "bloody borders" *between* civilizations. Trump administration civilizationalists have brought some of their harshest criticisms toward traditional allies *within the West*, reflecting the primary populist need for *domestic* political cohesion. This may reflect, as Brubaker argues, the fact that Trumpism was more thoroughly nationalist than civilizationalist, and thus very willing to criticize internal threats to the nation. Trump's civilizationalist appointees similarly engaged in unexpected partnerships with Russia and Saudi Arabia that rested more on populism's preference for strong man rule than shared civilization. In this sense, Trump was correct in his 2017 Saudi Arabia speech to claim, "This is not a battle between different faiths, different sects, or different civilizations."[101]

Analysis of populism's thin ideology also provides a more comprehensive picture of the ideological sources of religion in foreign policy than that offered by genealogical approaches to the study of international religious freedom. In many ways, the role of IRF policy in reinforcing populist boundary construction is consistent with work from scholars like Elizabeth Shakman Hurd, Winnifred Sullivan and others who point to IRF's role in recognizing and reifying certain forms of religion (particularly those with an affinity with Protestant Christianity). Incorporation of "good religion" and exclusion of "bad religion" similarly feature in existing analysis, and mesh with evidence from the Trump administration. As with civilizational theory, ironically, one dimension where this account is incomplete is in its general lack of attention to the *domestic* political logic of populism that drives this boundary construction. This explains why, for instance, Pompeo's remarks on the launch of his Unalienable Rights Commission's report so effortlessly blended exclusion abroad with attacks on domestic political critics. The domestic project, tied to the specific ideological needs of a particular populist leader rather than broader structural forces, was driving the rhetoric and policy variation all along.

Probably the largest additional insight that accounting for the ideology of Trump's populism adds to existing critical work is its attention to the anti-elitism of Trump-era variation. Indeed, much of Hurd's framework rests on the category of "expert religion," an explicitly elitist set of academics and public policy practitioners who respond to the "insatiable demand for knowledge about religion."[102] Hurd is undeniably correct that the growth of Bettiza's regime complex encouraged the growth of a network of such experts, perhaps even resembling an "epistemic community" with a certain vision of religion in the U.S. foreign policy bureaucracy. However, as Sanders's comments that opened this chapter indicated, there was an ideological project of undermining such authority during the Trump administration, and this project came with implications for the rhetoric, bureaucratic processes, and policy substance of religion in foreign policy. This move altered the elite project in unexpected ways.

Accounts of religious soft power and the bureaucratization of religion would similarly benefit from attention to the basically domestic logic of populist thin ideological construction. Bettiza's convincing story of the growth of the religion regime complex, for instance, provides limited guidance for understanding which portions of that complex would thrive under the Trump administration's new ideology. IRF's close ties to the ideological project of defining the populist in-group provides an explanation. Theories of soft power frequently involve an emphasis on shared cultural commitments that are broadly consistent with the populist project of in-group construction. However, the exclusionary dimension of Trump religious foreign policy, perhaps most obviously tied to the Muslim Bans and updates to counterterrorism policy, was largely about the domestic needs of the populist regime rather than calculations of the national interest or sincerity of belief on the part of a coreligionist.

From the earliest days of the transition, evidence mounted that the Trump administration would serve as a unique source of variation in the foreign policy bureaucracy, including how those institutions accounted for religion. In official remarks and substantive policy goals, the new administration made religion and foreign policy a key avenue for promoting the bounds around Americans faithful to populist rule and excluding foreign and domestic threats to that faithful people. While some have noted a "Christianization" of U.S. foreign policy, this was only one way in which religion and foreign policy factored into constructing populist identity boundaries. Next, I will turn to an implication of populism for foreign policy not directly tied to ideology, but with important implications for religion: the personalist structure of governance.

4

WHO NEEDS AN OFFICE?

Populist Personalism and Religion in the Bureaucracy

W hen Sarah Huckabee Sanders defended "the faith of the administration" in a 2018 press conference, her response also touched on populism's significant, if often overlooked, second dimension: personalism. What was important in evaluating the Trump administration, Huckabee Sanders insisted, was not "an office," but instead, the personal religious convictions of "people, front and center, speaking openly about their faith [within the White House]."[1] Formal, institutionalized bureaucracy was unimportant and might even prove to be an obstacle in understanding the role of religion once the populist movement came into power.

This chapter explores how populism's personalism impacted religion in the U.S. foreign policy bureaucracy. Turning to personalism is necessary because populism's thin ideology cannot explain, on its own, how the Trump administration altered the religion-foreign policy "regime complex" during its term in office. True believers in the thin ideology might have attempted to leverage every mechanism of the diverse U.S. foreign policy apparatus to reinforce religion-inflected identity boundaries. Another kind of true believer, ideologically hostile to all bureaucratic forms of power, might have entirely shut down or ignored religion in foreign policy agencies. However, because populism is less ideologically consistent than these extremes, the empirical record does not match either. Instead, certain bureaucratic offices related to religion saw increased attention while others withered, drew scrutiny from populist officials, or were bypassed entirely. Why? The answer lies in populism's personalism, which operates according to a strategic logic of connectivity to the populist leader, rejecting costs imposed by bureaucratic constraint but leveraging bureaucratic channels when convenient to the broader populist project.

While religion may have its most obvious role in defining identity boundaries around "the people," populism's distinctive personalism comes with important implications for religion in the bureaucracy. Offices perceived to represent potential or actual costly constraints, notably the Office of Religion and Global Affairs (RGA) and the elements of religion-related work at USAID, were indeed bypassed or confronted. However, bureaucratic channels under populist control received significant attention from the Trump administration, or in the case of the work to promote international religious freedom (IRF), saw their work altered to reflect populism's personalist style. Populism's personalist dimension is well-established in scholarly literature, but its implications for the study of religion remain largely unexamined.[2] Putting personalism at the center of blessing America First highlights the contribution of this approach.

POPULISM'S PERSONALISM AND FOREIGN POLICY

Populists come to power not only promising to embody and vindicate the people, but also to embody a personalistic politics that rejects institutional constraint. A strategic approach to populism highlights "the principal ways and means by which a political actor captures the government and makes and enforces authoritative decisions."[3] The key actor in this strategic approach is the populist leader, an individual politician who "contests, pushes aside, or dominates other types of actors, such as elite factions and organized political parties."[4] This leader draws on popular mobilization for authority, rather than a political party or any sector given "special weight." Personalist leaders "concentrate power and ignore or attack democratic institutions," in the process, threatening democratic breakdown.[5] Three indicators of populism as a personalistic political strategy could come with observable implications for religion and foreign policy: rejection of bureaucratic constraint, empowering of those with direct ties to the populist leader, and deploying a charismatic populist style in governance.

Personalism might matter in essentially a negative manner, by drawing the populist into confrontation with institutional constraint, eliminating or weakening bureaucratic capacity where existing institutions threaten to impose costs on populist governance. As Nadia Urbinati puts it, "[Populists] can change the constitution or gravely manumit the bureaucracy (both civilian and military) in order to make institutions directly reflect their irresponsibility."[6] Populist leaders have undermined or disregarded institutional constraints from the Turkish judiciary,[7] the independent human rights commission in the Philippines,[8] and EU bodies critical of Hungary and Poland.[9] In such contexts, costs imposed by existing institutions constitute a threat to the people, and thus populists have an easy justification for either dismantling or simply ignoring such institutional checks.

While evidence of such confrontations is quite common, it would be misleading to conclude that populists are normatively anti-institutional, refusing on principled grounds to wield levers of bureaucratized state power. Indeed, aspects of the bureaucracy useful to the populist's political interests may survive, and even thrive, while other bureaucratic channels are hollowed out or eliminated. Populists are not ideologically opposed to the existence of bureaucracy, for the same reason that they do not adopt *any* consistent ideological positions other than securing their personal political power. However, where bureaucracy imposes costs on populists in office, confrontation follows.

If personalism is occasionally negative, in its positive dimension it empowers individuals with direct, unmediated relationships with the populist leader. In Takis Pappas's formulation, "populist leadership exhibits highly centralized authority structure, the absence of clear bureaucratic characteristics, and the leader's untrammeled control over subordinates."[10] As Jan-Werner Müller sums up this dimension of populism, "populists in fact often want to create constraints, so long as they function in an entirely partisan fashion."[11] As Forest Colburn and Arturo Cruz put it, in analyzing Nicaraguan populism, personalism is "inherently oligarchic and profoundly antidemocratic" in its privileging of those with direct ties to the leader.[12] Robert R. Barr points to personalism's "loyalty to individuals rather than to ideologies, platforms, rules or any other impersonal factors."[13] And in Tatiana Kostadinova and Barry Levitt's formulation, "loyalty to the leader is the basis on which asymmetrical power relationships are established in a personalist party."[14] Populists in office may, at times, confront existing institutions, but they also frequently simply bypass them, sidestepping bureaucratization in favor of personal initiative taken by those with direct ties to the populist.

Finally, personalism is closely associated with a certain "populist style" centered on charismatic, individual leadership of the populist.[15] This style consists of discursive[16] and performative[17] characteristics. Stylistic analysis tends to emphasize "notions of conspiracy and emergency,"[18] "Manichaean discourse,"[19] and "heightened emotions."[20] Populism becomes a "performative relationship," with new media technology providing a "stage" on which populists enact their relationship with the people.[21] Such a populist style is at times analyzed in nearly religious terms, with populism approximating "the revivalist flavour of a movement,"[22] and the charismatic leader "seculariz[ing] the political theology of representation."[23]

Even before considering the implications for religion and the policy process, this strategic, personalist approach to populism comes with obvious expectations for Trump administration foreign policy, broadly speaking. As Angelos Chryssogelos observes, "populism's well known anti-institutionalist bent . . . unshackled by complex processes of rule-making" may have significant impact on foreign policy.[24] Indeed, Johannes Plagemann and Sandra Destradi find populism's impact on Indian foreign policy to be more substantial in "procedural aspects of foreign policy decision making" than the policy substance of those decisions.[25]

Rejection of costly institutional constraint, both domestic and international, was a regular feature of Trump's America First foreign policy. Domestically, Trump railed against the "deep state," that, as Stephen Skowronek et al. put it, allegedly "thwarts presidential authority and the popular will."[26] Abroad, Trump seemed to revel in rejecting international agreements like the Joint Comprehensive Plan of Action (JCPOA, or Iran Nuclear Deal) and the Paris Climate Accords. A draft executive order, leaked in the administration's opening weeks in office, declared a "moratorium on new multilateral treaties," and Trump withdrew from the United Nations' Human Rights Council.[27] He targeted NATO Article 5 security guarantees, and upended a spectrum of international trade agreements or negotiations, from the North American Free Trade Agreement to the Trans-Pacific Partnership. His administration slashed U.S. financial support for UN initiatives like the Relief and Works Agency for Palestinian Refugees, the UN Population Fund, and the UN Department of Peacekeeping Operations.

Domestically, appointments to key diplomatic and security posts lagged behind a typical presidential transition, and once in office, appointees often seemed at war with elements of their own bureaucracies perceived to constrain populist prerogatives. At the State Department, for instance, Secretary Tillerson pursued a "reorg" of his own department, rumored to include dramatic changes such subsuming USAID within the State Department, eliminating entire bureaus within State, and expanding the size and influence of the Policy Planning Staff at the expense of career bureaucrats.[28] Tillerson maintained a hiring freeze after it expired for the rest of the federal government, and attracted congressional criticism for temporarily suspending the entry of new A-100 classes to the Foreign Service, including the prestigious Rangel and Pickering Fellows programs.[29] At lower levels of the bureaucracy, inspector general reports documented "allegations of politicized and other improper personnel practices" at the State Department's Bureau of International Organization Affairs.[30] What Daniel Drezner terms the "shoddy caliber of those who worked for the Trump administration" further showed through in the confirmation failures, departures from government, and even criminal convictions of key appointees.[31]

While official diplomatic channels withered, unofficial diplomacy under the influence of individuals with personal ties to President Trump thrived. The most vivid early examples of this diplomatic personalism came in the appointment of Trump's daughter and son-in-law to White House portfolios with significant foreign policy responsibilities. According to a career White House staffer, both Ivanka Trump and Jared Kushner received their security clearances over the objections of career officials.[32] Each wound up in loosely defined but powerful White House roles with foreign policy responsibilities, particularly Kushner's portfolio on Middle East policy that reportedly bypassed bureaucratic channels at Rex Tillerson's State Department.[33] The blending of personalism with foreign policy was similarly evident in Ukraine-related initiatives that resulted in Trump's first impeachment. Trump campaign chair Paul Manafort and personal attorney Rudy Giuliani typify the personalist dimension of populism, with a blend of direct access, personal financial motive, and the political fortunes of the populist leader dominating over the formal foreign policy bureaucracy.[34]

Finally, the performative aspect of populism was a regular feature of Trump foreign policy. Trump's performances, first as candidate, then as president, were most visible at domestic electoral rallies. However, there was evidence of this dimension of personalism in the administration's foreign policy as well. Most prominently, Trump repeatedly expressed admiration for personalistic leaders around the world. Examples are almost too numerous to count, from Russian President Vladimir Putin's ability to "kill whoever"[35] to "somebody I've become very close to" in Turkey's President Edrogan.[36] World leaders reportedly understood that performative spectacle, with Trump at the center, became a key interest in U.S. foreign policy on his watch. North Korea, to give one example, threatened to withhold photo opportunities as "something [Trump] can boast of,"[37] while the French reportedly instrumentalized the spectacle of their annual Bastille Day celebrations to curry favor with the new president.[38]

In sum, populism's personalism matters for foreign policy. Whether in rejection of institutional constraint, promoting of those with direct ties to the populist leader, or preference for a style of charismatic performance and Manichean rhetoric, personalism was observable in several of the biggest-picture characteristics of Trump administration foreign policy. This chapter now turns to the impact of personalism on offices and foreign policy channels tied to religion.

PERSONALISM, RELIGION, AND TRUMP FOREIGN POLICY

Each of these elements of personalism (rejecting constraint, privileging direct ties, and deploying a populist style) stood out in religion and Trump administration foreign policy. Populism's thin ideology may have been of more obvious importance to religion, but its personalist dimension was just as impactful. Populism's extreme focus on personal ties and rejection of bureaucratic constraint helps to explain the nuanced

TABLE 4.1 Personalism, Foreign Policy, and Religion

	Dimension of Personalism	Foreign Policy Observable Implications	Illustration Tied to Religion
Reject Institutional Constraint	Bypass or confront costly bureaucratic constraints on populist discretionary decision-making.	Reduce the size of career foreign policy bureaucracy and delay appointment of senior officials. Replace officials who attempt to constrain populist initiatives.	Neglect of Office of Religion and Global Affairs. Intervention in USAID foreign assistance decisions related to religion and post-ISIS reconstruction.
Privilege Direct Ties	Centralized leadership structures consisting of personal loyalists.	Prominent foreign policy appointments to campaign loyalists. Diplomacy conducted by personal initiative, outside of official diplomatic channels.	Informal diplomatic missions of religious advisory board members. Structure and membership of Commission on Unalienable Rights.
Deploy Populist Style	Charismatic leadership performances featuring Manichean discourse.	Regular high profile, performative foreign policy events. Populist style in major foreign policy addresses.	Photo opportunities and rhetoric style on "Abrahamic" diplomatic trip to Saudi Arabia.

changes in the religion and U.S. foreign policy regime complex during the Trump administration.

In what follows, I track the importance of personalism across portions of the foreign policy bureaucracy. In contrast to populism's thin ideology, which had a particular effect on the *substance* of Trump administration foreign policy, personalism had strongest effect on the *process* through which the foreign policy bureaucracy operated. All corners of the religion-foreign policy regime complex bore the imprint of personalism, but unevenly. Table 4.1 summarizes the evidence presented in more detail in the remainder of the chapter.

RESPONDING TO INSTITUTIONAL CONSTRAINT: NEGLECT AND CONFRONTATION

While populism does not reject institutions or bureaucracy as such, its personalist dimension does reject costly constraint from formal bureaucratic processes. Religious allies lent moral legitimacy to a number of anti-institutional Trump foreign policy initiatives, including withdrawal from the Iran Nuclear Deal, eliminating funding to the UN Population Fund, and even stepping away from the Paris Climate Accords.[39] Religious endorsement of norm breaking, violation of precedent, and rejection of imposed bureaucratic burdens featured regularly in issues more directly tied to religion, as well. When the Trump administration decided, against the reported advice of multiple cabinet appointees and career officials, to move the United States Embassy in Israel to Jerusalem, it met with warm support from the administration's evangelical allies. In that example, rejecting institutional constraint also reinforced identity boundaries, described in chapter 3.

Beyond blessing these particular transgressions, rejecting institutional constraint came with implications for some offices of the religion-foreign policy bureaucracy. This showed through especially clearly in changes to the Office of Religion and Global Affairs (RGA) and controversies about religion and development assistance largely centered on the U.S. Agency for International Development (USAID).

Clear evidence of populism's heightened sensitivity to the potential for bureaucratic constraint emerged in the neglect of the RGA. As detailed in chapter 2, by late 2016, RGA consisted of nearly thirty staff, including four political appointees and a range of foreign and civil service officers, academic fellows, and support staff. Because RGA took shape under the suite of personal offices reporting to the secretary of state, there was an expectation that any change in administration would likely lead to changes within the bureaucracy. Former State Department staff like Peter Mandaville and Judd Birdsall argued in favor of "a range of possible organizational changes . . . that would preserve its clear utility while rendering its work even more efficient and effective."[40] A spectrum of religious and civil society organizations who had worked closely with RGA in its early years, from the Episcopal Church to the American Jewish World Service and the Islamic Society of North America, wrote to the Trump transition team in January 2017 that RGA was "an irreplaceable focal point" for increasing diplomatic engagement with religion.[41]

In spite of these efforts, as Trump administration appointees trickled into Foggy Bottom in the early months of 2017, it became clear that maintaining the bureaucratization of religion, which culminated with RGA's 2013 founding, would not be a priority. Secretary Tillerson wrote to Senator Bob Corker, chair of the Senate Foreign Relations Committee, that many special envoy positions "have accomplished or outlived their original purpose."[42] Tillerson went on to specifically name the special representative for RGA, special representative to Muslim communities (SMRC), and special envoy to the Organization of Islamic Cooperation (SEOIC) for removal of titles and absorption within the Office of International Religious Freedom.

By late summer 2017, RGA's staff capacity dropped below a half dozen, largely through neglect rather than direct confrontation. None of the office's open political appointments were initially filled. Career staff prepared for their next assignments, and replacements were either slow to arrive or never approved. Substantive work bypassed the office as well. Documents directly related to religious assessment or engagement that would have typically received clearance from RGA, the process of bureaucratic review that occupies significant time within State, were either never received or altered after clearance without recirculation. Staff were left to wait for opportunities for input on presidential remarks on core concerns of religion and foreign policy, like those delivered in Saudi Arabia in May 2017. The RGA office was eventually removed from the State Department's 7th Floor and out of the Secretary's Bureau on the organizational chart. Its function theoretically remained filled by a newly minted Strategic Religious Engagement Unit within the Office of International Religious Freedom, but with nothing like the capacity that enabled its initial structure to function.

On one level, this did represent a general normative skepticism of government bureaucracy, and therefore a turn against the "expert religion" that guided earlier bureaucratization.[43] Advocates of blessing America

First emphasized, instead, individual religious commitments of the administration's allies. Prominent populist allies advanced this view in conservative Christian news outlets. Evangelical advisory council member Johnnie Moore explicitly contrasted personal relationships with a more bureaucratized approach: "One of the problems with the United States government and with governments around the world that are flush with cash is that we end up with lots and lots of offices with lots and lots of employees and it just grows and it grows and it grows . . . Just because something has been, doesn't mean that it should exist."[44]

This conflation of general, anti-bureaucratic framing with religious authority impacted particular offices, including those tasked with diplomatic efforts to combat global anti-Semitism. Secretary Tillerson hesitated to fill the special envoy to monitor and combat antisemitism (SEAS) position and office, a remarkable proposal given the position's congressional legal mandate. In testimony before the House of Representatives Appropriations Committee's State, Foreign Operations, and Related Programs Subcommittee, Tillerson speculated that maintaining an SEAS position might somehow "weaken attention to those issues" in spite of potential "good intentions behind why they were created."[45] Hundreds of religious, scholarly, and civil society organizations objected, and bipartisan hearings in Congress reminded Tillerson of the SEAS position's legal mandate. The position was, as will be discussed in chapter 6, filled. But even floating the idea of dissolving the position reveals the pervasive populist instinct to be suspicious of bureaucratized offices and processes. Bible studies replaced bureaucratized structures, from cabinet officials to working-level staff in faith-based affinity groups.

However, it is important to note that offices perceived as likely to impose costs on the populist in office were most directly targeted for such anti-bureaucratic framing. Comments from administration religious loyalists made it clear that RGA was perceived as a source of potential constraint to populist prerogatives. Tony Perkins, religious right stalwart, and eventual Trump appointee to the U.S. Commission on International Religious Freedom, remarked that "RGA is used to pressure religious groups around the world to violate their tenets by approving of homosexual conduct and LGBT lifestyles. This is unacceptable."[46] Shaun Casey, RGA's founding leader, reported hearing similar complaints centered on RGA's alleged work as "the tip of the spear for Obama's global gay marriage campaign."[47] With this in mind, it was not ironic for the conservative *Christian Post* to ask: "Would eliminating State Department's Office of Religion and Global Affairs be a big deal?"[48] The conflation of the political priorities of a departed administration with the behavior of the permanent bureaucracy was a common feature of populist complaints about deep state obstruction, and took on a sacred tone in the hands of populism's religious loyalists.

In the end, populist perception of potential institutional constraint resulted in a zombie RGA office with extremely limited capacity and little autonomy from the administration's approach to promoting international religious freedom. This pattern of neglect owes more to populism's personalism than to thin ideology. It is perhaps noteworthy that the RGA office was not shuttered entirely, but instead allowed to wither through neglect. This was a distinction without much difference during the Trump administration but could lay the groundwork for future institutional revival. As will be discussed in more depth in chapter 5, career RGA staff were not passive observers in this process, and instead exercised constrained agency in preserving office functions in spite of this neglect.

If populist response to hypothetical constraint from RGA consisted mostly of neglect, much more direct confrontation took place in portions of the bureaucracy where attempts at constraint were more material. Foreign assistance partnership with religious organizations is not unique to populism. Government cooperation with faith-based organizations has expanded on a bipartisan basis in the past several decades.[49] However, populism's personalism encouraged bypassing or confronting existing bureaucratic structures in delivering such material assistance when any attempt was made to constrain rewards to populist loyalists. The use of material inducements to cement personal loyalty is consistent with comparative evidence of religion's role as a strategy of populist mobilization.[50]

One episode illustrates this pattern most clearly: the provision of development assistance to Christian charities in portions of the Middle East impacted by ISIS violence. The status of Christian minorities in the Middle East became a significant focus of charitable networks, including several tied to American Christian advocates of blessing America First. After the ISIS takeover of large portions of Iraq, religious minorities (both Christians and others like the Yazidi community) faced systematic violence that Secretary of State John Kerry deemed genocide. With battlefield gains in ISIS territory, the international community confronted massive reconstruction challenges, both in cities like Mosul and more sparsely populated areas of the Nineveh Plain. The Obama administration was a significant international contributor to reconstruction efforts, largely by directing over $100 million in USAID funding to United Nations Development Program (UNDP) stabilization initiatives in the country. While UNDP officials claimed to work closely with local Christian leaders on the ground, Archbishop Bashar Warda of Erbil complained, in 2017, that "almost none of this aid reached the Christians."[51]

The Trump administration moved, quickly in rhetoric and eventually in financial commitment, to reject this bureaucratic pattern, altering funding decisions to direct tens of millions of dollars directly to religious charities rather than large initiatives centralized via the United Nations. Vice President Pence remarked as early as mid-2017, "We will no longer rely on the UN alone to assist persecuted Christians . . . the U.S. will work hand in hand from this day forward with faith-based groups."[52] As President Trump himself put it, in discussing this funding with the 2019 Values Voter Summit, "My administration has provided more than a half a billion dollars in support of religious minorities and others suffering from atrocities in Syria and Iraq alone. Other Presidents would not be doing that. They'd be spending a lot more money, but they'd be spending it on things that would not make you very happy."[53] USAID established a Genocide Recovery and Persecution Response initiative that alone was responsible for roughly $350 million in funding "to help ethnic and religious minorities in northern Iraq heal and restore their communities."[54] Recipients of aid included multinational charities whose leaders had been sympathetic to Trump, like Samaritan's Purse and the Knights of Columbus, as well as local religious institutions like the Catholic University of Erbil, in Archbishop Warda's diocese. Populist officials did not seek to eliminate bureaucratized religious assistance, but instead to reject institutionalized constraints on their discretion.

It is important to clarify that funding religious charities to implement development projects is not, on its own, inconsistent with the preexisting approach to faith-based funding partnerships in international development assistance.[55] These funding decisions reflected populism's personalist approach because, at several steps, they brought political appointees, including senior officials, into potentially costly conflict with established bureaucratic processes. In spite of Pence's 2017 remarks, the foreign assistance process presented multiple barriers to simply delivering hundreds of millions of dollars to religious allies of the administration. Extensive reporting by *ProPublica* has documented that multiple religious proposals were initially rejected by career staff at USAID: In the words of one official, "You gotta have a good proposal . . . and they didn't meet the standards."[56] Representatives of one group complained, during congressional testimony, "The political appointees [are] much more willing to help us, [but] they have been unable to move the bureaucracy."[57] USAID Administrator Mark Green openly complained of "the often rigid processes of the federal bureaucracy have slowed implementation."[58] Career officials worried about restrictions on targeting groups for funding based on their religious affiliation, which could run afoul of USAID's requirement that grant-making "must not discriminate for or against an organization on the basis of the organization's religious character or affiliation," and reportedly rejected multiple applications from faith-based organizations.[59]

These constraints were characteristic of the development of religion as a tool of postsecular statecraft but yielded in the face of populism's personalism. When a *Wall Street Journal* opinion piece complained that "career staff at USAID have ignored Mr. Pence's words," the administration moved swiftly to remove the USAID career official helming the Middle East bureau, in favor of a political appointee.[60] One Foreign Service Officer remarked, "There was a very ideological focus on Christians [from political appointees] . . . we were trying to get them to focus on others in the minority communities that might need assistance."[61] Senior administration officials insisted, as Pence put it in remarks to the In Defense of Christians network, on working "hand in hand" with faith-based groups. This shift to direct funding reflected the rejection of potential constraint from international organizations as well. In that same speech, Pence lamented that "The United Nations too often denies [faith-based] funding requests . . . Our fellow Christians and all who are persecuted in the Middle East should not have to rely on multinational institutions when America can help them directly.[62] This then moved from high-level remarks to working-level funding decisions. A former lobbyist for Christian churches seeking USAID funding in Iraq was appointed as USAID's special representative for minority assistance in Iraq,[63] and remarked to the conservative Catholic EWTN network that he saw it as a strong suit that local Christian groups were "defining how we do our work," rather than being subject to governmental review.[64]

Both the organizational decay of RGA and the confrontation with standard faith-based funding practices at USAID are consistent with the personalist dimension of populism. Institutional costs and bureaucratic process will not constrain the agency of the populist leader, and so, in the realm of religion and foreign policy, such potential guardrails were actively or passively dismantled. Even elements of the religion-related bureaucracy more privileged by populist governance were not immune to this dynamic. While IRF-related diplomacy, in some ways, grew under personalism's sway, it would be difficult to argue that promotion of religious freedom truly constrained Trump's populist priorities when they came into conflict. Concerns about religious freedom in India never led to its designation as an IRF "Country of Particular Concern" by Trump's State Department, in spite of the recommendation of the U.S. Commission on International Religious Freedom. Instead, Trump and Indian Prime Minister Narendra Modi, a fellow populist with little tolerance for constraint by human rights institutions, staged mutual admiration celebrations across continents.

PROXIMITY TO THE POPULIST: DIRECT TIES AND RELIGIOUS DIPLOMACY

While populists reject institutional constraint, this does not entail an ideological opposition to every use of bureaucratized power. That would imply an ideological consistency that is at odds with populism's ad hoc, adaptable focus on the personal interests of the populist leader. During the Trump administration, elements of the religion-foreign policy bureaucracy persisted, but in service to those with personal access to the populist leader. The logic of unmediated connection was observable in several areas: informal diplomatic initiatives of White House religious allies, elements of the administration's promotion of International Religious Freedom, and the development of Secretary of State Mike Pompeo's Commission on Unalienable Rights. While some formal offices like RGA withered, religion did not disappear from the policy process. Rather, bureaucratization gave way to a more personalistic structure centered on direct ties to the populist president.

The Trump campaign's evangelical outreach director was among the earliest arrivals at the State Department, but did not assume the formal title of special representative for RGA.[65] Rather she assumed a more ambiguous portfolio including issues of gender, sexuality, and Christian minorities. The White House initially declined to appoint a director of its own Office of Faith-Based and Neighborhood Partnerships, instead preferring informal meetings with its campaign's evangelical advisory board, whose members bragged about "meetings at the White House and State Department that began or ended in prayer."[66] One of these faith advisors described the relationship as "informal . . . not down the road meeting with staffers, but actually in the heart of the conversation."[67]

These comments went on to draw an explicit contrast between the logic of bureaucratization that had prevailed for the last several administrations and the personalistic approach of populism present under Trump: "Just because the infrastructure is different, it doesn't mean the quality of the relationship is different; and on the contrary, it's actually better . . . One of the many things I like about this White House is that they are more reliant on their relationship with regular, everyday Americans and less reliant on the formal infrastructure of government."[68] This informal structure attracted legal action, alleging violations of the Federal Advisory Committee Act (FACA), which provides transparency standards for federal advisory bodies. Legal expert Robert Tuttle ironically remarked that the evangelical advisory board may not have risen to FACA's standard because, "It's just a group that [Trump] named and gathers together for the sake of having them praise him."[69] When the White House eventually issued Executive Order 13831, "Establishment of a White House Faith and Opportunity Initiative," more than two years after taking office, it drew prosperity gospel preacher Paula White from the ranks of the same campaign advisory board.[70] The contrast with steps promoting self-constraint in this area from the Obama White House, as discussed in chapter 2, is significant.

The importance of personalist White House ties translated into informal diplomatic initiatives bypassing the formal bureaucracy. Evidence of this type of ad hoc diplomacy abounded in Trump administration foreign policy, often tied to members of the campaign's evangelical advisory board. Religious allies, including Johnnie Moore and Michele Bachmann, traveled to Egypt for a meeting with authoritarian leader Abdel Fattah el-Sisi. Moore gushed that the meeting "was like we were best friends for our entire life."[71] When the U.S.-Saudi relationship came under scrutiny after the murder of journalist Jamal Khashoggi, a similar troop of religious advisors visited Saudi Arabia to meet with Crown Prince Mohammed bin Salman. At a time of grave allegations of extraterritorial, extrajudicial execution by Saudi authorities, these leaders announced that "we were encouraged by the Crown Prince's candor . . . we don't judge and hope not to offend."[72] Ralph Drollinger, a pastor who led a White House cabinet-level Bible study, similarly engaged in informal diplomatic initiatives, including outreach to the Ortega government in Nicaragua, against the advice career State Department staff.[73] Elsewhere, in Latin America policy, evangelical loyalists met with Brazilian President Jair Bolsonaro after his meeting with President Trump in March 2019, praising both for "really understand[ing] who God is."[74] Trump administration evangelical allies John Hagee and Robert Jeffress delivered prayers at the opening of the new U.S. Embassy in Jerusalem, in spite of contentious histories of comments about Judaism and Islam.[75] A similar group of evangelical pastors met with White House officials in March 2019 for informal, off-the-record consultations on the administration's pending Middle East peace plan.[76]

The importance of personal ties extended to administration engagement with religious media outlets. Christian Broadcasting Network (CBN) reporters regularly enjoyed extended interviews with senior officials, and State Department press corps members were passed over in favor of targeted calls with faith-based media outlets, which a former State Department spokesperson termed "PR malpractice."[77] Facing questioning about this unique access, department officials replied that, because the call "targeted 'audience-specific media,' it was not subject to normal transparency procedures."[78]

International Religious Freedom promotion provides evidence that personalism can show itself within the bureaucracy, not just outside of it, when institutions do not raise costs to populist governance. IRF is the clearest indicator that populist personalism does not necessarily require hostility to the exercise of bureaucratic power. Ambassador-at-Large

Sam Brownback was a fairly rapid nominee in a chaotic transition, and during his brief tenure in office, Secretary Tillerson "realigned" sixteen staff positions from other elements of the religion-diplomacy bureaucracy under the control of IRF.[79] Vice President Pence, Trump's bridge to conservative Christians, had long-standing ties to the IRF community. Secretary Pompeo signaled the impact of personalism on the structure of IRF in 2019 remarks, by reaffirming that IRF Ambassador-at-Large Brownback "report[s] directly to me," and that the IRF office would move within the State Department organizational chart, reporting directly to an undersecretary rather than the assistant secretary for Democracy, Human Rights, and Labor.[80] Pompeo justified these steps, first and foremost, because IRF "is a deeply personal [cause]" as "a Sunday school teacher and deacon at my church."[81] Appointees to the U.S. Commission on International Religious Freedom included Trump evangelical advisory board leader Johnnie Moore. As discussed in chapter 3, Trump's IRF activity was indelibly marked by populism's construction of identity boundaries. But personalism left a mark as well.

Trump, ever the personalist, made little effort to hide the fact that IRF initiatives were about personal loyalty and benefit. In his remarks to an American convening at the United Nations on international religious freedom, he began by boasting about "obliterating the Johnson Amendment," which does not deal with IRF, but does allow pastors to endorse political candidates without tax consequences.[82] Trump's special advisor on religious pluralism in the Middle East within USAID was reported to the agency's chief legal officer for potentially violating the Hatch Act while wishing for President Trump's reelection in front of several hundred people at a high-profile Ministerial on Religious Freedom.[83]

Prominent cases of IRF advocacy, most notably Pastor Andrew Brunson's release from Turkey, similarly demonstrated this personalism. Trump attorney Jay Sekulow referred to Brunson as "our guy," and negotiations over Brunson's release from Turkey reportedly centered on meeting the personalistic priorities of another global populist, Turkish President Recep Tayyip Erdogan, including his desire to have exiled Muslim leader Fettulah Gulen extradited from the United States to Turkey.[84] That particular diplomatic foray reportedly included the individual who perhaps embodied Trump's personalism in foreign policy better than any other: Rudy

Giuliani. In their Oval Office meeting after Brunson's eventual release, Trump opened, on camera, by making the point quite clear: "Can I ask you one question? Who did you vote for?"[85]

Further evidence of personalism empowering direct ties while bypassing existing elements of the bureaucracy can be traced to the Commission on Unalienable Rights convened by Secretary of State Mike Pompeo's Office of Policy Planning. The content of the commission merits attention in its own right, but in the context of this chapter, it provides illustrative evidence of personalism in effect. Pompeo created entirely new bureaucratic channels to ensure personal control and undercut potential existing checks in the bureaucracy. In both structure and content, the commission illustrated the importance of personalism in explaining changes from the Trump administration to the religion and foreign policy bureaucracy.

Pompeo launched the Commission on Unalienable Rights in summer 2019 to "provide fresh thinking about human rights discourse and where such discourse has departed from our nation's founding principles of natural law."[86] The group's draft charter specified that it would "report to the Secretary of State" and that the secretary would have personal authority to appoint and remove commission members.[87] Its chair, Prof. Mary Ann Glendon, is a distinguished scholar, but also the "beloved professor" of Pompeo (in his words).[88] Importantly, the commission was located *outside* of the typical State Department offices within the Bureau of Democracy, Rights and Labor (DRL) charged with monitoring and promoting human rights abroad. The entire endeavor was intended as a criticism of the international human rights bureaucracy, both its "international institutions [that have] drifted from their original mission," and the supposed "proliferation" of rights claims that these institutions had encouraged.[89]

This somewhat esoteric commission, staffed primarily by academics and with no specific policy mandate, is a particularly strong indicator of populism's bypassing of institutional constraint and minimizing costs. As a group of twenty-three senators wrote to Pompeo after the commission's 2019 launch, the secretary's office failed to respond in a timely manner to congressional requests for information. In the senators' view, "the Commission does not reflect the diversity of views required for any body tasked with advising the Secretary on human rights."[90] Senators raised concerns that "members are overwhelmingly clergy or scholars known to support discriminatory policies toward LGBT persons, hold views hostile to women's rights and reproductive freedoms, and/or support positions at odds with U.S. treaty obligations."

They further argued that "The Commission appears to be an effort to circumvent the Department's own foreign policy and human rights experts in an effort to pick and choose which rights the United States will respect." In a separate letter, a related group of members of Congress noted, "DRL is entirely absent from the Commission's charter," which also "makes no reference to the Universal Declaration of Human Rights or any international human rights treaty the United States has signed or ratified."[91] Public comments by commissioners clarified that bypassing the institutionalized human rights community, in fact criticizing that community, was a raison d'être for the commission that thought of itself as bringing back into line "a cadre of bureaucrats, judges, scholars and activists" who had, ironically, undermined human rights by invoking them too regularly.[92]

The commission's eventual preliminary report, issued in July 2020, and the remarks from Secretary Pompeo that accompanied the report's release, further clarify the extent to which the commission was intended to bypass, or even confront, the institutionalized human rights bureaucracy. From its introduction, the report ties "erosion of the human rights project" to "disappointment in the performance of international institutions" and "overuse of rights language."[93] On substance, the commission critiques the establishment human rights community for "cloak[ing] contestable political preference[s] in the mantle of human rights." On process, the report goes after the international institutions that are a focal point of such establishment human rights work, arguing that "programmatic bias in the United Nations Human Rights Council, and in the UN more broadly," required the Trump administration to withdraw from institutionalized participation in human rights advocacy for the greater good of the human rights agenda itself.[94]

In sum, while one could read the Commission on Unalienable Rights as illustrating populism's thin ideology, with its valorization of the American rights tradition and exclusion of those who criticize American behavior, it provides important, but easily overlooked, evidence of the manner in which the Trump administration's personalism reshaped religion in the bureaucracy. At times this meant explicit criticism, for example, criticism of international organizations responsible for supposed "prolif-eration" of rights. But personalists can, and do, work through the bureau-cracy at times, when they can create channels under their direct control and free from oversight of existing offices or career staff.

All presidents appoint loyalists to key administration positions. As I explored in chapter 2, religion in the foreign policy bureaucracy was not immune to this. However, populism's personalism goes beyond, to reject constraint and create new personalistic processes prioritizing direct con-nection above all else. If Trump's populist strategic logic neglected or even confronted institutions that tried to constrain his rule, it also layered on additional personalistic religious diplomacy both within, and in parallel to, that official bureaucracy.

STYLE, PERFORMANCE, AND RELIGIOUS DIPLOMACY

A final element related to populism's personalism is the existence of what scholars term its unique "style" of performative politics.[95] Personalism brings with it a performative approach to build direct ties with the masses, often centered on the charisma of the populist leader. These performances frequently highlight threat and crisis, as well as norm violation or "bad manners" on the part of the populist leader.[96] If there was a style of the regime complex that Gregorio Bettiza documented in religion and U.S. diplomacy before Trump's election, it would center on bureaucratic performance and what Elizabeth Shakman Hurd calls expert religion.[97] That style is a world away from the performances for which Trump gar-nered a reputation on the campaign trail and in office.

Foreign policy in general, and religion and foreign policy in particu-lar, became characterized by this performative element of populism as Trump and his key appointees settled into the presidency. This was per-haps most visible in Trump's first trip abroad as president, the visit to Saudi Arabia, Israel/Palestine, and the Vatican, analyzed in chapter 3. The substance of the trip fits well within populism's thin ideological bound-ary drawing, but explaining its style requires attention to the performa-tive dimension of populism. The visit produced some of the most theat-rical images of the early Trump presidency, perhaps none more striking than the glowing orb that Trump laid hands on with Egyptian President Sisi and Saudi King Salman on his Riyadh stop to address "the heart of the Muslim world."[98] His remarks that day featured populist identity themes, but also repeated references to the bombastic, crisis-driven style of populism. Trump praised Salman's "extraordinary words" and the "splendor," "grandeur," and "magnificen[ce]" of the country within the speech's first paragraph. He remarked on the size of the gathering and his personal relationships with those gathered, and he invoked vivid images of "streams of innocent blood," "plague," and a "battle for souls," in keeping with the populist style's crisis-driven approach.

Beyond this initial adventure, performance of populist style appeared in the Trump administration's approach to IRF, particularly public events. The most regularly cited IRF centerpiece of the Trump administration was a series of "ministerials," or high level diplomatic convenings, on the topic. Pompeo's remarks at 2018's inaugural ministerial in Washington D.C. were steeped in the populist style, extolling the meeting as "fantastic" and response to it as "overwhelmingly positive," while going on, à la a Trump campaign rally, to cite the number of countries represented at the meeting. The trend continued at the second ministerial, where Pompeo opened his remarks noting "the remarkable growth in attendance . . . there are hundreds more attendees . . . it is the largest event ever hosted by a U.S. Secretary of State ever. It's truly remarkable."[99] The remarks concluded by noting, "I am sure that the next ministerial will be even bigger than this one."[100] These remarks bear the imprint of populist performance, highlighting style as substance.

Among Trump's most common populist performances in office was the signing ceremony, in which he brandished legislation or executive orders bearing his exaggerated signature for the press, while loyalists crowded around. While not unique to religion or foreign policy, this seemingly sacred populist ritual did extend to documents related to religion and foreign policy, including the signing of the "Muslim Bans" early in his presidency, and a photo opportunity around his signing of the Iraq and Syria Genocide Relief and Accountability Act that prominently featured not only appointees like Tony Perkins, but also Archbishop Warda himself.[101]

It is somewhat more challenging to evaluate the impact of this sort of populist style on the substance of religion and foreign policy. Margaret

Canovan links populist style to "solutions that are simple and direct," which would be consistent with, for example, assuming that simply insisting on referring to countering Islamic extremism would meaningfully increase American security.[102] Steps like moving the American embassy in Israel would similarly seem in keeping with the populist style shaping the substance of religion and foreign policy. At a minimum, they serve to focus religion and foreign policy on the person of the populist leader, bypassing the bureaucratic style that dominated in religion and foreign policy in the pre-Trump period.

IMPLICATIONS: PERSONALISM, INTERNATIONAL RELATIONS, AND THE RELIGIOUS FOREIGN POLICY AGENDA

Personalism, a constitutive dimension of populist governance, was observable across diverse facets of the religion-foreign policy bureaucracy during the Trump administration. The variation documented in this chapter helps to explain why the thin ideology of populism described in chapter 3 left an uneven imprint across the bureaucracy. I conclude by turning to two final questions. First, how does personalism interact with some of the other approaches to understanding religion in the foreign policy bureaucracy prominent in international relations scholarship? Second, what did this introduction of personalism, a concept heavily tied to the *process* of foreign policy, mean for the *substance* of religion and foreign policy in the Trump administration?

This book's opening chapter pointed to several existing approaches to analyzing religion in U.S. foreign policy, including civilizational theory, critical/genealogical approaches, scholarship emphasizing bureaucratic complexification, and theories of soft power. Highlighting personalism's role in populist foreign policy complements civilizational or soft power approaches, revealing elements of variation that those approaches leave largely unexamined. As described at some length in chapter 3, civilizational theory does indeed help to explain religion's place in Trump administration foreign policy, as a part of constructing thin ideological boundaries. However, civilizational theory is less useful in explaining the nuanced variation across the bureaucracy, particularly anti-institutional behavior, bypassing formal channels, and the importance of direct ties to the populist leader. Agreeing on civilizational boundaries may have helped individuals build personal ties to the populist, but this does not explain why the populist prefers to govern via personal relationships in the first place.

Likewise, studies of soft power have something important to contribute to the variation analyzed in this chapter. Pastors utilizing faith relationships with policy makers abroad to gain access and then engage in a kind of shadow diplomacy is quite consistent with soft power accounts. However, a turn to personalist theories of populism clarifies the way in which soft power operated in the Trump administration. Actors empowered to deploy soft power were not, primarily, endowed with this capability because of their moral authority or religious credibility, but because of their personalistic ties to the White House built on the campaign trail. Soft power theory is also not particularly equipped to grapple with the anti-institutional aspects of recent variation. Why, for instance, did the Trump administration cripple the RGA office, rather than staffing it with officials from the campaign, dedicated to deploying forms of religious soft power? Understanding populism's deep hostility to institutional constraint completes the story.

While different in their approaches, scholarship offering genealogical approaches to international religious freedom[103] and scholarship focused on documenting bureaucratization of religion in the foreign policy process[104] face a shared question from personalism in foreign policy. Hurd's emphasis on expert religion and Bettiza's grounding in theories of "epistemic communities" foregrounds the importance of networks of scholars, policymakers, and think tank analysts in generating the knowledge that governed religion in the foreign policy bureaucracy. Generally, each tells a story of increasing bureaucratic complexification under expert guidance, with the potential effect of creating what Hurd calls "governed religion."[105] Dismantling of bureaucratic offices, bypassing of established diplomatic channels, and prioritization of informal agents empowered by personalistic ties to the executive suggest a different set of forces at play. This is not to suggest that either account is inaccurate in its characterization of the post-Cold War quarter century. But explaining the nature of recent variation requires a turn to analyzing the personalist governance that Trump's populism brought to office.

A second concluding question asks what is at stake in this attention to personalism in the foreign policy process. Understanding changes to relatively obscure bureaucratic offices may have some intrinsic worth, but what does it mean for substantive decisions tied to religion in U.S. foreign policy? While personalism does not point to particular substantive foreign policy outcomes as directly as populism's thin ideology, it does impact the types of foreign policy issues likely to feature in religion and diplomacy.

First, personalism's style and rejection of bureaucratic constraint may encourage religion to be implicated in foreign policy decisions with shorter time horizons and less complex implementation challenges. The Trump administration's decision to relocate the U.S. Embassy in Israel to Jerusalem provides one example of a theatrical decision, tailor-made for the populist style, that both rejected long-standing objections from elements of the bureaucracy while also sidestepping many of the protracted challenges involved in actually arriving at any sort of rejuvenated peace process between Israelis and Palestinians. The theatricality of decisions like the embassy move seems to contrast with many longer-term diplomatic engagements with religion that emerged during the period of bureaucratic complexification in the pre-Trump era. Integrating religion into international public health policy via the PEPFAR program, for instance, relied on extended coordination with the legislative branch, implementation through various government agencies, and dialogue with a spectrum of professional development and public health associations. Such "slow boring of hard boards," to borrow from Max Weber, is out of step with religion in populist foreign policy.

Second, personalism's emphasis on the person of the populist leader may implicate religion in higher-profile diplomatic controversies than the relatively mundane diplomacy that constituted much of the bread and butter of religion-related diplomacy in the pre-Trump period. Both for the populist, and those opposed to populist politics, foreign policy outcomes impact not only the U.S. national interest or normative, humanitarian concerns, but first and foremost, the strength of the populist leader.

Refugee and asylum policies, for instance, have always involved close integration with religious actors, most obviously in coordination with the various domestic resettlement agencies with ties to faith-based organizations.[106] However, during the Trump administration, populism's personalism meant that substantive policy decisions (and resistance to those decisions) occupied direct attention from White House advisors and drew thousands of protesters into the streets of American cities in response. If religion and diplomacy was, at a certain level, boring during the late Obama administration, this was certainly not the case under Trump's personalism. This was not only because of populism's contentious ideology of division, but also because every foreign policy initiative, every change to the bureaucracy, served as a reminder of the personal power of the populist himself, for good or ill.

PART III

PREEXISTING CONDITIONS AND POPULIST CONSTRAINT

5

FAITH IN A DEEP STATE?

Bureaucratic Preservation in a Populist Transition

"First day of the Trump presidency. Eerily quiet on the 7th Floor and in the RGA suite." So began my reflections on the evening of January 23, 2017, as the Trump administration started its term in office. My own time as a fellow in the Office of Religion and Global Affairs (RGA) had roughly six months remaining, and it was highly uncertain what those months would hold for the office, or American diplomacy more broadly. Chapters 3 and 4 told the story of how the Trump administration's populism eventually reshaped religion in the foreign policy bureaucracy, including the RGA office. I now turn to a different question. Why did Trump and his loyalists generally succeed in the changes they brought to religion and foreign policy? This section will explore three potential constraints on populist change: agency on the part of career officials (chapter 5), existing political institutions regulating foreign policy and the religion-state relationship (chapter 6), and public opinion, especially among populism's supporters (chapter 7).

Turning to the first potential source of resilience in the face of populist change: working-level, career staff in offices like RGA. This is an especially appropriate task because the behavior of nonpolitical appointees within the federal bureaucracy was a regular bogeyman for Trump and his acolytes, even before career officials wound up central to his first impeachment. Commentators, some optimistically and others with outrage, speculated that a "Deep State," a term once largely utilized by scholars of places like Turkey and Egypt, might check the ambitions of the new populist president, especially in the realm of foreign policy.[1] RGA was an intriguing site to observe this possibility because of its relatively recent creation during a Democratic administration by Secretary John Kerry, and the extent to which campaign promises of candidate Trump seemed to implicate existing RGA work in areas as diverse as refugee policy, the Paris Climate Agreement, and countering violent extremism. Would RGA become a nest of deep state resistance during the early months of the Trump presidency?

While it is certainly true that populism's identity-based exclusion and personalism provoked frustration, anger, and even occasional tears in the initial months of the transition, the RGA suite was far from a hotbed of deep state subversion. Here, I document a more nuanced, improvisatory set of responses from staff in RGA in early 2017. Those who remained on the 7th Floor encountered a great degree of uncertainty about both the substance and process of their work. How would the role of religion in populist rhetoric on the campaign trail translate into substantive policy once in office? What would populism's personalism mean for the process-bound foreign policy bureaucracy? And what about significant areas of foreign policy that seemed relatively isolated from populism's twin concerns with identity and personal power?

In this environment, I argue that staff in RGA adopted varied strategies aimed at what Daniel Drezner terms institutional survival, "maintain[ing] its organizational integrity and continu[ing] to advance its initial set of ideas even after its political patrons lose power."[2] Strategies chosen reflected both norms among career staff and dimensions of populism itself. First, populism's ideological thinness meant that, in significant areas of foreign policy, RGA staff could work with a kind of "bounded persistence," as existing initiatives did not attract personal attention from the White House or key appointees. Second, in response to populism's personalistic dimension, staff attempted a process of "mutual adaptation," simultaneously adjusting internal processes in a more personalistic environment while attempting to apply the office's core approach to certain policy spheres perceived to be personal priorities of key populist actors. Finally, it was in response to elements of populist identity construction, especially related to exclusion, that staff demonstrated the most significant dissent, what I term "channeled constraint," predominately via established bureaucratic procedures and norms rather than overt resistance.

As noted in the Introduction, the responses documented in this chapter are largely focused on the RGA office in the initial six months of the Trump presidency. This raises reasonable questions about the generalizability of these patterns across other portions of the bureaucracy and beyond the term of Secretary Tillerson. While chapters 3 and 4 are intentionally structured to incorporate empirical material from religion-related offices beyond RGA, the responses observed in this chapter are, by their nature, more particular. Detailed attention to observed dynamics within a single office brings benefits of measurement validity. RGA would seem to be a most likely case for deep state constraint, given the office's history of work on multiple policy areas that ran directly counter to populist priorities. This approach does admittedly mean that this chapter does not set out to assess potential responses from career staff in offices that attracted significantly more direct attention from the populist administration, particularly the Office of International Religious Freedom (IRF). There is certainly anecdotal evidence of career staff facing complex incentives in those offices as well. Recall, for example, the reported career consequences facing staff who objected to redirecting USAID funding in Iraq directly to churches. But a more comprehensive look at career staff response to populist change across diverse offices remains beyond the scope of this analysis.

During this transitional period, RGA staff exercised a significant amount of agency, and, on the whole, utilized it in attempts to preserve the form and function of the RGA office. The nature of populism, particularly its reliance on personalism and skepticism of bureaucratic constraint, meant that, during Trump's term in office, these actions were of questionable effect in altering either populism's exclusion or personalism. However, in the longer run, they may have contributed to a foundation for institutional restoration in a post-populist period.

POPULISM AND BUREAUCRATIC RESPONSE

Even before the drama of Trump's first impeachment, where testimony from career national security officials featured prominently, populist concerns about an alleged deep state were regularly aired in public. The term has its roots in elite military, economic and governmental networks in places like Egypt and Turkey that prevent duly elected public officials from implementing policy. In the American context, Trump and his allies alleged that similar officials, largely career staff in executive branch agencies, represented "a conspiracy of powerful, unelected bureaucrats secretly pursuing their own agenda," and thwarting the populist president in the process.[3] Press Secretary Sean Spicer remarked that State Department career officials should "either get with the program or they can go."[4] While Stephen Skowronek et al. are right to observe that "presidential impatience with administrative resistance and conditions on their control of the executive branch has flared repeatedly in recent years," there is little doubt that Trump's populism dialed up the nature of this confrontation, thus setting the stage for potential resistance.

Needless to say, the United States is not Egypt, and there is limited reason to accept the claim that State Department officials, including those in RGA, represented the ideal type of deep state conspiracy seen in other cases.[5] With that said, the significant populist variation discussed in chapters 3 and 4 does raise an important question: how did career officials respond to the twin populist projects of constructing identity boundaries and implementing a personalistic structure of governance? Posing the question in this way highlights the agency of career staff left behind when Obama administration political appointees departed after the 2016 election. It also provides a link to a long literature on bureaucratic responsiveness, including response to areas of policy disagreement.[6] Scholars of bureaucracy are well acquainted with the possibility that career officials may not approve of priorities set by elected superiors, whether on rationalist or normative grounds. State Department officials are certainly high on the list of dissenting bureaucrats, with a diverse history of disagreement, whether to the George W. Bush administration's Iraq War or the Obama administration's response to the Syrian civil war. The populist changes during Trump's time in office provided ample opportunity for further disagreement.

RGA staff occupied a tenuous place during this period. RGA closely matches Drezner's description of an "embedded" "missionary institution." Its approach was missionary in that by 2016 its staff possessed "a coherent set of preferences over means and ends," in this case related to appropriate steps to assess and engage religion in diplomacy.[7] Moreover, RGA "tried to prevent the introduction of additional normative or material goals in order to avoid value conflicts or tradeoffs."[8] When such offices are embedded within existing agencies, survival is never a guarantee, particularly after initial political patrons leave the scene. The Trump transition thus represented a twin challenge to RGA staffers. On the one hand, elements of Trump's populism, especially related to identity construction, ran headlong into the coherent preferences of RGA's approach to assessment and engagement, which was pragmatically rooted in a pluralism quite different from populist exclusion. Moreover, populist personalism introduced significant uncertainty over the nature of decisions that would determine whether newer offices like RGA would survive, much less thrive, in the new administration.

Some of the core choices available to bureaucrats, like career RGA staffers, closely reflect options long considered by scholars of bureaucratic politics, including Albert Hirschman's classic *Exit, Voice and Loyalty*.[9] Like Marissa Golden, the categories of bureaucratic response discussed below borrow from Hirschman's work, although are not a systematic test of his framework's claims.[10] Furthermore, drawing inductively on observed behavior during the transition period, this chapter adds a response option open to bureaucrats confronting what Hirschman calls decline: persistence.

"Voice" may most closely resemble the claims of more conspiracy-minded critics of the deep state. As Golden summarizes, "Voice covers any type of resistance other than exit undertaken by agency careerists; in other words, it is any expression of dissatisfaction or resistance from within."[11] There are numerous specific forms of voice documented by students of bureaucratic politics, including foot-dragging, whistleblowing, and internal dissent. Some forms of voice may respect existing procedural rules, such as filing policy dissents through approved bureaucratic channels, while others may involve violation of bureaucratic norms or even law, such as the leaking of sensitive documents. Voice brings obvious potential costs to career bureaucrats, even in nonpopulist times. This may involve facing rational consequences in the form of restricted career prospects, as well as more normative costs, such as disapproval from fellow career staff who continue to abide by procedural norms. For these reasons, much of the voice that this chapter documents is what I refer to as "channeled constraint," taking place via less costly channels than open rebellion.

In contrast to voice, Hirschman identifies the fact that, even in environments in which citizens or low-level bureaucrats are quite dissatisfied, some may continue to display loyalty to newly elected officials. "Loyal civil servants comply with the directives of presidents and their designated deputies and actively and responsibly implement the administration's policies."[12] In the context of the Trump State Department, I refer to loyalty as "mutual adaptation." The roots of adaptation are diverse. Some career officials may share the policy preferences of incoming political elites. Some may act simply out of rational self-interest, in pursuit of career advancement or other material incentives. Some may abide by strict normative commitments to implementing the policy preferences of elected officials that render voice too costly. The status of offices like RGA as one of Drezner's "missionary" organizations raises another possibility: staffers dedicated to the preservation of vulnerable embedded offices during times of political transition may engage in loyalty in part to ensure their office's survival. This explanation blends material calculation with an essentially normative dedication to bureaucratic, rather than individual, preservation.

Hirshman's categories do not explicitly account for a final category of bureaucratic behavior that merits discussion in the context of a populist transition—persistence. Persistent behavior essentially ignores the signals sent by newly empowered political appointees, instead continuing in existing work that does not directly run counter to expressed preferences of political appointees. I refer to bounded persistence because this response takes place within limits set by populist incumbents. Persistence differs empirically from both voice and loyalty. It does not involve active participation in furthering the policy ends of political appointees, which characterizes loyalty. However, it also does not involve open contestation of those goals, as is the case with voice. Instead, persistence represents a kind of bureaucratic muscle memory, continuing to operate in the absence of clear guidance to the contrary. Persistence may be an attractive option in missionary agencies for several reasons. It represents an attempt to "expose others [in this case new political appointees] to the ideas the missionary institution is supposed to encourage."[13] Bureaucrats thus choose this approach both because of a sincere dedication to their institution's mission, as well as the lower risk to the office that it represents in comparison to voice.

TABLE 5.1 Bureaucratic Responses to Populist Variation

	Response	Impact of Populism	Indicators Related to RGA Work
Bounded Persistence	Continue preexisting foreign policy work, in process and substance.	Encouraged by populism's limited policy priorities.	Development of a work stream on religion and electoral institutions.
		Inhibited by populist-driven reductions in staff capacity.	Expanding diplomatic training in religion and foreign policy.
Mutual Adaptation (Loyalty)	Engage with appointees of populist leader.	Populism's personalism lends importance to policy priorities of key loyalists.	Outreach to new populist officials for education on office's structure and function.
	Adapt existing mission to populist policy priorities.		Added emphasis on assessment and engagement related to Trafficking in Persons.
Channeled Constraint (Voice)	Express dissent via formalized bureaucratic channels.	Most likely in foreign policy areas impacted by populism's thin ideology.	Dissent channel to "Muslim Ban" executive orders.
	Assessment of external religious dissent to populist policy.	Personalism raises potential costs of this response, if activated.	Maintaining communication with faith-based partners regarding changes to environmental policy.
Exit	Departure from government or active areas of religion and diplomacy.	Most likely in presence of both populist ideology and direct attention from elites empowered by personalism.	Departure of career officials involved in Paris Climate Agreement.

Table 5.1 summarizes these categories and provides illustrative indicators from early 2017.

Of Hirshman's classic categories, I have yet to discuss exit. Exit was certainly a possibility for career officials during the Trump administration, and departures from government service took place in several prominent bureaus of the State Department.[14] Some staff left out of frustration with the substance of government decisions, while others found budgetary support for their positions removed (for instance, the elimination of special representatives and associated staff described in chapter 4). Others simply left religious diplomacy, either because of the regular nature of Foreign Service rotations into new posts or because they proactively sought policy areas less tied to populism's ideology of exclusion. Patterns of exit are worth noting but receive limited further attention for a simple reason: individuals who exited religious diplomacy (or government service entirely) had less agency over the office's activities in the midst of the transition. Departed colleagues did provide listening ears and advice on office preservation but operated at a distance from the substance and process of populist foreign policy. The primary goal of this chapter is to document the responses of staff, in place, who guided RGA's initiatives during the transition, and those who exited had less influence in this regard.

How might constraint, adaptation, persistence, and exit relate to the twin dimensions of populism: constructed identity boundaries and personalistic structure of rule? In summary, the costs of constraint become most necessary to bear in the presence of populism's identity-based exclusion. In these policy spheres, bureaucrats are likely to be required to violate their office's missionary purpose, while also finding it difficult to simply avoid the question entirely. In contrast, forms of adaptation are most likely in the presence of personalism, but weaker focus on identity boundaries. In these cases, career staff may cooperate with new political players without violating the normative mission of their organization, also conforming to powerful bureaucratic norms of service to elected officials. Persistence is likely in the *joint absence* of populist personalism and identity construction. This may initially seem like a residual category, unlikely to occupy much space. However, due to populism's ideological thinness and the relative lack of political experience on the part of some populist officials, there are substantial foreign policy spheres that, at least for a time, remain largely below the radar of populists in office. In these diplomatic niches, persistent bureaucrats may have significant ability to

Ideological Boundaries

	Strong	Weak
Strong	*Exit*	*Mutual Adaptation*
Weak	*Channeled Constraint*	*Bounded Persistence*

(left axis label: **Personalism**)

FIGURE 5.1 Dimensions of populism and predominant bureaucratic responses.

preserve their office's core functions away from populist view. Exit is most consistent with strong operation of both populism's identity-based ideology and personalist structure, which implicates career officials in policy decisions running counter to their missions and removes the ability to avoid attention of populist officials with significant discretion over policy (figure 5.1 summarizes these expected patterns). To be clear, while these are general expectations, individual actors retained discretion over their responses in the workplace. One would expect, however, that offline responses may incur costs. For instance, a career official confronting a policy matter of strong personalist concern via constraint is likely to provoke populist reaction.

In sum, constraint, adaptation, persistence, and exit coexisted at the State Department, and in a missionary office like RGA. All are much more nuanced than the myth of a deep state that preoccupied Trump administration loyalists. These strategies may be deployed variably by career officials depending on the nature of the populist interests in a given policy sphere. Table 5.1 summarizes the operation and evidence of these mechanisms. The rest of this chapter now turns to detailing their operation in RGA in the initial months of the Trump administration.

(BOUNDED) PERSISTENCE: STAYING BELOW POPULISM'S RADAR

Earlier chapters discussed the ways in which populist boundary construction and personalism came with implications for religion and Trump administration foreign policy. Without minimizing the importance of those areas, there were significant regional and functional spheres of U.S. foreign policy that were largely irrelevant to the Trump administration's populism. Especially in the early months of the administration, as the pace of political appointments lagged, there was ample opportunity to muddle ahead in several areas of ongoing work. This was the case in the functional portfolio related to governance issues that occupied a majority of my time in the RGA office. This continuity was bounded, particularly because of staffing limitations that were, themselves, endogenous to populism's personalism. However, bounds did not preclude substantive work, and enabled staff to preserve some of RGA's function, even in a highly uncertain information environment.

Some of this persistence directly built on initiatives already well-established in RGA by early 2017, such as anti-corruption policy and work to counter wildlife trafficking. By early 2017, RGA's anti-corruption work was fairly well advanced in the Nigerian context, and so the office's primary responsibilities involved lending support as needed to the ongoing work of diplomats in the field. This included confronting several practical challenges as the anti-corruption engagement deepened, including maintaining engagement from busy religious leaders and considering how to monitor and evaluate the effects of programs carried out in cooperation with religious networks. In the most tangible sign of this continued engagement, RGA's acting special representative returned to Nigeria in July 2017 to lend additional encouragement to the religious leader network in their partnership with civil society organizations.[15]

Beyond Nigeria, RGA explored the possibilities of similar work in other contexts where the template of religious engagement could hold promise. In part because of the strong working relationships that RGA had developed in the Bureau of African Affairs, cases on the subcontinent provided several opportunities. The 2016 Ghana election, for instance, brought opposition candidate Nana Akufo-Addo into office, trumpeting themes of both interfaith cooperation in the diverse country and addressing endemic corruption that impedes equitable economic growth. In this environment, working with diplomats in the field on religious assessment and engagement held significant potential.

Governance work developed in new areas as well, such as a focus on the impact of religion on efforts to strengthen electoral institutions and avoid election violence. Strengthening democracy remained a priority of

American diplomats in various regions, and there was an obvious opportunity to bring RGA's assessment and engagement tools to bear on the issue. Like much of RGA's work, the impact of religion on elections would be politically ambivalent, at times a tool for hardline candidates to whip up anti-minority sentiment, but, at others, a resource to integrate high-credibility local leaders into efforts to fortify political institutions during times of instability. During this period, elections loomed especially large in some prominent cases in sub-Saharan Africa, notably Kenya, seeking to avoid a replay of 2007's election violence, and the Democratic Republic of the Congo, where uncertainty loomed over the political future of then-President Joseph Kabila. In 2017, while religion had become more closely integrated into areas of development assistance like those combatting HIV/AIDS, there was limited similar progress related to the significant diplomatic and foreign assistance attention that the United States has historically placed on strengthening global democracy.

Over the course of 2017, RGA worked with colleagues in the State Department, USAID, and organizations like the United States Institute for Peace to develop an initiative designed to address this shortfall. Background conversations with colleagues in and out of government revealed exactly the sort of conditions tailored for an RGA contribution: significant, largely ad hoc, responses from practitioners in the field, a lack of formal guidance, and a consistent sense that missing out on religion's importance was undermining effective diplomatic and programmatic response. Anecdotal evidence of religion's relevance abounded. Houses of worship served as registration centers and polling places in a wide variety of contexts. Religious networks mobilized hundreds of thousands of domestic citizen election monitors in the Philippines. Catholic bishops in the DRC organized domestic election observation, while some in the Muslim community expressed concerns about the inclusivity of that process. Some Buddhist clergy in Sri Lanka promoted voter registration efforts, while others allied themselves with Sinhala nationalist politicians seen as hostile to diversity on the island. In other settings, programs designed to increase voter registration had to contend with traditional gender roles closely implicated with religion. Supporters of anti-democratic leaders claimed that the very idea of democracy ran counter to religious beliefs. And in repeated conversations, practitioners were concerned that the most common approach in their organizations was to avoid the subject of religion, whether for fear of stirring up more trouble or personal discomfort with the topic.

These background conversations culminated in a roundtable workshop with approximately thirty participants from the State Department, USAID, and various contributors from democracy promotion organizations like the Carter Center, International Foundation for Electoral Systems, and Freedom House. The agenda devoted time to the assessment of religion's impact on elections and engagement with religious actors, both in peaceful contexts and those where election violence looms. Attendees particularly wrestled with questions of impartiality and credibility of religious leadership, which may vary within a given country and significantly impact any religious assessment and engagement strategy. While the relationship between Islam and elections receives the lion's share of attention, participants agreed that the challenges and opportunities were just as pronounced in various religious contexts, whether Christian-majority portions of Latin America, Buddhist-majority Sri Lanka, or Hindu-majority India. The consultation readout compiled best practices as well as potential challenges in religious engagement, recommended assessment principles, and included implementation opportunities for governmental and nongovernmental organizations. While my own term in government was drawing to a close, the next steps for a fully functional RGA office would have been fairly straightforward: conduct a religious electoral assessment in partnership with an interested post, and then develop and implement an engagement strategy for the post, based on the assessed dynamics. In many ways, the dynamics in the workshop room in July 2017 bore little imprint of any populist change.

Beyond the governance portfolio, RGA staff also continued to prioritize the important work of institutionalizing its approach to the training of fellow diplomats during this transitional period. While RGA was accustomed to participation in the Foreign Service Institute's (FSI) cornerstone Religion and Diplomacy class by this time, 2017 saw several opportunities for more narrowly tailored training engagements. In January, RGA staff piloted a half-day training in the main State Department building, rather than within the more isolated context of FSI, and later in the winter, RGA joined training courses focused on African politics to add a session on religion and diplomacy in the region. RGA's training template provided a fairly clear model that could be adapted to more specific regions and functional areas, and discussions began about training tailored to issues like combatting trafficking in persons. RGA also remained engaged in the cornerstone FSI Religion and Diplomacy course, with active participation across multiple days in May 2017. With limited involvement at RGA by new political appointees, the content and structure of these trainings was largely similar to patterns developed over the first three years of RGA's existence.

These stories of bounded continuity in some of RGA's early 2017 work raise an obvious question: was a populist difference detectable in these elements of RGA's work, or did staff effectively insulate this work from populism's identity construction and personalism? In sum, these initiatives remained largely free of populism's identity boundaries, but were bounded by its personalism, mainly in the form of reduced office capacity due to the lack of direct personal ties necessary for influence under populist rule. In these early months of the transition, staff did not need to take steps to minimize the influence of populist boundary construction; there was little to no involvement in these streams of work from political appointees associated with the new administration's identity construction. Aside from one question from a transition staffer about obstacles for faith-based organizations in receiving governance programming grants from the U.S. Government, there was little active participation from the new administration in this work.

Continuity in one important area of RGA's work, internal training, did involve effectively avoiding the topic of populist identity construction. While the RGA content for diplomatic training changed little (if at all) in early 2017, contributions from new administration officials certainly did. Remarks in trainings referenced the universality the need for God in human hearts, referenced only conservative Christian organizations as potential resources to diplomats in the field, and criticized prominent civil liberties organizations for supposed hostility to religion. Religion's impact on foreign policy was stressed as a real priority to the Trump administration, but attention then focused on Christian persecution in the Middle East, links between religious freedom promotion and counterterrorism, and the relative rarity of atheism around the world. Subsequent training sessions led by career staff existed in parallel with these remarks, unaffected but in clear tension with some of the identity-construction offered by new appointees.

The persistence of governance work was also bounded by populism's personalism. In the absence of strong, personalistic ties to key White House loyalists, RGA's personnel capacity diminished rapidly during the early months of 2017. While the potential for additional work related to governance was latent during this period, regional staffers responsible for Africa, Europe, and the Western Hemisphere departed the office. Questions about the general State Department hiring freeze and uncertainty about the future of S bureau offices delayed the potential addition of new staff responsible for those regions and others. Phone conversations with colleagues in Latin America related to religion and wildlife trafficking, and Sub-Saharan Africa related to religion and anti-corruption efforts, revealed clear opportunities for the sort of assessment and engagement advising that had become RGA's basic work plan by late 2016. But reduced staff capacity, uncertainty at embassies abroad about incoming political appointments, and restrictions on expenditures for foreign travel made these sorts of proactive engagements effectively impossible. With no indication from key White House figures that such topics would be an administration priority, initiatives could limp along, but without the capacity built in RGA's first three years of existence.

MUTUAL ADAPTATION:
ENGAGING POPULIST PERSONALISM

In contrast to areas of bounded continuity that largely attempted to "stick to knitting" while paying limited attention to populist change, RGA staff also exercised agency in active adaptation to a new environment. Adaptation took place through two channels. First, adaptation had a relational component, as political leadership arrived in key posts. RGA staff leveraged ties with more senior career foreign policy officials who would likely have some influence in structural decisions about the State Department's future structure. Staff simultaneously attempted rapid learning about the nature of incoming political appointees, and exercised agency to ease their transition into relevant work in Foggy Bottom. Second, RGA adapted its substantive policy focus, highlighting the relevance of its approach to policy spheres likely to be a high priority to the incoming administration that did not run counter to the office's missionary goals.

Unlike areas of bounded continuity, these adaptations involved real updates in RGA's work, either in its form or substance. However, it is important to be clear that these adaptations were intended to preserve RGA's core approach to assessment and engagement. Career staff shared a substantive commitment to this approach and calculated that this set of adaptations was most likely to increase the office's odds of survival in the midst of the significant uncertainty associated with the transition. For this reason, adaptation was most feasible in policy spheres that were at some distance from populist identity construction, but of personal interest to key loyalists.

First, and most consistently, RGA staff laid the groundwork for the office's preservation by leveraging ties to more senior, career foreign policy officials likely to have a role in guiding any transition, regardless of party. In addition to senior relationships within the State Department itself, staff and office supporters also conducted bipartisan outreach to potentially sympathetic House and Senate offices in leadership positions on relevant foreign policy committees. Meetings between career staff in RGA and senior career State Department colleagues began almost immediately in January 2017, and occurred regularly throughout the early months of the transition. These colleagues advised RGA staff on how to make the case for the office's utility in the most compelling way possible and advised RGA leadership about the very structure of the State Department, as Secretary Tillerson's "reorganization" loomed and rumors swirled about the elimination of entire bureaus, or even the merging of the State Department with USAID.

In this poor information environment, senior ties within government helped clarify the likely nature of upcoming variation. It became apparent that the goal of preserving the office's "mission and function" would be prioritized, while accepting change to its form and location. This, of course, left significant uncertainty. Would the functionality of the office truly be preserved if staffing levels declined precipitously? Would the mission of the office be preserved if its location changed to report within IRF? Relationships with career officials were of limited use in answering these sorts of crucial questions because they themselves likely had limited clarity on decision-making plans in the new populist environment.

Career RGA staff were aware of this, and again exercised agency in attempting to build relationships, provide information, and ease the transition of incoming Trump administration appointees. Even before the inauguration, staff closely monitored foreign policy appointments and discussed how to frame RGA's work to them, to clarify the office's function. Some candidates reportedly considered for the secretary of state role, notably Mitt Romney and Bob Corker, had well-established ties to either religious politics or the foreign policy bureaucracy, while others, including eventual nominee Tillerson, had less obvious work experience in RGA's core area. As nominations and appointments were formalized, RGA staff tracked the likely personal priorities of those like Tillerson, as well as short-lived National Security Advisor Mike Flynn. Staff engaged in similar background research as the transition's landing team arrived at the State Department. While the overall pace of political appointments at State was notoriously slow under the Trump/Tillerson regime, there were several early arrivals with substantive ties to religious politics, most prominently the campaign staffer responsible for maintaining the Trump evangelical advisory board.

This process of adaptation to political appointees entered a new phase once they began to arrive in the building. Some arrived in the State Department in the earliest days of the transition, and fairly quickly began to meet with career staff. The National Prayer Breakfast, an annual event of particular importance in evangelical circles, took place in early February and provided a further opportunity for career staff to build ties with incoming appointees.[16] RGA staff hosted an informal welcome breakfast for new arrivals in the administration's opening weeks, with the goal of promoting awareness about the office's structure and mission. Staff drafted and circulated pieces on RGA's potential future structure to potentially relevant transition officials. As transition staff at State settled into more permanent roles, RGA regularly incorporated them into relevant work, for instance by facilitating involvement in an in-house session on religion and conflict mediation that combined practitioners from religious organizations, career staff from relevant country desks at State, and new appointees.

This adaptation was not always smooth and, at times, thrust RGA staff into the role of minimizing potential stumbling points for the new administration. Trump officials and religious loyalists regularly boasted of prayer in White House and State Department meetings, and career staff took steps to increase pluralism in this practice. Staff found themselves actively mediating the White House's decision not to include a mention of Jews or anti-Semitism in its January 2017 statement on International Holocaust Remembrance Day. In preparing for meetings with external religious leaders critical of aspects of the Trump administration, especially tied to migration and refugee policy, office staff prepared briefing materials to manage potential conflicts that could arise. When political appointees outside of the State Department complained about which religious leaders were afforded meetings with senior officials, RGA staff clarified the official process for requesting such meetings, the bureaucratic steps that went into preparing briefing materials, and likely questions. When documents that should have had RGA clearance were either altered (or simply not provided), RGA staff stressed the utility of this process in making sure that communications were in sync and mistakes avoided. When Secretary Tillerson refused to keep with bipartisan tradition in hosting a diplomatic reception in celebration of the end of the month of Ramadan, RGA staff worked to clarify to S Bureau staff that such a reception was primarily a diplomatic tool to engage with relevant representatives of foreign governments based in Washington, D.C., not a matter of domestic coalition maintenance.

A second mechanism of adaptation moved from cultivating personal relationships to the substance of the policy work prioritized in a shrinking RGA office. Perhaps the clearest evidence of adaptation in RGA's substantive work was the development of a stream of engagement related to combatting trafficking in persons (TIP). While discussions about partnering RGA with the State Department's TIP office preceded the Trump administration, these efforts received a boost with the new administration's early emphasis on the trafficking issue. The contours of the issue seemed to provide an opportunity for RGA staff to demonstrate the office's approach to the new administration. Given the relative lack of personal ties to the new populist leadership, this opportunity was attractive to RGA's career leadership, who were attempting to demonstrate the nonpartisan nature of the office's potential contribution.

Work to combat human trafficking enjoyed relatively bipartisan support in Congress long before Trump's term in office, with the Trafficking

Victims Protection Act of 2000, for instance, enjoying overwhelming support in its original passage and several subsequent revisions. The Office to Monitor and Combat Trafficking in Persons was subsequently created at the State Department to report on the issue and direct foreign assistance to programs designed to combat both sex and labor trafficking globally. Countering TIP attracted bipartisan support, not only on moral grounds, but also because of the links between trafficking and various forms of international criminality and weak governance that run against U.S. security and economic interests. Faith-based organizations have a long history of working to combat human trafficking.[17] At a staff level, multiple career staff in the State Department TIP office had experience involving religion and diplomacy, including working ties to IRF. Although TIP work was not a major focus of RGA's limited staff capacity during the Obama administration, initial conversations in late 2016 had probed potential partnership.

Early in the Trump administration, it became clear that TIP issues would be a personal priority of key administration loyalists, notably Ivanka Trump and Vice President Mike Pence. While the substantive nature of this issue could have made it a fit for RGA adaptation regardless, RGA staff were aware that the incoming administration was likely to increase focus in this area. As early as February 2017, White House officials conducted prominent listening sessions with anti-trafficking advocates, and President Trump issued a related executive order that month. When Trump visited the Vatican in May 2017, a trip that many expected to be fraught with controversy over issues like climate change and refugee assistance, Ivanka Trump attempted to build bridges in a side meeting with the Catholic Community of Sant'Egidio, discussing cooperation in anti-trafficking efforts. In June 2017, Ivanka joined Secretary Tillerson for the launch of the State Department's annual report on the issue. By September 2017, she would announce to the annual United Nations General Assembly a grant of $25 million in U.S. foreign assistance to fund anti-trafficking work around the world.[18]

As part of ongoing efforts to demonstrate RGA's utility to the new administration, career staff accelerated efforts to develop a line of religious engagement work on TIP issues. While this kind of engagement could have developed in a nonpopulist administration, signals about the personal importance of the issue to key officials around President Trump attracted special attention from RGA staff. They met several times with career colleagues involved in combatting trafficking to develop coopera- tion between the offices. This represented a logical extension of RGA's work in governance across bureaus such as Conflict & Stabilization Oper- ations and Population, Refugees and Migration, which shared space in the State Department's organization chart. The template provided in RGA's anti-corruption work, for instance, provided a kind of proof of con- cept for value that RGA could bring to TIP's work.

Over the course of these planning sessions, staff clarified that involve- ment in TIP work could draw on both RGA's assessment and engagement capabilities. On the assessment side, diplomats in the TIP office and in global embassies charged with TIP monitoring could benefit from under- standing the nuanced ways that religion contributes to and potentially mitigates human trafficking. TIP is, in many ways, a clear issue to illus- trate the ambivalence of religion. Some religious practices and networks have, at times, been seen as a source of trafficking, for instance in the movement of young Quranic students in Senegal, while others have been seen as a source of victim reintegration assistance, as in Indonesia.[19] TIP also presents strong evidence of the multifaceted nature of religion's impact on politics. At times, official statements from national-level reli- gious leaders are important to track, but the lived religious experiences of grassroots women's organizations may be just as important in track- ing religion as a source of resilience.

Turning to engagement, embassies and consulates could receive advice on approaches to integrating religious networks into efforts to combat TIP. Such engagements exist in multiple locations, from Thailand to Ghana, and RGA could work with TIP to advise on applying similar techniques in other environments.[20] As in RGA's anti-corruption work in Nigeria, any engagement would need to reflect local circumstances given religion's con- textual impact on issues like trafficking. Religious organizations are probably most prominently associated with efforts to end sex trafficking, but religious dynamics may be closely tied to labor-based human traffick- ing. Work against TIP also highlights RGA's common advice to consider not just male hierarchs, but also the role of women as religious leaders. For example, Sr. Gabriella Bottani, one of the State Department's Human Trafficking Heroes in 2019, directs a global network of women religious combatting trafficking across multiple continents.[21]

Moving from engagement in the field to RGA's common role in DC-based policy convening, office leadership discussed adapting its training modules for a session with DC-based TIP staff, where this core approach (blending assessment with engagement) would be narrowly tailored to the specifics of TIP policy. Such a workshop would then provide career TIP staff with the tools to develop religious engagement approaches in their work directly with global diplomatic posts. RGA frequently promoted ties between State Department officials and D.C.-based nonprofits and faith-based organizations, and a similar model could have applied to TIP work. Prominent antitrafficking organizations like International Justice Mission have a Christian orientation, while several more general faith-based development organizations like Catholic Relief Services have significant human trafficking programs. Domestic public diplomacy associated with TIP could also have a religious element, for instance through networks of religious colleges or seminaries with student groups engaged in advocacy against TIP.

How much of a difference did populism make to the nature and effects of these attempts at adaptation? First, populism's personalism presented a clear challenge to the relational side of adaptation. RGA's early 2017 career leadership developed strong ties to senior career officials in the State Department, as well as bipartisan awareness of the office's function and utility on Capitol Hill. However, such relationships were of limited use given the realities of populist rule. Career colleagues joked that Congress would have little fall back if the White House ignored them. Instead, populism's personalism meant that direct ties to those like Vice President Pence and core Trump loyalists around the White House became key to influence over the future of the bureaucracy, religion included. Staff worked to cultivate these ties, but they were very weak, especially in comparison to offices like IRF. Trump loyalist Johnnie Moore was likely being sincere when he asked in early 2017, "What is the Office of Religion and Global Affairs actually doing?"[22] Trump administration loyalists, including those tied to the evangelical advisory board, had much deeper direct ties to other streams of the religious regime complex, particularly international religious freedom and the more Islamophobic portions of the counterterrorism community. Policy adaptation did have some effect, as religious engagement in TIP work was acknowledged in meetings like those of Ivanka Trump with Sant'Egidio and the recognition of Sister

Gabriella Bottani as a "Anti-Trafficking Hero" by the Department in 2019. But TIP was, in some ways, exceptionally well-tailored for adaptation, and more difficult to replicate in other policy spheres.

Second, populism's identity-based foreign policy content limited, without eliminating, the potential for adaptation in the office's policy agenda. On the one hand, populism's ideological thinness meant that, aside from core campaign issues tied to migration and refugees, there was not a clear policy agenda to which RGA staff could adapt. TIP was in some ways an exception to a general rudderlessness on many of the everyday policy issues that flew below the radar of a populist campaign for office. Even TIP essentially attracted RGA attention because of populism's personalistic dimension, with the daughter of the populist incumbent sending credible signals of the issue's importance. Several of the foreign policy issues that were of clearest importance to the incoming populist on identity grounds clearly ran afoul of existing RGA approaches to religion and U.S. foreign policy. In an environment, where the Policy Planning Staff advocated for an "Islamic Reformation" and White House officials considered changing Countering Violent Extremism to Countering Islamic Extremism, RGA's ability to adapt without violating core elements of its mission was limited.

CHANNELED CONSTRAINT? RESPONDING TO POPULIST IDENTITY BOUNDARIES

Trump administration fulminations against the deep state centered on the alleged role of career staff in directly thwarting the legitimate foreign policy authority of duly appointed executive branch officials. While immediate, emotional responses to the 2016 election were indeed common within the State Department, it did not follow that career staff then united to craft a shadow foreign policy, undermining Trump administration goals. In RGA, staff generally acted via approved channels and through activities consistent with the mission of the office. More overt dissent did, at times, take place in the State Department, particularly through leaks to reporters. But with RGA vulnerable to closure and largely bypassed by the new administration, there was limited opportunity for systematic forms of foot-dragging or whistleblowing that sometimes arise in the literature on dissent and bureaucratic politics.

In policy areas where populist identity boundaries operated most strongly, RGA staff primarily took action consistent with the office's mission of serving as a point of assessment and engagement between faith-based organizations and U.S. officials on foreign policy matters of mutual concern. In the early months of 2017, assessing religious dynamics related to foreign policy decisions meant tracking criticism, both in the U.S. and abroad, of many early Trump administration decisions. Turning to engagement, RGA's role as a convenor of domestic, faith-based organizations was hardwired into its bureaucratic raison d'être, a key part of what Elizabeth Shakman Hurd describes as "expert religion."[23] This convening function meant that the office's staff had an obligation to pass along policy concerns and facilitate meetings at both working and high levels of the State Department. Two particular areas of RGA work provide insight into how this channeled constraint operated during the early months of the transition: the executive orders related to refugees and visa policy constituting the "Muslim Ban," and withdrawal from the Paris Climate Agreement.

As mentioned in chapter 3, in the immediate aftermath of President Trump's January 2017 inauguration, draft executive orders related to refugee resettlement and visa access began to circulate through the foreign policy bureaucracy and the press. Very quickly, on Friday, January 27th, Trump formally issued the first of what would become a series of slightly updated executive orders on these topics. Executive Order (EO) 13769, "Protecting the Nation from Foreign Terrorist Entry into the United States," had two primary targets: suspending entry and visa issuance from a subset of Muslim-majority countries, and temporarily halting refugee admission into the country.[24] The EO was widely understood to deliver on the call of then-candidate Trump for a "total and complete shutdown of Muslims entering the United States," also frequently referred to as the "Muslim Ban."[25] The order's substance quickly drew protesters into the streets around the country, and its ambiguities, especially about travelers in transit to the United States, resulted in chaos at major U.S. international airports.

The draft and final executive orders did indeed land like bombs in an already uncertain State Department. They directly implicated several different aspects of RGA's existing work, and raised concerns related to its future implementation. The general issue of migration policy is a concern to countless religious organizations based in the United States, and the particular issue of refugee resettlement involves religious charities worldwide who interact with the U.S. Government. Of the nine agencies officially contracted by the government to resettle refugees within the United States, six have religious ties. RGA's founding Special Representative Shaun Casey did extensive public diplomacy related to refugee resettlement during his term in office, reflective of these close ties.[26] On substance, several dimensions of early order drafts raised concerns within RGA. Drafts had various, awkward wording that implied that religious-based exemptions to the refugee ban would only be granted "provided that the religion of the individual is a minority religion in the individual's country of origin," effectively ruling out Muslim applicants facing persecution in Muslim-majority countries. The fact that only Muslim-majority countries were mentioned in the parts of the initial order related to travel bans raised obvious concerns. So did calls for "uniform screening standards" intended to weed out "those who would place violent ideologies over American law." In practice, these seemed to raise serious concerns about potential religious discrimination in the screening process.

All of this gave ample reason to expect resistance to this policy approach from within the State Department more broadly, and RGA in particular. What stands out in the response was how efforts to respond to what many viewed to be slapdash policy making generally took place *within* typical bureaucratic channels and drawing on established office functions. Foreign Service Officers and other staff at State view candid debate over proposed policy to be central to their jobs, not antithetical to them. This showed through both in a prominent "dissent channel" cable formulated in the days around the initial EO, as well as RGA's primary internal response: compiling criticisms of the EO from relevant religious leaders in the United States and assessing them for department leadership. Supporting a dissent channel cable, providing assessments of external criticism from religious leaders and faith-based organizations, and facilitating meetings with groups opposed to the policy development are all entirely consistent with the established mission and approach that had developed within RGA by late 2016.

Most directly, staff across the State Department responded by organizing the largest dissent channel memo in the history of the department, with over one thousand signatories. The dissent channel, initially established in response to concerns that diplomats lacked an avenue for lodging disagreements during the Vietnam War, is an institutionalized means of registering the substance of a policy disagreement from Foreign Service Officers or other State Department employees. Dissenters should be protected from retaliation and are entitled to receive a response from the department's Policy Planning Staff. The leaked memo objected to the executive orders on both principled and pragmatic grounds. Pragmatically, authors objected that the bans would "sour relations" with "much of the Muslim world, which sees the ban as religiously-motivated," raising the prospect of both diminished security cooperation and economic costs.[27] On principle, the ban's singling out of Muslim-majority countries seemed to run counter to "the concept that we are all equal under the law and that we as a nation abhor discrimination." It is important to note that this form of dissent was *not* extralegal or some deep state act of refusing policy implementation.

RGA's more specific response to the EO was tied directly to its mandate to serve as a point of contact between religious organizations, both in the United States and abroad, and U.S. diplomats to ensure high-quality communication over areas of mutual concern. With this function in mind, RGA staff (even before the EO was officially issued) began to receive objections and criticisms from religious leaders and organizations. Compiling these statements was consistent with RGA's assessment mission, as it involved analysis of the status of responses across the U.S. religious landscape, as well as its engagement function, as it involved passing along policy feedback from valued institutional and individual partners. Examples of such criticism were abundant. The Hebrew Immigrant Aid Society, an official refugee resettlement agency, officially sued the Trump administration in federal court.[28] Criticism went far beyond resettlement organizations, including "top evangelical leaders from all 50 states call[ing] on President Trump and Vice President Pence to support refugees."[29] Mormon leadership also expressed concern. Assessment also noted that some in the evangelical world like Franklin Graham publicly supported the EO.

Beyond passing on assessment documents on these patterns of critique and (more limited) support to senior career State Department officials, RGA found itself regularly managing the fallout from the EO in face-to-face engagements throughout 2017. At a working level, RGA hosted listening sessions with faith-based organizations of various traditions who expressed opposition to elements of the policy. This opposition stretched well beyond Muslim American organizations or organizations that worked primarily in refugee resettlement. Religious freedom advocates expressed concern that the policies would undermine U.S. Government credibility in IRF promotion; counterterrorism experts worried that the EO would undermine relationships with Muslim partners; and contacts at faith-based, anti-trafficking organizations expressed concern that the restrictions could impede their ability to engage with the U.S. Government in TIP work. At a higher level, RGA staffed a meeting between Secretary Tillerson and Bishop Oscar Cantú, then Chair of the Committee on International Justice and Peace of the United States Conference of Catholic Bishops, where migration policy featured on the agenda.[30]

To be clear, this sort of channeled constraint did, at times, coexist with more open resistance outside of institutionalized channels. Most prominently, the content of the dissent to the Muslim Bans was leaked to the press, presumably by a disaffected career staffer, which resulted in extensive media coverage of the unprecedented number of career staff who had signed the memo. There was communication between anonymous State Department staff and reporters in other areas that touched on RGA work as well. For instance, Secretary Tillerson's spring 2017 decision to decline RGA's proposal to hold the department's customary Ramadan reception received press coverage.[31] Reporters on the Foggy Bottom beat clearly had plenty of internal sources willing to voice unattributed frustrations with both populist identity-based exclusion and personalism. In a public appearance at a faith-based conference on refugees and migration in early 2017, staff appeared in a nonspeaking role. However, in the context of an RGA office that was vulnerable to closure, and largely bypassed by the new administration, these episodes did not live up to conspiracies of deep state resistance.

A similar pattern played out in another area of Trump administration departure from the policy priorities of the Obama administration: the Paris Climate Agreement. As with refugee policy, candidate Trump openly broadcasted his hostility to the Paris Agreement, tying it to a general populist rejection of multilateralism and international constraint. While

Trump administration action to fulfill these pledges once in office moved more slowly than refugee restrictions, in early June 2017 Trump officially announced a pullback from participation in the Paris Agreement, remarking, "I was elected to represent the citizens of Pittsburgh, not Paris."[32] Somewhat lost in the theatrics that day was the fact that, due to the structure of the Agreement, Trump actually could not technically begin the process of withdrawal until 2019, and in the end only completed that process in late 2020, as his term drew to a close. However, Trump could and did take more immediate action related to key funding mechanisms associated with the Agreement, in particular the Green Climate Fund (GCF). This fund, primarily intended to assist developing countries in adaptation to and mitigation of climate change, was a key commitment of the Obama administration, which rushed through a final tranche of GCF funding in its final days in office, bringing the U.S. contribution to $1 billion. Still, this fell well short of the total U.S. pledge of $3 billion, and the Trump administration had authority to halt future transfers on its watch.

Integrating religious assessment and engagement into environmental diplomacy was a well-developed portfolio of work within RGA by late 2016. In his 2013 remarks launching the office that would become RGA, Secretary Kerry referenced the role of religious leaders in contributing to environmental diplomacy by reminding adherents to be "safe guarders of God's creation."[33] RGA's work in this area grew along with U.S. engagement in the process leading to the Paris Agreement. Many global religious leaders were active supporters of that process, including Pope Francis, whose 2015 encyclical *Laudato Si'* developed a theological foundation for international action to "care for our common home." At high levels, faith-based organizations have contributed to multiple rounds of conference of parties (COP) meetings related to the United Nations Framework on Climate Change, and grassroots, Indigenous cultural and religious leaders are central to environmental advocacy from South America to Southeast Asia.

As the Trump administration took steps away from the Paris Agreement, RGA's engagement function again drew it into facilitating information flows between religious partners critical of this move and relevant career U.S. diplomats. This included assessment briefings for diplomats on dynamics in environmental diplomacy in the evangelical community, both in the United States and internationally through networks like the World Evangelical Alliance's diverse work on environmental policy issues.

Most substantively, RGA continued to facilitate engagements between interagency U.S. officials responsible for the Green Climate Fund and faith-based organizations involved in environmental diplomacy and development projects.[34] In the early days of the Trump administration, these meetings involved updates about staffing of these issues on the U.S. Government side, communication from faith-based groups on their efforts to lobby the new administration to remain committed to the Green Climate Fund, and an array of questions on the GCF's proposal and funding process. In later meetings, still held before the official Trump administration Paris Agreement announcement in early June, participants continued to share technical updates on the GCF's funding operations while also exchanging information on potential policy change, with the cautionary proviso that great uncertainty remained during this period about the likely future trajectory of U.S. commitment.

What to make of these efforts during this transitional period? In all, it seems clear that the immediate response of career officials in RGA was more nuanced than the deep state resistance alleged by some (and wished for by others). Staff adopted varied responses with the shared goal of preserving office principles and functionality. Even in areas like the Muslim Ban and walking away from the Paris Agreement, which directly challenged preexisting policy work in the office, the predominant response in RGA was to continue to serve its function of providing assessment of religious dynamics and engagement of religious actors. RGA did not create faith-based resistance to the Muslim Ban. But it did assess this resistance and report on it to impacted colleagues. In a new, personalistic environment of foreign policy via Twitter, there was limited opportunity for more substantial resistance.

In terms of evaluating the overall effectiveness of these efforts, populism's personalistic dimension raises real questions about short-term impact. The faith-based criticisms of the Muslim Ban, for example, were not voiced by the evangelical leaders with most direct personal loyalty to the White House, but instead by Trump-critical evangelicals like Russell Moore. In contrast, leaders like Franklin Graham and Ralph Reed were either sympathetic to or enthusiastically supportive of Trump's steps.

Pastor Robert Jeffress, for instance, praised Trump for stepping away from international action against the "imaginary crisis" of climate change.[35] Even dissent had unclear effect, with White House Press Secretary Sean Spicer seeming to relish the opportunity to criticize "career bureaucrats" who "should either get with the program or they can go."[36] Given the relative lack of connection between RGA staff and those closest religious loyalists to the populist leadership, there was little real possibility that channeled constraint would actually alter the substance of populist policy goals.

CONCLUSION: EVALUATING "DEEP STATE" EFFECTS

How should one interpret the overall effects of these bureaucratic responses to the populist transition of early 2017? It would be difficult to argue that RGA staff altered any populist policy priorities. The office shrank dramatically in size and bureaucratic location, on its way to absorption within IRF. The period produced some high-quality gallows humor among staff, but not some conspiracy of highly effective deep state resistance. To return to Drezner's work on missionary institutions, RGA did not "thrive" during this period, which would require "espoused norms and principles [to] closely correlate with the state's observed policy outcomes."[37] It barely survived, although it did indeed accomplish this in its altered form as a "Strategic Religious Engagement Unit" within the IRF office.[38]

And what might this chapter's findings imply about other offices within the religion/foreign policy bureaucracy? The framework set out in figure 5.1 could also apply to other offices. It seems likely, for example, that IRF experienced populism's personalism more intensely, due to the issue's importance to key Trump loyalists, thus making persistence below the populist radar a less likely outcome. Staff likely faced judgment calls about whether administration initiatives involved identity-based exclusion in such a way that ran counter to their office's mission (provoking exit), or whether it was plausible to minimize populist ideology's influence (encouraging mutual adaptation). Career staff at USAID seem to have attempted forms of constraint in response to populist moves to direct foreign assistance to religious in-groups, but then to have faced serious consequences when their constraint attracted personalist attention from Vice President Pence and others. What seems apparent is that all of these steps, in the short run, had limited capacity to eliminate populism's influence over religion in the bureaucracy of U.S. foreign policy.

The longer story may be more complex in time. RGA's survival, even in vestigial form, could provide raw material for revitalization in a post-populist period. The adaptation work of RGA staff to build relationships where possible with incoming political appointees may have demonstrated the value of a religious engagement approach to some open-minded appointees. Areas of bounded persistence surely showed that RGA's model, particularly when focused on governance-oriented issues like anti-corruption and trafficking in persons, is viable in a way that can transcend the partisan nature of a given administration. Channeled resistance to populist identity construction may have maintained relationships between career staff and partners in civil society who had the ability to push for institutional preservation from outside government. However, in the short term, it is difficult to see actions from career staff as having obstructed populist priorities in religion and foreign policy.

6

SALVATION IN INSTITUTIONS?

American Secularism, Executive Power, and Populist Change

B
eyond the personal agency of career staff, another source could have constrained populist change in religion and foreign policy: checks encouraged by the structure of existing political institutions. Scholars frequently note that aspects of judicial review and separation of powers, which might limit the extent of variation that a leader like President Trump could bring to religion and foreign policy, are significantly more robust in the United States than other cases where populists have come into power. In one version of this (relatively) more optimistic account, Kurt Weyland and Raúl Madrid argue, "The federal and presidential system of government enshrines a firm separation of powers . . . the legislature and judiciary, in addition to independent federal agencies and state and local-level authorities, all have considerable influence in the US system, including the power to block or modify presidential initiatives . . . President Trump faces a set of rather firm institutional constraints."[1]

While these claims are fairly convincing in some areas of governance (such as the performance of electoral institutions in 2020), there is mixed evidence of their effect in limiting populist change in religion and foreign policy. As scholars of institutional change have noted, the nature of political institutions varies even within a single country, providing "soft spots" that encourage change.[2] Ultimately, whatever the strength of such institutional checks in other policy spheres, soft spots abounded in religion and foreign policy, for reasons that predate the Trump administration. First, in spite of the common metaphor of a "wall of separation between church and state," America's legal regime of secularism provides relatively few bright lines on religion and foreign policy, particularly under the Supreme Court's current "accommodationist" majority.[3] Furthermore, especially in the realm of foreign policy, executive branch dominance has grown, relative to the legislative and judicial branches. Where legal standards were clear and other branches of government empowered, existing institutions did, in fact, provide some stability to the religion-foreign policy bureaucracy, and populism had more limited effects. But, on the whole, supposedly coequal branches faced obstacles responding to the change documented in chapters 3 and 4 due to institutional conditions in place before Trump's election.

The chapter moves forward in four parts. First, it draws together scholarship on institutional change, American legal secularism, and executive branch dominance to motivate the claim that institutional checks are likely to be a relatively weak constraint on populism in religion and foreign policy. Second, it turns to evidence from an earlier period, during the emergence of religion across the foreign policy bureaucracy, that the limited nature of institutional constraint existed even before the Trump administration's arrival in office. Third, it examines evidence from the Trump administration itself, which reveals that the conjunction of legal flexibility and executive dominance proved a weak constraint on the substantive and procedural changes that Trump's administration made to religion and foreign policy. Finally, it explores some limited areas where institutional checks did operate, because of robust legal standards and clear empowerment of other branches of government. This suggests that more overt institutional checks could, in the future, help to stabilize religion and foreign policy in a post-populist period.

POPULISM, FOREIGN POLICY, AND INSTITUTIONAL CHECKS

Trump's populism, both in its construction of identity boundaries and personalistic structure of governance, seemed of a type with leaders like

Viktor Orbán in Hungary and Jair Bolsonaro in Brazil who weakened democracy from within once in office. However, there are obvious differences between the United States and these cases, which have caused some to be more optimistic about America's democratic prospects. Madrid and Weyland argue, "Political institutions in the United States are much stronger and more resilient than those in Latin American and East-Central Europe."[4] This argument echoes James Mahoney and Kathleen Thelen's observation that institutions with "low level(s) of discretion" and "strong veto possibilities" are less likely to experience dramatic displacement, even if revisionist actors come to power.[5] Scholars have devoted extensive attention to "path dependence" of political institutions,[6] including the role of "increasing returns" in imposing costs on those seeking change.[7]

In the United States, "the entrenched system of checks and balances imposes firm constraints on populist machinations and illiberal initiatives."[8] Even scholars more circumspect about the United States's prospects admit that "institutional and political checks in the United Sates make an outright reversion to authoritarian rule far less likely than in the middle-income backsliders."[9] To be more specific, "the United States' federal system of government and independent judiciary should provide more robust defenses against backsliding."[10] Others point to Congress, "without a doubt, the world's most powerful legislature" as a "substantial check on executive authority."[11] In addition to these structural features of American institutions, the U.S. Constitution "cannot be easily overhauled" because of the document's demanding amendment process, which contrasts with more easily replaced documents in other settings experiencing backsliding.[12] For all of these reasons, a populist like Trump could face real costs in implementing either the identity-based exclusion or personalism of populist rule. These institutionalist hopes seemed to be, at least partially, born out in the chaotic closing days of the Trump presidency, when decentralized electoral institutions and diverse courts generally held the line in the face of a final populist bid to undermine the democratic transition of power.

Notwithstanding the influence of these institutional advantages in certain spheres, it bears noting that their causal expectations are not equally clear in all areas of governance. The increasing returns that scholars see as a source of institutional path dependence may not be particularly powerful in religion-state relations. Institutional features like federalism may be largely irrelevant in areas like foreign policy. Separation of powers and checks among the federal branches cannot be taken for granted, and presidents may enjoy particular advantages in certain policy spheres. The supposed clarity of constitutional constraints in the United States may be uneven in the areas of constitutional law most relevant to religion and foreign policy. Finally, even in areas characterized by clear standards and veto possibilities, populist actors pursuing change do have the potential for meaningful effects, whether by allowing existing institutions to "drift" from their original functions or "layering" their own initiatives alongside them.[13]

In short, there is good reason to suspect that the intersection of religion and U.S. foreign policy reflects an almost ideal case of a policy sphere that would *not* be subject to robust institutional constraint, whatever advantages the United States may enjoy in other policy spheres. This is not due to any change brought on by the Trump administration, but preexisting trends in the development of American political institutions that had been building in the decades before Trump's unexpected 2016 election. Indeed, these trends were present in the development of religion in the foreign policy bureaucracy, even before that election. First, constitutional guidance on religion-state relations (what I will term legal secularism) is notoriously flexible, and jurisprudence was in a multi-decade process of becoming more accommodationist before Trump's election. Second, foreign policy may be the area of presidential power least constrained by federalism or separation of powers across branches of government. For both of these reasons, Trump and his advisors may have even had strategic incentives to *prioritize* religion and foreign policy for implementing their populist vision, as costs imposed were likely to be far lower than other areas of policy change.

Americans are accustomed to invoking the rigid image of a wall of separation between church and state from Thomas Jefferson's letter to the Danbury Baptists. However, it is a deeply misleading metaphor on several levels. The phrase does not appear in the Constitution or First Amendment, thus limiting its relevance to constraining later decisions, and it implies a solidity that simply cannot be squared with the record of jurisprudence over the past several decades. The Constitution itself says notoriously little about religion, other than a ban on religious tests for office, and the First Amendment's statement that the government should "make no law respecting an establishment of religion or prohibiting the free exercise thereof." Both the Establishment Clause and Free Exercise Clause of the Constitution have been subject to intense, shifting litigation over the course of the past quarter century, with neither providing the sort of bright lines likely to constrain populist manipulation. Scholars distinguish separationists from accommodationists, or what Noah Feldman terms "legal secularists" and "values evangelicals," groups with radically distinct legal approaches to the religion clauses.[14] At the level of the Supreme Court, especially, a general drift away from the separationist approach of legal secularists diminished the likelihood of institutional constraint from the country's highest court.

As Kent Greenawalt observes, "Establishment Clause issues have been among the most controversial decided by the Supreme Court in the last half century."[15] Establishment Clause decisions provided some of the highwater marks of strict separationism in the post-World War II period, perhaps most famously *Engle v. Vitale*'s prohibition on prayer in public schools. In that era, the Supreme Court developed the multipronged "Lemon test" that it would then frequently use to strike down forms of government assistance for religion. However, this separationist interpretation of the Establishment Clause was weakening for several decades before Trump's election. Instead, justices with more accommodationist views have argued that state involvement with religion is often consistent with the Establishment Clause, provided it takes place on a neutral basis. Whether symbolic actions like opening council meetings with community-led prayer (*Town of Greece v. Galloway*), or financial support via school voucher programs largely used to send students to religious schools (*Zelman v. Simmons-Harris*), the Supreme Court's recent majority has been less likely to rule out government initiatives that may be seen as benefiting religious institutions, especially when such support is generally available to other varieties of institutions.

The Free Exercise Clause has been subject to similar inconsistency during this same time period. To what extent does the government owe religious minorities special protection from laws that may impede their exercise of religion? Separationist majorities were frequently sympathetic to such claims in cases involving questions like the mandatory Pledge of Allegiance (*West Virginia v. Barnette*) or requiring school attendance through adolescence (*Wisconsin v. Yoder*). However, a shift took place here as well, most notably in *Employment Division v. Smith*'s insistence that minorities are not *entitled* to an exemption from a neutral governmental law of general applicability. In the years before the Trump administration, the Supreme Court was closely divided in several cases related to such free exercise claims, leading legal scholar Winnifred Fallers Sullivan to argue for the "impossibility" of any consistent approach to religious freedom in the American legal context.[16] Courts would still, at times, unite in defense of minority exemptions (2015's *Holt v. Hobbs* decision, for instance). However, exemption claims increasingly came from members of the U.S. Christian majority, what Lewis calls the "rights turn" in conservative politics, further muddying expectations about how the Free Exercise Clause might operate in the face of populist manipulation by a president from the conservative party.[17]

The Supreme Court, even in the immediate pre-Trump era, did (at times) arrive at unanimous agreement on cases related to the Establishment or Free Exercise Clauses, such as 2012's *Hosanna-Tabor Evangelical Lutheran Church v. EEOC*. The Constitution's religion clauses are not a total blank slate that populists could rewrite in their entirety. However, sharp disagreement between separationists and accommodationists, and the Supreme Court's general drift towards accommodation under a conservative majority, should make us skeptical that constitutional law in this area would provide the sort of entrenched or robust check on machinations of a determined populist executive.

Skepticism about institutional checks should be even stronger in the realm of foreign policy because of general executive dominance in this sphere. As James Goldgeier and Elizabeth Saunders observe in analyzing the longer-term roots of Trump's assertions of executive power related to foreign policy: "In reality, the problem goes well beyond Trump . . . [constraints on the president] have been eroding for decades."[18] It is for precisely this reason that Daniel Drezner highlights "the carnage suffered by American foreign policy [under Trump], the arena where the powers of the other government branches have receded the most."[19] As Aaron Wildavsky argued over fifty years ago, "Since World War II, Presidents have had much greater success in controlling the nation's defense and foreign policies than in dominating its domestic policies."[20] In the mid-1990s, Paul Peterson similarly argued for "the President's dominance in foreign policy making," in contrast to gains in congressional authority in the aftermath of the Vietnam War.[21] Linda Fowler has documented significant declines, for example, in foreign policy and national security oversight activities by the most relevant Senate committees, the very bodies that should "exert substantial pressure on administration officials to disclose information in ways that most individual lawmakers cannot."[22]

More recent polarization in Congress has further diminished the Senate's ability to fulfill some of its foreign policy responsibilities, which encourages presidents to bypass the legislature entirely in making decisions regarding the use of force or major foreign policy negotiations. President Obama's commitment of the United States to the Paris Climate Agreement, for instance, involved only executive action, rather than Senate approval. Goldgeier and Saunders further argue that expertise on foreign affairs has declined among members of Congress, with structural changes in the nature of committee assignments interacting with polarization to create change: "Congress has relinquished its authority on foreign policy and trade to the executive branch—and would have trouble reclaiming it even if it wanted to."[23]

Scholars of the Supreme Court have likewise (generally) argued for significant limits on judicial checks in this realm. Kimi Lynn King and James Meernik, although measured in their own treatment of this claim, call it "axiomatic that decisions with foreign policy implications are infrequent and that the Supreme Court 'almost always' supports the Executive."[24] Justices may avoid intervention because they perceive foreign policy claims as policy disputes unsuitable for judicial review, or outside of court competence. As Thomas Franck sums up, "No one, however critical of U.S. officials, seriously suggests that the judiciary should make foreign policy. No one thinks judges can, or should, interfere at moments when national survival depends on instant response."[25] Even prominent recent cases tied to the Global War on Terror, notably the *Hamdan v. Rumsfeld* decisions contesting the use of military commissions, largely relied on conflicts with non-constitutional law, rather than wide-ranging checks on executive authority. As with congressional authority, there may be areas where courts do feel empowered to review executive actions related to foreign policy and national security, but on the whole, we should expect this area to be significantly less constrained than other areas of executive action.

It is important to note that, even within religion and foreign policy, specific institutional contexts vary across offices, which should provide different responses in the face of populist change. Certain positions or offices enjoy explicit congressional mandates, empowering actors in other branches with increased capacity to respond to populist change. The International Religious Freedom Act provides the clearest example in this regard. Likewise, some legal standards related to religion and foreign policy provide lower executive discretion when compared to the Establishment and Free Exercise Clauses. Scholarship on institutional change suggests that populist actors might still pursue change in these areas but are less likely to replace existing institutions entirely, instead having more gradual effects that may increase resilience in a post-populist period.[26]

In sum, analysts optimistic about American democracy because of structural features of political institutions, particularly separation of powers, checks and balances, and stability of the constitutional framework, may have a point in policy spheres as diverse as provision of education, oversight of policing, or organization of elections. However, many aspects of religion and foreign policy did not enjoy these advantages, for reasons that predate the Trump administration. In fact, the very combination of constitutional flexibility and executive dominance in foreign policy contributed to the rise of the religion regime complex in the first place.

INSTITUTIONAL FLEXIBILITY AND THE RISE OF RELIGION IN FOREIGN POLICY

From its earliest stages, religion's growth in the foreign policy bureaucracy demonstrated executive branch predominance and the flexibility of the legal institutions of American secularism. Portions of Gregorio Bettiza's religion and foreign policy regime complex reflected discretion on the part of the president or secretary of state, and while officials consistently referenced the need to uphold constitutional boundaries between religion and state, specifics on where lines would be drawn regularly left ambiguity. While not the intention of the officials who advocated for the religion bureaucracy's growth, these conditions did, after Trump's election, mean that bright lines of institutional constraint were generally lacking. With that said, certain elements of the religion-foreign policy bureaucracy did have more institutional rigidity than others, largely due to clear legal standards or congressional mandates, which set them apart even in the pre-populist period.

As various offices tied to religion began emerging in the foreign policy bureaucracy in the 1990s, the network of academics and policymakers who guided the bureaucratization could not agree on the extent to which the First Amendment, particularly the Establishment Clause, was relevant to the conduct of American officials in these areas. The Chicago Council on Global Affairs' Task Force on Religion and the Making of U.S. Foreign Policy, for instance, included a recommendation that the president of the United States "clarify that the Establishment Clause of the First Amendment does not bar the United States from engaging religious communities abroad in the conduct of foreign policy, though it does impose constraints on the means that the United States may choose to pursue this engagement."[27] That report repeatedly references "legal uncertainty" about the applicability of First Amendment guarantees abroad, and calls for "comprehensive and definitive consideration of this question" from the executive branch."[28]

Even among that Task Force's members, however, this relatively benign claim provoked some dissent, with a group of five members appending a statement that "no administration should impose constraints on American foreign policy that are imagined to derive from the Establishment Clause."[29] This uncertainty about the extent to which domestic constitutional principles apply to foreign policy would persist in other advisory groups, with the 2012 White Paper from the Interagency Working Group on Faith-Based and Other Neighborhood Partnerships observing, "special circumstances [apply] to programs operating in foreign countries . . . additional considerations may be implicated."[30] The 2012 White Paper from the State Department's Religion and Foreign Policy Working Group requested "guidelines for civil society on complying with the Establishment Clause [in engagement with the State Department]."[31] The 2013 U.S. Strategy on Religious Leader and Faith Community Engagement claimed that "U.S. officials will ensure that engagement efforts are consistent with the U.S. Constitution and other laws," but provided no specific public guidance beyond that general claim.[32] And the Obama administration's eventual final rule on USAID participation with faith-based organizations explicitly cemented a distinct treatment for foreign programs from domestic ones: "In the international context, therefore, the notice and referral requirements are unworkable and could place an excessive burden on faith-based organizations."[33]

Beyond questions about the basic applicability of American legal secularism to foreign policy, the development of Bettiza's regime complex was heavily tilted towards the executive branch. In both the case of USAID's faith-based office and the Office of Religion and Global Affairs (RGA) at the State Department, bureaucratization took place under the umbrella of what was called the "faith-based initiative" of the George W. Bush administration. Bush's Executive Order 13199, among the first of his presidency, was a matter of executive discretion and was subsequently updated by President Obama under similar executive authority, especially in Executive Order 13559. The Obama administration's reorientation of counterterrorism efforts, both at home and abroad, under the umbrella of Countering Violent Extremism (CVE) was similarly executive branch driven.

With that said, certain elements of religion in the foreign policy bureaucracy did experience either clearer legal boundaries or explicit congressional empowerment. Work promoting international religious freedom had significantly more legislative involvement, from its congressional mandate under the original International Religious Freedom Act to more recent updates in the Frank Wolf International Religious Freedom Act of 2016. Even here, the executive enjoyed significant privileges, for instance in the qualifications of the individual appointed to the ambassador-at-large for International Religious Freedom (IRF) position and the location of that office within the State Department's bureaucracy. Religious freedom advocates would routinely complain that, once in office, presidents failed to nominate qualified candidates to the role in a timely manner. But the office's legislative grounding at least provided Congress a focal point for oversight. Some more specific elements of religion in foreign policy similarly had clearer legislative backing, like the mandate to monitor and combat anti-Semitism, or judicial standards such as those involved in designating Foreign Terrorist Organizations (FTO). Religion was largely a matter of executive branch discretion in the years before Trump's election, but that discretion was more constrained in some areas than others.

Early evidence from RGA illustrates the interplay of legal flexibility with an absent legislative mandate. In remarks at RGA's founding (as the State Department's Office of Faith-Based Community Initiatives), an array of senior administration officials reflected on the flexible legal context in which RGA operated. All insisted that RGA's work would take place within the bounds of the Establishment Clause, while also contending that religious engagement was not inconsistent with these obligations. White House Director of Faith-Based and Neighborhood Partnerships Melissa Rogers articulated the basic rationale for the office's existence: "As the State Department does its work around the world, it must have a firm grasp of [religious] dynamics and it must know how to address them in ways that are informed and intelligent."[34] After describing the areas of RGA's focus, Rogers clarified that "a guiding principle for all of this work will be that our actions must be consistent with the United States Constitution . . . Our precious religious freedom guarantees of the First Amendment mean that we must observe some special rules when we engage religious actors and matters, such as ensuring governmental neutrality toward faith."[35] RGA's Special Representative Shaun Casey similarly remarked that "our engagement efforts will be consistent with the United States Constitution and other laws, both in terms of the spirit and letter of the law." At the same event, Secretary Kerry insisted, "We approach this with the full recognition and understanding of Thomas Jefferson's understanding and admonition about the wall of separation . . . But what we are doing is guided by the conviction that we have to find ways to translate our faiths into efforts that unify for the greater good. That can be done without crossing any lines whatsoever."[36]

RGA's unclassified "Religion and Diplomacy: A Practical Handbook" similarly attempted to formalize this ambiguous approach. The Handbook includes a section on the Establishment Clause, beginning with Former Secretary of State Madeleine Albright's observation: "The constitutional requirement that separates state from church in the United States does not also insist that the state be ignorant of [religion]."[37] The Handbook goes on to note that courts "generally require" federal activities to have secular purposes, no primary effect on religion, and avoid excessive governmental entanglement. Here, the Handbook reflects standards tied to the Supreme Court's Lemon test, in spite of the fact that parts of that test had themselves come under question in the Supreme Court in recent years.[38] The Handbook advises that "U.S. government employees can and should engage with religious actors (in addition to non-religious actors) on the entire range of U.S. diplomacy and development objectives," but also notes that "diplomatic engagement, public diplomacy, and foreign assistance programs abroad must generally comply with the Establishment Clause requirements and requirements of Executive Orders."[39] The section concludes with advice on consulting the Office of Legal Adviser or USAID's Office of the General Counsel with particular questions.

By late 2016, this generally flexible approach had taken fairly routine form in RGA's working level advising and engagement. In preparation for the 2016 Religion and Diplomacy Conference, the large-scale gathering that in some ways marked RGA's organizational peak, staff prepared to answer questions about the Establishment Clause's applicability by insisting that "Many engagements with religion are permissible within [constitutional] parameters . . . such as peacebuilding, capacity building, interfaith activities, educational programs, community development, governance, and humanitarian efforts." In advising on integrating religion into diplomatic efforts to combat wildlife trafficking, for instance, guidance from the Office of the Legal Adviser highlighted the need to be precise about assessing *religious dynamics* and engaging *religious actors*, while maintaining flexibility over the meaning of the term "religious." Concern existed that any attempt to more comprehensively define that core term would itself become a form of endorsement or "approved religion." Further ambiguity remained over the role of the U.S. government in supporting the crafting of religious messages related to areas of diplomatic concern. All parties agreed, on both principled and pragmatic grounds, that the government should not be in the business of drafting religious

| | | Legal Standards | |
		Rigid	Flexible
Legislative Mandate	Present		*International Religious Freedom; Monitoring Antisemitism*
	Absent	*Foreign Terrorist Designation*	*Office of Religion and Global Affairs; USAID Faith-Based Office*

FIGURE 6.1 Institutional constraint, religion, and foreign policy.

statements against corruption, for example. But questions of disseminating such messages, or even supporting non-religious NGOs who worked with religious leaders to craft messages on topics like addressing environmental protection, raised questions that remain unresolved.

Establishment Clause guidance is messy, even in areas of significant Supreme Court jurisprudence like school prayer, and was thus even less clear-cut in the realm of religion and foreign policy. In practice, by late 2016, staff in religion-related offices in the State Department and USAID had productive working-level relationships with government attorneys, although areas of ambiguity certainly remained. As my notes summarize one such meeting, with a lack of clarity, there was a lot of need for consultation. Figure 6.1 summarizes areas of institutional flexibility across bureaucratic offices, as well as some where standards of judicial review or legislative empowerment were relatively stronger.

INSTITUTIONAL FLEXIBILITY
AND POPULIST CHANGE

From the earliest days of his administration, Trump and his senior advisors made it clear that he would assert both flexibility in American religion-state relations and executive dominance in national security, to reject any constraint on his actions related to religion and foreign policy. He frequently promised to "destroy" the Johnson Amendment, which restricts partisan activities on the part of tax-exempt organizations, including churches. And after asserting, "Our Constitution is great" in a July 2016 interview with Chuck Todd, Trump went on to state that he viewed equal religious protection "differently."[40]

Institutional flexibility directly contributed to the fates of formal bureaucratic offices and positions related to the religion regime complex. The White House faith-based office had existed across administrations of both parties, but ultimately rested on executive orders under both the Bush and Obama presidencies. When Trump simply declined to staff this office in the first half of his term, there was no legal obstacle to his decision. When, instead of formally staffing that office, Trump continued to rely on informal networks of evangelical advisors, there was limited legal recourse. Americans United for the Separation of Church and State notified White House officials that they believed this arrangement to be in violation of the Federal Advisory Committee Act, arguing: "It is clear that the President's Evangelical Advisory Board is doing substantive work with the Trump administration behind closed doors—without any sunlight for the public to understand how and why decisions are being made."[41] But White House loyalists simply took the almost surreal step of claiming that such a board did not exist. Johnnie Moore, a member of the apparently nonexistent board, responded to Americans United's claims by insisting, "The truth is, there actually isn't a board . . . there is no formal faith advisory board of any sort at the White House."[42]

There was, similarly, little prospect of a formal check on changes to religion in the foreign policy bureaucracy. RGA's staff capacity was not legislatively mandated, but rather reflected discretion on the part of Obama administration appointees. There was no legal obstacle to eliminating the special representative for RGA, special envoy to the Organization of Islamic Cooperation (SEOIC), or special representative to Muslim communities (SRMC), each of which existed at the discretion of past presidents or secretaries of state. Secretary Tillerson "notified and reported to [Congressional] Committees on certain organizational changes to special envoys and related positions," but had no legal obligation to maintain the titles of special representatives listed above. As USAID officials faced Trump administration pressure to award development assistance directly to Iraqi Christian grant applicants (see chapter 4), existing bureaucratic procedures were, similarly, not robust enough to prevent change. ProPublica's extensive reporting shows that, after initial rejection of certain grants on procedural grounds by career officials, Trump administration political appointees systematically took steps to overcome this attempted constraint, including changing the staffing of key offices, placing political appointees in grant evaluation meetings normally controlled by career experts, and restructuring the goals of funds designated to flow through the United Nations Development Program. None of this required clear violation of any law or regulation; USAID's spokesperson insisted that these grants "follow[ed] all federal regulations."[43] While some areas of religion and foreign policy brought more clearly institutionalized checks, on the whole, the secular flexibility and executive deference that predated the Trump administration provided little constraint once he arrived in office.

No area of Trump foreign policy illustrates the frailty of these constraints more clearly than the set of executive orders restricting access for Muslims to the United States. The executive orders known as the "Muslim Ban," first issued in the opening weeks of the administration, were the most contentious early episode in Trump administration foreign policy. As detailed in chapter 5, these executive actions did indeed provoke dissent from within the career bureaucracy, although norms among career government officials channeled the effects of such resistance. Perhaps other branches, particularly the courts, would operate as checks on the combination of exclusion and personalism embodied in those orders?

In short, in spite of early victories in federal district and appellate courts, the eventual outcome was largely cosmetic changes to early administration orders and the eventual vindication of the Trump policies in the Supreme Court's encompassing *Trump v. Hawaii* decision. In both the Supreme Court's eventual ruling, as well as amicus briefs filed by outside parties in advance of the decision, both of the points cited above show through clearly: the flexibility in interpretation of the First Amendment's religion clauses, and the deference of the court to executive branch authority in matters of national security. Institutional constraints on populism need to be made of sterner stuff.

As soon as leaked versions of the executive order appeared on the internet in late January 2017, legal challenges began to mount. A draft order justified the visa bans as targeting individuals who value "religious edicts over American law," language that invited legal challenge and was quickly replaced with "violent ideologies" before the order's initial issuance.[44] The initial order singled out only Muslim-majority countries for its visa ban. It halted the U.S. refugee resettlement program, and directed that, when refugee admissions restarted in the future, executive agencies were "to prioritize refugee claims made by individuals on the basis of religious-based persecution, provided that the religion of the individual is a minority religion in the individual's country of nationality,"[45] awkward language seemingly intended to privilege Christians for protection. While the words "Islam" and "Muslims" did not appear in the order's January version, the intent was clear, particularly with authorship reported to rest with anti-immigrant officials Steve Bannon and Stephen Miller. As Trump advisor Rudy Giuliani bragged in the days after the order's January issue, "[The

President] called me up, he said, 'Put a commission together, show me the right way to do it legally' . . . and what we did was we focused on, instead of religion, danger."[46]

Early legal challenges won several temporary victories related to the order, mostly in the form of injunctions restricting its enforcement until courts could fully consider the legal merits of the challenges. In one prominent example, a federal district court in Virginia granted a preliminary injunction against the January 27th executive order, citing *Larson v. Valente* in finding, "The clearest command of the Establishment Clause is that one religious denomination cannot be officially preferred over another."[47] That court found that the "readily discoverable fact[s]" of the executive order's history revealed that it intended to discriminate against Muslims. It drew on Establishment Clause jurisprudence from *McCreary Co. vs. ACLU of Kentucky* to observe "the world is not made brand new every morning."[48] Citing statements from both Trump and Giuliani, the court found "direct evidence of animus" that ran afoul of the Establishment Clause, even though the order did not target all Muslims for exclusion. Rather than refusing to defer to national security powers of the presidency, the district court instead "question[ed] whether the EO was animated by national security concerns at all, as opposed to the impermissible motive of, in the context of entry, disfavoring one religious group, and, in the area of refugees, favoring another refugee group."[49] The court found, "the only evidence in this record concerning national security indicates that the EO may actually make the country less safe."[50] Similar arguments appeared in appellate responses. For example, the Ninth Circuit Court of Appeals rejected the claim of absolute executive authority over immigration and national security policy, instead finding, "it is beyond question that the federal judiciary retains the authority to adjudicate constitutional challenges to executive action."[51] The Fourth Circuit Court of Appeals likewise left in place lower court injunctions, citing the "animus toward Islam" in the orders.[52]

While not an exhaustive analysis of court decisions related to the Muslim Bans, these decisions, at both the district and appellate levels, seem to provide evidence of courts acting in precisely the way that institutional optimists might predict: drawing on the First Amendment's guarantees regarding establishment and/or free exercise to resist populist variation to religion in the foreign policy process. Similarly, these courts drew on landmark cases like *Hamdan v. Rumsfeld* and *Hamdi v. Rumsfeld* from the post-9/11 era to brush aside claims of broad executive exemption from judicial review in the realm of national security.

Notwithstanding this early evidence, the story was far from complete in district and appellate rulings. In the face of bids for judicial constraint, the populist executive updated the orders to provide them with a veneer of legitimacy, and in the end, the Supreme Court accepted those cosmetic changes in deciding to let the orders stand. In doing so, the Supreme Court's conservative majority drew on flexibility in constitutional law, both in its treatment of religion and its executive deference, which had been building for years before Trump's election.

The Trump administration made several revisions to the original January 2017 executive order, intended to remove the most obvious constitutional weaknesses while maintaining its populist intent of exclusion. As Stephen Miller put it shortly after the first revision, "Fundamentally, you're still going to have the same basic policy outcome for the country, but you're going to be responsive to a lot of very technical issues that were brought up by the court."[53] The first revision, Executive Order 13780, removed language seeming to privilege Christians in the refugee resettlement process, while simultaneously denying that the original language had any such effect. It also removed Iraq from the countries facing travel bans, although only Muslim-majority countries remained on the list. When this second order was also enjoined by federal courts, the order's third and final issuance took place in September 2017, via Presidential Proclamation 9645. This proclamation added non-Muslim-majority countries North Korea and Venezuela to the list subject to travel bans. By the time the Supreme Court eventually considered Proclamation 9645's constitutionality, consolidating various cases under the heading of *Trump vs. Hawaii*, Sudan and Chad had also been removed from the visa ban.

Oral arguments before the Supreme Court in *Trump vs. Hawaii* clarified the flexibility in secular institutions and executive deference in areas of national security that would ultimately undercut attempts to limit populist policy variation. Representing the Trump administration, the solicitor general foregrounded executive powers related to national security, arguing: "The proclamation reflects a foreign policy and national security judgment that falls well within the President's power."[54] Even Neal Katyal, counsel representing opponents of Proclamation 9645, conceded, "We wouldn't have a problem with [the policy] if it was tailored to a crisis," and "Presidents have a wide berth . . . if there's any sort of emergency," before arguing that Proclamation 9645 failed to meet that standard.[55]

The First Amendment's religion clauses were no more rigid a constraint. Justices indicated disagreement over whether the Establishment Clause or Free Exercise Clause should be considered the primary basis for a challenge. Justice Gorsuch questioned whether Establishment Clause concerns applied in a "purely international application," and expressed doubts about what Establishment Clause standards would even apply in the case, given the Supreme Court's recent hesitancy to invoke earlier criteria like the Lemon test and associated "reasonable observer" standards.[56] Katyal insisted that "all tests point in the same direction" because the case rested on "denigration of religion" on the part of government. But the solicitor general called even this into question, claiming: "The President has made crystal clear on September 25th that he had no intention of imposing the Muslim ban."[57]

The intersection of executive deference and secular flexibility showed clearly in the eventual 5-4 majority decision upholding the final proclamation. Chief Justice Roberts, writing for that majority, first turned to the authority of the executive branch, especially in areas of national security and immigration, writing that the relevant portions of the Immigration and Nationality Act "exude deference to the President in every clause."[58] The majority goes on to dismiss the claim that the president failed to offer a compelling justification for his policy choice: "Plaintiffs' request for a searching inquiry into the persuasiveness of the President's justifications is inconsistent with the broad statutory text and the deference traditionally accorded the President in this sphere."[59] The majority later goes on to complain, "[plaintiffs'] understanding of the President's authority is remarkably cramped."[60]

Establishment Clause protections offer no firmer ground for the plaintiffs in the view of that majority. Strikingly, the majority explicitly blends their rejection of Establishment Clause claims with executive deference, claiming that the fact that "the plaintiffs seek to invalidate a national security directive" must "inform our standard of review [of the First Amendment claims]."[61] Instead of searching for evidence of animus against Islam, the majority only required a governmental, rational basis for Proclamation 9645 that was "reasonably understood to result from a justification independent of unconstitutional grounds."[62] The majority found alterations in the policy (from its initial form) persuasive evidence of a lack of anti-Muslim animus, including the fact that some Muslim-majority countries had been delisted, as well as the development of a waiver process. In dissents, the skeptical minority of justices pointed to similar arguments as lower courts who had blocked the proclamation: that it was "motivated by anti-Muslim animus . . . far more harrowing [than acknowledged by the majority opinion]" and that national security justifications were nothing more than "window dressing."[63] Justice Soto-mayor's dissent pointedly notes the flexibility of religious animus standards, which were "less pervasive" yet essential in deciding the recent *Masterpiece Cakeshop v. Colorado Civil Rights Commission* case.[64]

After eighteen months of public protest, legal contention, and impact on human lives, the Supreme Court's majority in *Trump v. Hawaii* eventually made it clear that existing legal checks would not automatically eliminate the exclusionary changes of the Trump presidency. Separation of powers and First Amendment guarantees did provide vehicles for making claims, focal points for opposition, and even high-profile platforms for judicial dissent. The policy itself changed to a limited extent, with successive versions of the executive order becoming more sophisticated in shrouding anti-Muslim sentiment in bureaucratic legitimacy. However, on the most crucial question, the final Presidential Proclamation remained in place, removed only after President Biden's inauguration in 2021. It was the ballot box, not judicial review, which reversed populist manipulation of religion in the bureaucracy.

EVIDENCE OF CONSTRAINT? CONGRESSIONAL MANDATES AND CLEAR LEGAL STANDARDS

Thus far, this chapter has made a case that institutional checks on executive power were not, and should not have been expected to be, a particularly strong constraint on populist changes to the place of religion in U.S. foreign policy. The nature of preexisting institutions matters, and due to both executive dominance and constitutional flexibility, the religion regime complex was perhaps uniquely vulnerable to manipulation.

With that broader point in mind, turning to some areas of seeming continuity in the regime complex helps to highlight the fact that institutions do, in fact, have the capacity to channel populist energies—where they are structured to increase leverage and provide clear guidance. As scholars of institutional change note, the strength of potential veto points and the level of discretion in interpretation are variable, and come with implications for institutional outcomes and the strategies that change agents pursue.[65] There is evidence that congressional oversight and clearer legal standards did alter the effects of populist change in certain, relatively limited areas. While this does not change the overall assessment of populist success here, it may point to important lessons moving forward: where clearer congressional and legal standards exist, populists may face more costs for their governance decisions, and potentially alter their strategies in response.

The role of congressional oversight showed through most clearly in a relatively small portion of the religion-foreign policy bureaucracy: the Office of the Special Envoy to Monitor and Combat Antisemitism (SEAS). The SEAS position, while located within the RGA suite by the end of the Obama administration, was distinct in its history and legislative foundation. The 2004 Global Anti-Semitism Review Act, motivated by the fact that "acts of anti-Semitism in countries throughout the world, including some of the world's strongest democracies, have increased significantly in frequency and scope over the last several years," mandated both the existence of an Office to Monitor and Combat Antisemitism in the State Department, as well as a special envoy to lead that office.[66] The bill had bipartisan sponsorship in both the Senate and House versions, and passed by unanimous consent in the Senate and without objection in the House.[67] It proceeded through the Senate Foreign Relations Committee and House International Relations Committee, two of the very bodies that, in general, scholars have pointed to as less active in foreign affairs in recent years.

This legislative mandate provided a focal point for both congressional and interest group pressure on the Trump administration and Tillerson State Department as the SEAS position, like so much of the federal bureaucracy, sat vacant in the early months of the administration. Early rumors regarding Tillerson's reorganization of the State Department included the potential removal of the SEAS position. In testimony to the House Appropriations Committee, Tillerson raised the prospect that roles like SEAS might "weaken attention to those issues," ostensibly by removing their content from within the larger regional bureaus of the State Department.[68] However, in contrast to positions that Tillerson would later eliminate, including the special representative for RGA, his prepared answers to congressional questions on SEAS insisted, "The Special Envoy to Monitor and Combat Anti-Semitism is a statutorily-required position that will be maintained within the Department."[69] Tillerson similarly communicated to Senator Bob Corker, then chair of the Senate Foreign Relations Committee, that the SEAS position would be "retained" with the office and shifted within the organizational chart, in contrast to other eliminated envoy positions. Corker's statement in response to this announcement implicitly raised the importance of SEAS's congressional mandate, contrasting it with "over two-thirds [of envoys] which were created administratively," that is without congressional mandate.[70]

In spite of these assurances, the SEAS position lingered, unfilled, throughout the Tillerson term in the secretary's suite. This drew consistent pressure from bipartisan members of Congress, former officials in the special envoy role, and outside interest groups, who repeatedly referenced the position's statutory mandate. In response to the role's vacancy, bipartisan congressional allies acted to preserve the position, most notably in introducing, and eventually passing, new legislation—the Special Envoy to Monitor and Combat Antisemitism Act—to elevate the position to the ambassadorial level, require Senate confirmation of the position, and mandate its reporting directly to the secretary of state.[71] In February 2019, more than two years into Trump's term in office, and long after Tillerson's service ended, the administration eventually appointed attorney Elan Carr to the position.

The relative consistency in the SEAS position illustrates that, when a clear legislative mandate existed, elements of the bureaucracy were indeed more likely to persist in the face of populist skepticism. To borrow from Mahoney and Thelen's framework, populist officials behaved more like "subversives . . . disguis[ing] the extent of their preference for institutional change by following institutional expectations and working within the system," rather than overturning existing institutions openly.[72] Even in this area, populist neglect did have an impact, with Carr not coming into office until more than halfway through Trump's term. But the relative continuity in office may also help to explain why this fairly small component of the regime complex was able to recover quickly from populist neglect, with President Biden announcing Professor Deborah Lipstadt's nomination roughly six months into his term.

If Congress could serve as a constraint in some areas, another hypothesized source of constraint should be legal institutions less open to interpretation than the Establishment and Free Exercise clauses. As already argued, the religion clauses of the Constitution and Bill of Rights did not prove particularly constraining, due to long-standing flexibility that Trump and his advisors exploited in areas like the Muslim Ban. However, in some areas where legal standards were clearer cut, including a history of judicial review related to foreign policy, constraint could exist for reasons beyond the nature of American secularism. Evidence exists that this type of mechanism played out in one discrete area where the Trump administration declined to follow through on wishes from some of its most exclusion-minded members: designating the international set of organizations known as the Muslim Brotherhood as a Foreign Terrorist Organization (FTO).

Designating the Muslim Brotherhood as an FTO was a long-standing goal of foreign policy advisors who wound up in senior positions surrounding President Trump, including National Security Advisor Michael Flynn, and advisors like Sebastian Gorka. While such advocates claimed links between the Brotherhood and an array of conspiracies and violent plots, others suspected that the FTO designation would have been used as grounds to investigate Muslim associations in the United States with potential ties to Brotherhood-affiliated organizations. It would have been entirely consistent with the use of foreign policy to construct populism's identity boundaries, in this case signaling that inclusion in the American political community was highly limited for Muslims.

Several reports, from the early days of the Trump presidency through later years, indicated that executive orders had been drafted that would lead to an FTO designation.[73] In his Senate confirmation testimony, Rex Tillerson jointly referred to ISIS along with "al Qaeda, the Muslim Brotherhood, and certain elements within Iran" as "agents of radical Islam."[74] The first set of reported executive order drafts was during roughly the same time period as the Muslim Ban executive orders, so there was no reason to doubt the administration's willingness to follow through on campaign rhetoric about the Brotherhood. Members of Congress, in both houses, filed legislation in support of such a move.[75] Reports indicated that career officials within the State Department and National Security Council argued against the designation decision,[76] but it is not obvious why such careerist objections would, on their own, have carried the day. Similar appeals did little to slow the Muslim Bans.

The likelihood of significant legal impediments to the designation would, in this area, have increased costs to the administration for implementing this populist change related to religion and foreign policy. FTO designations take place through the State Department under the authority of the Immigration and Nationality Act (INA) but are subject to certain due process guarantees that can be litigated in federal courts. In one high-profile case, an Iranian group known as the People's Mojahedin Organization of Iran engaged in years of legal action contesting the process through which it was designated an FTO, including winning some decisions that found due process failures on the part of the State Department in the designation process.[77] While the secretary of state has authority under the INA, the designation must demonstrate that the organization meets certain legal standards: being a foreign organization, engaging in terrorist activity as defined under law, and threatening U.S. national security by such actions.[78] As analysis from Middle East policy experts observed in January 2017, "There's no reason to think the D.C. Circuit would simply roll over for a plainly deficient record."[79]

While it is difficult to test the counterfactual in a direct way (that without such legal constraints the administration would have moved forward) there was significant reason to suspect that legal obstacles under the INA's authority would have been very real, in contrast to the much more flexible First Amendment constraints that faced the Muslim Bans. First and foremost, it is not clear that the Muslim Brotherhood is in any legal sense a single organization. Numerous academic and governmental assessments have pointed to the fact that the Brotherhood has developed quite differently, in different contexts, after its Egyptian founding, from the terrorism of Hamas against the Israeli state, which has already earned it a FTO designation, to the peaceful participation in government in Tunisia after that country's Jasmine Revolution. As William McCants and Benjamin Wittes observe, the Supreme Court's jurisprudence, upholding restrictions on material support of terrorist groups, ultimately rests on the fact that such groups engage in terrorist activities, not simply that they hold objectionable ideas.[80] It is at least plausible that fairly rigid legal standards tied to the FTO designation process thus signaled to populist officials that this one initiative would provoke some costs via court losses, beyond the general costs to U.S. national interests that the policy could have imposed.

To be clear, stronger veto points and clearer legal standards do not mean that institutional change is impossible. Scholars of institutional change point out that, in such environments, institutions are more likely subject to "layering," where existing institutions persist but "[veto players] cannot necessarily prevent the addition of new elements."[81] This closely fits the eventual outcome of the IRF office in the bureaucracy. With a clear congressional mandate, like the SEAS position, there was little prospect of the IRF office meeting RGA's fate. As documented in chapters 3 and 4, the IRF office persisted in its congressionally mandated functions, and even grew in capacity during this period. Very much in keeping with these expectations, however, populist change agents were very capable of layering additional functions onto the office to match their priorities, in this case via the "ministerial" initiative, marked by populism's personalism and tied to actors lending their moral blessing to populism's identity boundaries.

The persistence of the SEAS position and lack of follow-through on the Muslim Brotherhood designation at least demonstrate that, in spheres where more explicit institutional checks existed through congressional oversight or clear jurisprudential standards, populist variation was limited. The IRF office's development serves as a useful reminder that even such limitations do not eliminate the potential for populist actors to pursue other varieties of institutional change to serve populism's twin goals of identity bounding and personalist governance. On the whole, however, these were exceptions to the rule when it came to religion and the foreign policy bureaucracy. Veto points were generally weak and legal standards open to discretion, facilitating the change, documented earlier, to the structures and substance of religion in U.S. foreign policy.

———— ❧ ————

Populist changes to both the process and substance of religion and foreign policy were relatively uninhibited by features of American institutions like separation of powers and judicial review. American institutions may enjoy advantages in certain spheres that make them more resistant to populist-driven backsliding than cases like Brazil or Hungary. Fairly isolated examples like the SEAS and the Muslim Brotherhood FTO designation show that, at times, such constraints may have correlated with elements of religion and foreign policy that remained fairly consistent throughout the Trump administration. But in several other areas, from executive authority over the structure and staffing of key offices to eventual judicial vindication of the substance of the Muslim Bans, supposedly strong institutions provided little resistance. An honest assessment of trends related to religion and foreign policy, even before Trump's election, should make this result less than shocking. The religion regime complex in foreign policy was always closely tied to executive dominance in foreign policy, and the wall of separation more flexible than in separationist mythology.

7

A FAITHFUL AUDIENCE?

Public Opinion and Trump's Religious Foreign Policy

A final constraint on blessing America First could have come from the populist's key audience: the American public. To this point, the story of blessing America First has mostly focused on elite, bureaucratic politics, through policy outcomes like the Muslim Ban and bureaucratic processes like dismantling the Religion and Global Affairs (RGA) office. Courts, Congress, and career government officials had limited capacity to halt these populist changes, notwithstanding some areas of continuity in favorable institutional conditions.

I now turn to a final potential source of restraint on blessing America First: the general public. Populism's key political logic is essentially domestic, centered on maintaining the power of the populist leader through manufacturing identity boundaries and deploying a personalistic structure of rule. The populist leader is nothing without an audience, and in theory, should be quite sensitive to audience costs while governing. Religious leaders considering blessing America First have their own audience costs in mind, as political activism could impact their own moral authority. How could audiences, in campaign rallies or in congregational pews, factor into elite-level stories of State Department offices and ministerial diplomatic meetings?

Two related, but distinct, logics could link relatively obscure changes in religion and foreign policy bureaucracy to audiences for political populists and their religious elite allies. First, the general public could act as a stabilizing force by rejecting either populist identity boundaries or personalist attacks on institutional constraint. Robert Putnam and David Campbell argue that "American Grace" consists of an appreciation for religious pluralism that seems to run counter to populist exclusion, while other scholarship has identified religion's role in promoting institutional trust.[1] Some of Trump's actions documented earlier in this book, most prominently the "Muslim Bans," provoked nationwide public protest. At the same time, Trump's populist base could share his hostility to institutional constraint and his core supporters could endorse populist in-group and out-group boundaries. Blessing America First might provoke resistance from outsiders, but simultaneously solidify core support.

A second possibility shifts the source of constraint. Instead of looking for potential limits on the populist, it is plausible that the religious leaders most actively blessing America First could, themselves, have risked their public credibility, thus having some incentive to restrain the populist executive to preserve their own moral authority. When Trump's religious allies rushed to his defense in areas related to national security, what effect did this have on their moral authority? While the United States has long been noted for its religious exceptionalism,[2] a burst of recent scholarship has highlighted secularization in the country, as well as the role of conservative religious politics in causing this change.[3] Such negative reaction to blessing America First is plausible, but another possibility exists: Trump's religious foreign policy allies may have alienated those outside their political orbit, but actually reinforced their moral authority among political fellow travelers in their pews. Trump's religious allies could have built their support among the president's loyalists, while simultaneously alienating other Americans.

To test these possible paths of constraint from the general population, I turn to analysis of an original survey designed to probe popular responses to blessing America First. In sum, survey evidence shows that Trump's core supporters were uniquely hostile to career government bureaucrats, and that both ideological boundaries and rejection of institutional constraint were strongly associated with support for President Trump. Results are especially strong in relating Trump support to hostile attitudes towards the federal bureaucracy of career civil servants, suggesting that Trump faced minimal costs for his efforts that weakened the existing religion-foreign policy bureaucracy in favor of more personalistic initiatives. The results linking Christian nationalism to deep state hostility provide new evidence of the enmeshing between that religious ideology and newer elements of populist politics.

More nuanced results emerge when turning to an experiment that tests the *effects* of clergy blessing America First. Consistent with the overwhelming focus of populism on the direct, unmediated populist-voter relationship, receiving support from clerical endorsers had no effect on the political support Trump enjoyed, either in the general population or among his core supporters. Trump's supporters endorsed the former president, regardless of what type of elite was advocating for him.

However, being exposed to religious advocacy for Trump's national security behavior did affect the religious legitimacy of those pastors. Their moral authority *increased* among Trump's core supporters, while *decreasing sharply* among those outside of Trump's base. This suggests that religious leaders blessing America First may have had incentives to lend moral authority to populist foreign policy, while at the same time provoking resistance to religious politics beyond their core loyalists. Blessing America First served as yet another source of polarization within American religion, building narrow bases of clergy support while alienating the wider public.

This chapter is structured in four sections. The first briefly reviews existing scholarship on public opinion, populism, foreign policy, and religion, with special attention to recent work that has argued that politicized religion may have as much of an effect on religion as it does on politics. I then examine an original survey designed to test the potential effects of blessing America First on public opinion. Next, an initial section of results from that survey tests the potential links between Trump's religious foreign policy and his political support. And finally, I move to an experiment testing the causal effect of blessing America First on religion and polarization in the United States. Taken as a whole, results suggest that populism's instrumentalization of religion and foreign policy faced little constraint from core supporters. Instead, it likely reinforced religious polarization in the country, with troubling implications for the future of American religious exceptionalism.

PUBLIC RESPONSE
AND POPULIST RELIGIOUS FOREIGN POLICY

The general public deserves attention in analyzing the origins and effects of blessing America First. Foreign policy may not typically rank high on surveys of voter priorities, but both populist leaders and religious clergy need to be keenly aware of their audiences, and the impact that political actions may have on those relationships. The public could plausibly punish a populist directly at the ballot box for changes involving religion and foreign policy, or indirectly discourage blessing America First by granting lower moral authority to the clergy who endorse populist foreign policy.

In spite of predictions from some of the founding fathers of postwar political science that the general public lacks anything approaching coherent views on U.S. foreign policy, recent research has probed the mutual links between national-level foreign policy decisions and public opinion, in nuanced ways.[4] Public opinion potentially constrains elite foreign policy decisions[5] but may also be molded by elite cues.[6] Two things could be simultaneously true: foreign policy could factor into domestic political strategy and that strategy could have effects on public opinion.

Focusing on audiences is especially justified because of the populist nature of Trump administration religious foreign policy. Whether in foreign or domestic policy, populism is, first and foremost, a variety of rules centered on the bonds between the populist leader and "the people," however defined. As Kurt Weyland points out, "Populists constantly commission surveys and brandish their popularity ratings as political weapons."[7] The performative style of populism reflects the importance of direct, unmediated connection with the population through personal performance at rallies or, today, through mass media.[8] There is every reason to suspect that these comparative scholarly insights apply to the instrumentalization of religion in Trump administration foreign policy. Many of the most notorious populist claims about America First took place not in the context of wonky policy speeches or vetted statements of foreign policy doctrine, but instead in campaign rallies and press events. Trump's vow, at a South Carolina rally, to implement a "total and complete shutdown of Muslims" entering the United States most dramatically captures this point.

Recent research on the intersection between religion and Trump's rise reinforces these instincts. First and foremost, a substantial body of research has documented the extent to which religion shapes foreign policy attitudes and correlated with Trump support. Beyond the general link between white evangelicalism and support for Republican candidates,[9] a series of studies has shown that Trump's base largely consisted of "Christian nationalists" who conflated Christianity with American identity and expressed a preference for privileging Christianity in American law.[10] Second, some public opinion evidence has indicated that Trump changed American religion itself. Exemplary in this regard is the finding from the Public Religion Research Institute that white evangelicals showed a dramatic decrease in their concern about immoral decision-making in the personal lives of politicians between 2011 and 2016, after Trump's national political rise.[11]

A first pathway linking these research trends to populist foreign policy focuses on popular responses to the populist himself. Does Trump's populist foreign policy approach, both in its identity-based boundaries and personalist structure of rule, provoke public blowback? Or could it serve as a means of building his core domestic political support, especially among his religious base? International relations scholars have shown that elements of "Moral Foundations Theory" from social psychology correspond "strongly and systematically to foreign policy attitudes."[12] Public opinion scholarship in religion and American politics has found similar ties between religion and American exceptionalism, as well as preemptive use of military force.[13] Aspects of American evangelicalism have been shown to increase support for Israel,[14] as well as skepticism of international diplomacy to address climate change.[15]

More directly tied to the subject matter of America First foreign policy, James Guth documents the affinity between white evangelicals and elements of populism,[16] while other researchers have shown ties between Christian nationalism and both American exceptionalism and anti-Muslim sentiment.[17] Moreover, Christian nationalism has been shown to correlate with conspiratorial politics in ways that could drive support for Trump's rejection of supposed deep state constraint.[18] In short, there is good reason to suspect that relationships exist in public opinion data between Christian nationalism, elements of America First foreign policy, and most importantly to the populist, personal political support for President Trump.

To be clear, tests in most of this existing research are correlational, rather than causal, in nature. This is a challenge for much of the foreign policy public opinion literature, which is "explicitly about a particular top-down causal mechanism, rather than a simple correlation, yet [relies] on observational data where questions of directionality are difficult to disentangle."[19] One approach to address this shortcoming is to use survey experiments to carry out more direct causal tests. In this case, one test might be whether rallying religious supporters brought Trump unique support for his populist foreign policy approach, when compared to any other elite endorsing the president's foreign policy. On the one hand, we might expect this to be the case. Christian nationalists are more supportive of religious leaders being involved in American politics, and religious-partisan cues have been shown to effect candidate perception for copartisans.[20] At the same time, some research on populism might temper our expectations. Weyland, for example, insists that "[populism] pushes aside, or dominates other types of actors, such as elite factions," rather than relying on elite endorsement.[21] If this is the case, it could be that religion correlates with America First foreign policy, but endorsement from religious leaders does little to increase this support.

Turning to an experimental approach is worthwhile for further reasons: Trump's instrumentalization of religion may generate constraint through a second pathway—impacting the moral authority of his religious endorsers. Integrating religion into populist politics could change American religion, generating constraint from religious leaders who risk having their own moral authority undercut. The strongest theoretical foundation for this claim comes from comparative research that has documented the fragility of religious leaders' moral authority in politics. As Anna Grzymała-Busse argues, "Because it relies on the perception that the churches are national representatives and righteous defenders of the common good, political moral authority . . . is a brittle resource."[22] Cases in countries such as Ireland, where religious elites previously enjoyed "moral monopolies," show that authority can crumble in the face of the failure to cultivate it on the part of religious elites.[23] Grzymała-Busse continues with words that echo criticisms of Trump's religious apologists: "Pursuing narrowly self-interested, parochial, or local interests also risks dissipating this valuable capital."[24] Even highly religious individuals may hesitate to support religious leader involvement in politics,[25] and unwanted clerical cues may cause blowback from audiences more skeptical of the religious messenger.[26] Religious leaders, aware of these dynamics, might have reason to rein in populist excesses.

Early evidence, generally consistent with this dynamic, emerged in the rapid growth of the religiously unaffiliated (commonly termed the "nones") in the opening decades of this century. Michael Hout, Claude Fischer, David Campbell, Geoffrey Layman, and John Green among others, have documented the extent to which declining American affiliation may be a reaction to conservative religious politics.[27] This research primarily focuses on domestic policy issues tied to gender and sexuality as the source of popular blowback, but it is entirely feasible that, given the salient links between Trump foreign policy and religion, blessing America First could have a similar effect today. At the same time effects could be contingent, reflecting our polarized religious politics. The late journalist Michael Gerson observed that, with Trump's election, "[Evangelicals] have become another Washington interest group, striving for advantage rather than seeking the common good."[28] To formalize Gerson's logic, it is plausible that blessing America First may build moral authority among a narrow base of political loyalists, while driving polarization and rejection from those outside the populist camp.

SURVEY DESIGN

To test these potential links between elite-level religious foreign policy under the Trump administration and constraint via popular support, an original survey, with an embedded survey experiment, collected information from a representative sample of American voters. Qualtrics fielded the survey of roughly 1,700 U.S. adults in late October/early November 2022. The sample was constructed such that it was largely representative of the U.S. adult population based on age, race, education, and sex. Survey design incorporated three additional steps to ensure the quality of the data. First, the survey required respondents to pass multiple attention checks; if they failed a single check, they were not allowed to complete the survey. Second, analysis removed all respondents who sped through the survey. More specifically, if respondents spent less than ten minutes on the survey, which was designed to take twenty minutes, they were removed from the sample.[29] After taking these steps, the final sample size was 1,673. Third, the survey used embedded timers to ensure that subjects stayed on the screens for an adequate time to complete required reading.

The survey's first goal was to document indicators of support for populist dimensions of foreign policy: identity boundaries and personalist rejection of institutional constraint. First, to capture populism's thin ideology, the survey included feeling thermometers tied to two groups who were consistently excluded from the political community by Trump and his foreign policy loyalists: Muslims and international organizations. One feeling thermometer asked directly for perceptions of Muslims (from 0 [cold/negative] to 100 [warm/positive]), and another asked about the respondents' views of the United Nations. The Muslim feeling thermometer's mean score of 53.8 approximates results from the Pew Research group, which found a mean in 2019 of 49, while the mean rating of the United Nations was slightly higher (54.2).[30] Although the items are correlated with one another ($r = .27$, $p = 0.000$), they operationalize attitudes that are substantively different on their face, so they are treated separately in the analysis that follows rather than being combined into a single index.

Second, the survey turned to populism's strategic dimension, by measuring a preference for personalist rule and a rejection of institutional constraint. The instrument contained a basic feeling thermometer asking subjects to express their rating of "Government Employees." Additionally, Trump's foreign policy personalism frequently centered on combat with an alleged deep state opposed to his election. To operationalize these ideas, the survey included a battery of items related to the personal authority of former President Trump over government bureaucrats. Subjects were asked to evaluate the following statements on a five-point scale, ranging from "strongly disagree" (1) to "strongly agree" (5): 1) New presidents should have the power to replace nonpartisan government officials with members of their own political party; 2) Unelected officials in the federal government have too much influence in determining government policy; and 3) a deep state worked to undermine Donald Trump during his presidency. All three correlate strongly with one another ($p = 0.000$), so they

TABLE 7.1 Summary Statistics of Dimensions of Populist Support

	N	Mean	SD	Min	Max
Muslims Feeling Thermometer	1673	53.8	29.3	0	100
UN Feeling Thermometer	1673	54.2	30.0	0	100
Government Employees Feeling Thermometer	1673	54.8	28	0	100
Deep State Index	1671	2.98	.88	1	5

are combined into a *Deep State index* in later analysis. Table 7.1 provides summary statistics for these primary variables of interest.

The survey's next goal was to probe potential sources of constraint by testing relationships between Trump voting and support for the various populist dimensions of his foreign policy. In keeping with the hypothesis that populists engage in various policy initiatives to build domestic support, the primary dependent variable testing this hypothesis was whether a respondent voted for Trump in the 2020 election.[31] Data collection for this dependent variable consisted of two steps. First, subjects were asked if they voted in the 2020 U.S. presidential election, and then those who voted were asked to select their candidate from a list that included Trump, Joe Biden, Joe Jorgensen, Someone Else, and a "Can't Remember" option. Roughly 43 percent of the sample of 2020 voters reported voting for President Trump, which slightly underperforms his popular vote share of 46.8 percent. This is perhaps unsurprising given the events of January 6th, 2021, and Trump's declining popular support numbers for a time after leaving office.[32]

Beyond these core variables related to populism and Trump foreign policy, the survey included standard demographic measures (sex, age, race, Hispanic/Latino identification, education), along with those for partisanship and political ideology. To operationalize religion, the instrument included a common, multi-question measure to categorize individuals into religious traditions (Catholics, evangelicals, Jews, etc.), along with a distinct measure of religious service attendance. The instrument also included a common battery of questions to operationalize "Christian nationalism," which a diverse array of studies has linked to support for the Trump administration, its Islamophobic policies, and the violence of January 6th, 2021.[33]

In addition to variables used for observational hypothesis testing, the survey contained an embedded experiment to test the effects of religious endorsement of Trump's populist foreign policy behavior. All subjects read a hypothetical, but true-to-life, newspaper headline and introductory article section related to the investigation into President Trump's handling of classified national security documents. This subject matter is substantively linked to the populist nature of Trump's foreign policy behavior, as the rejection of constraint tied to the security clearance and document classification process was a constant theme of his presidency, from early controversies about security clearances for family members to the ongoing criminal investigations of post-presidency document security. This subject matter was also chosen because of its timely nature, given the survey's time in the field, when compared to other examples of populist foreign policy from earlier in his administration.

To introduce experimental variation, subjects were randomly assigned to one of two conditions, with each group receiving a slightly varied article. Experimental variation consisted of a straightforward "messenger test" to explore the unique implications of religious leader support for America First foreign policy. Half of participants experienced the "Leader" condition, which can be thought of as a control, in which the messenger rallying in Trump's defense is identified simply as a leader. The other half experienced a second, "Christian Pastors" condition, in which clergy messengers are identified as the source of the Trump support. Postsurvey analysis reveals balance between two groups on major covariates like age, gender, ethnicity, partisanship, and religiosity.[34] See the two mock newspaper articles in figure 7.1.

The research design is intended to pose a tough test of potential clergy endorsement effects. It compares coverage of religious leader support of Trump not to the absence of all news coverage of Trump's supporters, but instead to the absence only of religious messengers in that coverage. It also is entirely possible that individuals in the "Leader" condition were exposed to information that would resemble the Christian Pastors treatment outside of the study, via real-world coverage of controversies over the Mar-a-Lago document investigation.[35] If present, this dynamic would water down

SPLIT A	SPLIT B
The Examiner	**The Examiner**
Leaders defend Trump amid classified document investigation	**Christian Pastors defend Trump amid classified document investigation**
By Steven Fischer, September 30	By Steven Fischer, September 30
Former President Donald Trump remains the target of criminal investigation involving his handling of highly classified national security documents. Supporters of this investigation have argued that it should continue because the former president needs to be held accountable.	Former President Donald Trump remains the target of criminal investigation involving his handling of highly classified national security documents. Supporters of this investigation have argued that it should continue because the former president needs to be held accountable.
Opponents of the investigation rallied yesterday to support the former President. They argued that the investigation should stop immediately because it is politically motivated and dividing the nation.	Opponents of the investigation, including a group of Christian pastors, rallied yesterday to support the former President. They argued that the investigation should stop immediately because it is politically motivated and dividing the nation.

FIGURE 7.1 Experimental design.

any differences between the two randomized groups, which should increase our confidence in any differences that do emerge in the data between the two groups.

The survey then used two questions as dependent variables after exposure to this newspaper article. One was designed to measure support for former President Trump, in keeping with the hypothesis that populists might build networks of religious elites to buttress their popular appeal with coreligionists. The survey measured respondents' answers on a scale from (0) "The classified document investigation should continue because former President Trump needs to be held accountable" to (10) "The classified document investigation should not continue because it is politically motivated and divides the nation," with (5) centered as "Believe both equally." As we would expect, in the control condition this variable was highly correlated with partisanship ($r = 0.56$, $p = 0.000$).

The second dependent variable pivoted to a second potential source of constraint: moral authority of pastors themselves. Negative reaction to

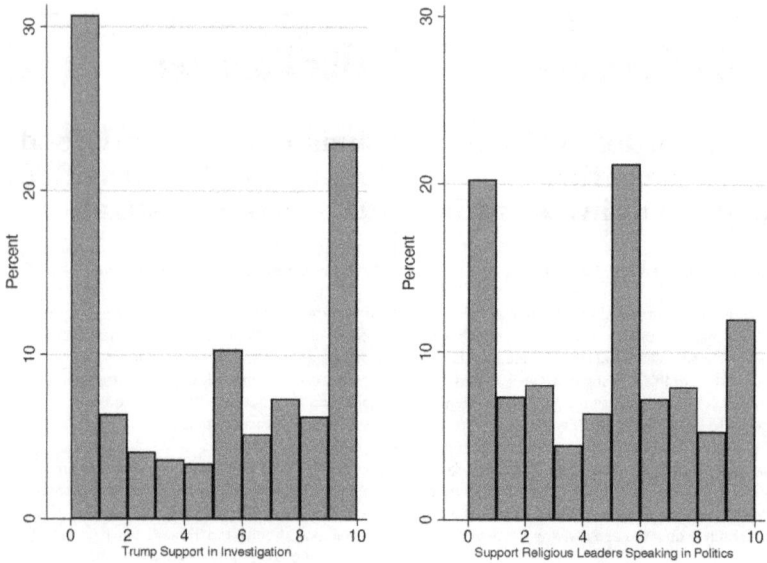

FIGURE 7.2 Distribution of experiment dependent variables (control condition).

blessing America First could provide clergy with incentives to avoid rallying in defense of populist foreign policy. This measure draws on an approach used regularly in survey research, including repeatedly in Pew Research Group polling.[36] Respondents' support for religious leader involvement in politics was measured from (0) "Religious leaders should keep out of political issues" to (10) "Religious leaders should speak out about political issues," with (5) centered as "Believe both equally." In the control condition, this dependent variable was also linked to partisanship, although to a weaker extent than the dependent variable measuring Trump support ($r = .138, p = 0.001$).

The distribution of these two dependent variables from the control condition is presented in figure 7.2. This gives a baseline of public opinion on these two issues, without religious endorsement for Trump's actions. This figure serves two purposes. First, it demonstrates that variation exists among U.S. voters in evaluating both the personalism of the Trump administration and the involvement of religious leaders in public life. Second, the variable related to supporting Trump in the classified document investigation is significantly more polarized, in the control condition, than that for the involvement of religious leaders in politics, where a neutral response of "5" is actually the modal position in the sample.

TESTING OBSERVATIONAL LINKS BETWEEN POPULISM, RELIGION, AND TRUMP SUPPORT

A first step in linking the personalist rejection of institutional restraint to religion and Trump support is to test the potential relationship between religious variables and the deep state index. Based on recent research, we have strongest expectations that Christian nationalism would correlate with this hostility to career national security officials, with mixed expectations regarding more traditional religious variables like religious tradition and attendance at religious services.

Figure 7.3 provides a visualization based on the results of regression models testing the relationships between religious variables and the deep state index.[37] The model presented in the graph includes controls for major demographic and political variables that might also impact the deep state index.[38] Both indices have been rescaled 1 to 5 to allow easier visualization of the substantive effect. The primary finding shows strong, consistent links between Christian nationalism and the deep state index. In all models, results are highly statistically significant ($p < 0.001$). Rather than a source of constraint on populist initiatives, this core group of religious supporters seems disposed to share deep state hostility. In keeping with scholarship from Samuel Perry, Andrew Whitehead, and coauthors, the importance of evangelical identification is minimal once Christian nationalism is included in the models.[39] It is worth noting that, with the inclusion of controls, religious service attendance becomes negatively associated with the deep state index, although with an estimated coefficient that is modest in size compared to Christian nationalism. This may be some evidence that certain dimensions of religiosity in the United States continue to provide the civic trust and habits of institutional participation that have traditionally fueled more optimistic stories about religion making American democracy work.[40]

Substantively, Christian nationalism is doing a significant amount of explanatory work in accounting for variation in the deep state index. In

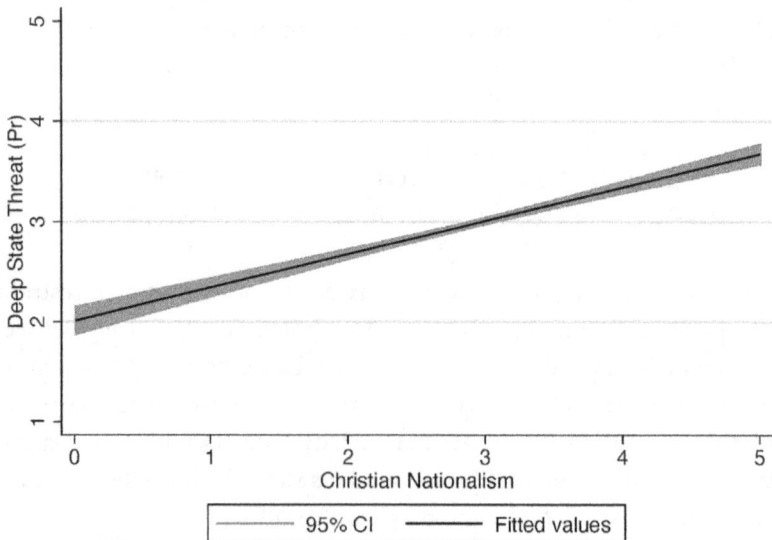

FIGURE 7.3 Christian nationalism and deep state threat.

the models without additional controls, it is the only statistically significant variable of a model with an r² of 0.2, and the inclusion of political
controls that are also correlated strongly with the deep state index only
increases that r² to 0.28. Moving from the twenty-fifth percentile of
Christian nationalism (2.17 on the scale) to the seventy-fifth percentile,
corresponds to a shift of .5 on the deep state index, over half a standard
deviation, even while taking into account the influence of other control
variables. Clearly Trump administration rhetoric targeting career national
security officials resonated strongly with the administration's staunchest
religious allies in the general population.

While this relationship between Christian nationalism and attacks on
career government officials is substantial, it is one step removed from the
core populist concern: maintaining personal support. Thus, as a next step,
analysis shifts to explaining the dependent variable most directly operationalizing that idea—having voted for Trump in the 2020 election. To
what extent are measures linked to the two dimensions of populism in
foreign policy (thin ideological boundaries and personalist political strategy) also linked to having voted for Trump in his reelection campaign?

While not conclusive, significant results in this area would increase confidence that the populist maneuvering documented in earlier chapters of this book was consistent with a political strategy of building domestic support in the electorate. If so, there is little reason to think that public opinion would serve as a direct limitation on blessing America First.

Figure 7.4 visualizes the results of regression models testing the relationships of four variables related to populism and foreign policy to voting for Trump in the 2020 election, with several control variables included.[41] The first row of graphs in figure 7.4 highlights indicators tied to populism's personalism. The independent variables of interest are the deep state index, as well as a feeling thermometer for government employees. Both the deep state index and anti-government employee sentiment correlate consistently with Trump support. In models with full controls, results are statistically robust ($p < 0.01$).[42] Party identification, ideology, and Christian nationalism strongly predicted Trump support as well, but including them in the models does not eliminate the significant link between the indicators of populism's personalist political logic and support for Trump in 2020. Again, these relationships are not necessarily causal, but demonstrate an affinity between Trump's core supporters and a crucial dimension of populist foreign policy related to religion.

The second row of graphs turns to variables most closely tied to Trump's ideological boundaries in foreign policy: attitudes towards Muslims and the United Nations. Both anti-Muslim sentiment and anti-UN sentiment correlated consistently with Trump support. Regardless of what controls are present, results are statistically robust ($p < 0.01$). Several controls again behaved as expected, with party identification, ideology, and Christian nationalism all strongly predicting Trump support. However, even after accounting for these factors, the additional indicators of support for Trump's foreign policy hostility to Muslims and multilateral organizations maintained an independent relationship to increased voter support.

Substantively, the four relationships plotted in figure 7.4 demonstrate an important effect in increasing the likelihood of Trump voting in 2020. To give two examples to illustrate this point, moving from the twenty-fifth percentile on the deep state index to the seventy-fifth percentile increased the share of Trump voters from .37 to .46, and those at the ninetieth percentile and above were more likely than not Trump voters. Rejection of

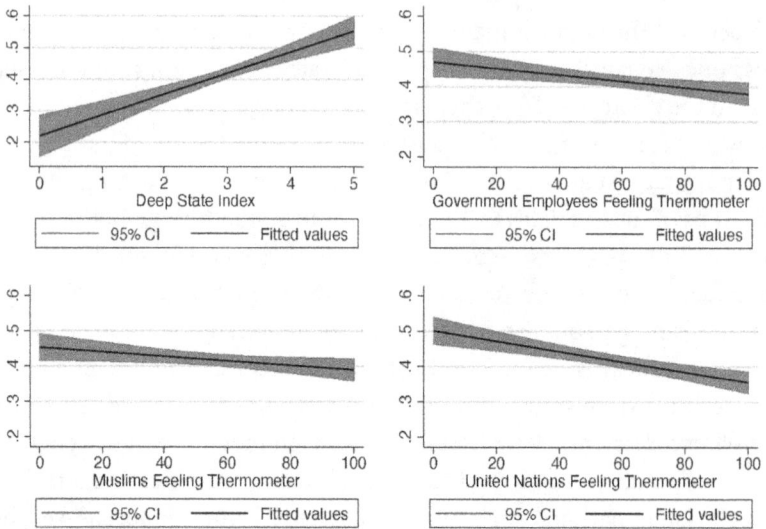

FIGURE 7.4 Populism, foreign policy, and Trump voting.

multilateral organizations like the UN had a similar substantive effect, with a shift across similar percentiles moving Trump support from .38 to .44. Again, while only correlational in nature, these substantive results indicate that the Trump administration's foreign policy combination of personalism with ideological exclusion of groups like Muslims and "cosmopolitan" international organizations was consistent with preferences among its core voters. With core voters linked to support for religious dimensions of America First, there is little support for the hope that public opinion could constrain populist action.

TESTING EXPERIMENTAL EFFECTS OF RELIGIOUS ENDORSEMENT

These observational results give credence to the hypothesis that the Trump administration enjoyed grassroots support for its populism in religion and foreign policy, and thus public opinion was unlikely to provide any check on blessing America First. This sets the stage for a tougher experimental test of two potential effects when religious elites rallied to support Trump's foreign policy. First, it is plausible that religious endorsement for America First brought unique political dividends to the president. This would strengthen the political incentives to engage in blessing America First. Second, blessing America First could undermine the moral authority of religious leaders in the public eye, potentially inflicting costs on those clerical voices most supportive of the populist project in foreign policy.

In sum, experimental results show that clergy endorsement brought little unique political benefit to Trump, but significantly polarized popular views of religious authority of clergy in public life. In response to blessing America First, Trump voters granted *greater* moral authority to clergy. However, non-Trump voters expressed significant *blowback* to these clergy endorsements. In the end, exposure to blessing America First left Americans more polarized over the political role of religion, with significantly more extreme anti-religious views expressed by non-Trump voters. However, the positive response to religious endorsement may explain why certain clergy had narrower incentives to bless America First, rather than constrain it.

First, and most briefly, did clergy endorsement increase support for ending the classified document investigation of Trump, when compared to a control condition in which the endorsement came from unidentified leaders? As figure 7.5 visualizes clearly, the answer is no. Estimated treatment effects among all subjects are effectively zero, as well as when subjects are broken down by 2020 vote choice. No estimate even approaches conventional levels of statistical significance, and there is no meaningful difference in how Trump supporters or opponents responded to religious endorsement. This negative result is substantively consistent with a core claim of scholars of populism: support for populist leaders is unmediated by traditional elites in parties, interest groups, or other social sectors, including organized religion. It also should raise questions about whether any resistance from clerical elites to populist initiatives was likely to provoke unique public outcry, although the research design does not directly test this claim.

The results, however, show a quite different pattern when the focus turns to the dependent variable related to the moral authority of clergy. As the right panel of figure 7.5 demonstrates, in the sample as a whole, clergy endorsement was estimated to have a negative effect on clergy moral authority, although with modest levels of statistical significance ($p < 0.09$). This raises the question of why clergy would have supported Trump in his populist national security initiatives. Why defend the president if one's moral authority in public life suffers as a result? Could this be some evidence that clergy had incentives to limit their faith-based endorsement of America First?

The nuanced answer lies in the different responses of Trump voters and non-Trump voters. The right panel of figure 7.5 makes it clear that clergy endorsement drove down moral authority among those who opposed the president in 2020, but actually *increased* clergy moral authority among Trump voters ($p < 0.07$). It seems that two things could be true at the same time: blessing America First could drive down clergy moral authority overall, while strengthening the hand of clerical loyalists among core populist supporters. This result is confirmed in interaction models reported in Appendix Table 4, where Trump voters are shown to have responded in a statistically distinct way to treatment than non-Trump voters ($p < .01$). This pattern may help to explain the confidence of Trump's religious endorsers, in spite of real blowback from sectors of the American public. Blessing America First brought polarization to a question about religion in public life where, as figure 7.1 showed earlier, relatively less polarization existed before.

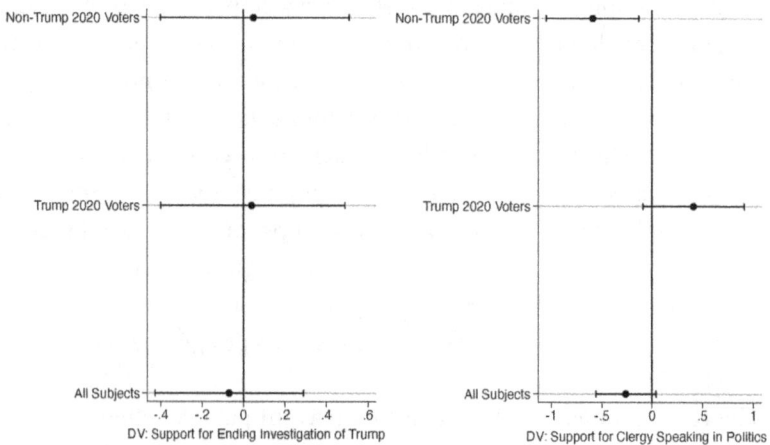

FIGURE 7.5 Experimental effects of clergy endorsement.

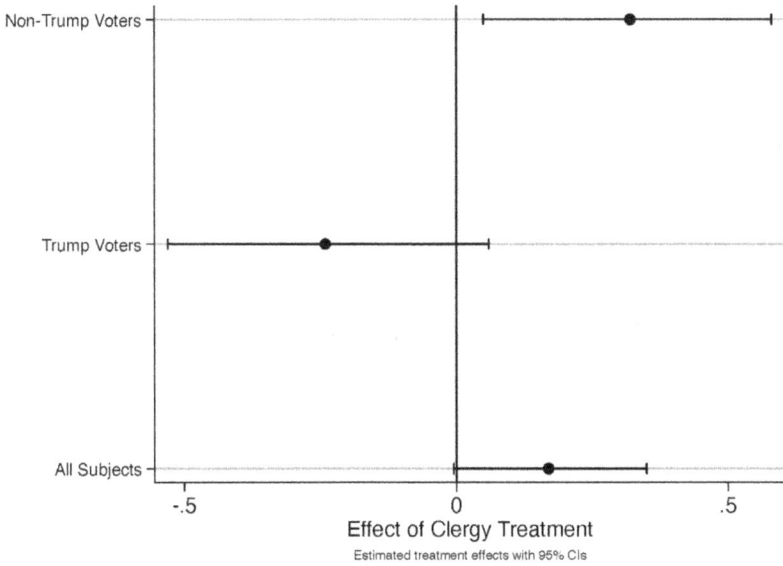

FIGURE 7.6 Extremism in attitude to clergy moral authority.

As a final test, another indicator of polarization over clergy moral authority might be if clergy defenses of Trump drove subjects to increasingly extreme positions at either end of the 0 to 10 scale of clergy moral authority. "Folding" the clergy moral authority scale into a new variable, where a higher value indicates a *more extreme response* at *either end* of the original scale, gives one way to test this possibility. Figure 7.6 depicts the result: for all voters, the clergy endorsement did increase extremity ($p < 0.057$), but the effects were primarily clustered among Trump's opponents ($p < 0.018$) rather than his supporters, who actually were estimated to become modestly less extreme in their response ($p < 0.12$).[43]

CONCLUSION: COULD THE PUBLIC CONSTRAIN BLESSING AMERICA FIRST?

How do these findings change the way we should understand the process of blessing America First foreign policy? They clarify that initiatives like the Muslim Ban made perfect sense in terms of the domestic populist project of the Trump administration, even if their impact on America's security and economic interests may have been costly. Furthermore, the experimental results indicate that the effects of blessing America First may have further polarized the political role of clergy in the country. Blessing America First seems to generate blowback, but in such a polarized manner that it would be unlikely to restrain Trump's religious loyalists.

First, observational results show the consistent domestic public support that Trump was likely to have received from his base for the various dimensions of his populist foreign policy agenda tied to religion. At a basic level, there is a strong correlation, undocumented to this point in public opinion scholarship, between hostility to career government bureaucrats and the Christian nationalist ideology that has repeatedly been shown to be among the strongest predictors of support for the former president. To put it another way, the ideological boundaries associated with Trumpism actually seem to correlate with support for its personalist political structure. This is consistent with other recent scholarship that shows strong correlations between Christian nationalism and other dimensions of what might be thought of as the "cutting edge" of alt-right politics: conspiratorial beliefs, white racial identity, and perceived victimhood.[44] This suggests a future spot in the diverse American religious marketplace for ideas blending anti-institutional, conspiracy-minded cues with religious justification. On a perhaps slightly more optimistic note, once controlling for Christian nationalism, religious service attendance did correspond to decreased deep state threat, so some resources may still exist for drawing religion into efforts to strengthen governmental institutions.

The consistent positive relationships between Trump-voting in 2020 and indicators tied to populist foreign policy lend further support to the idea that Trump correctly understood that he was unlikely to bear any domestic cost for his confrontations with the career bureaucracy, Muslims, and "cosmopolitan globalists." If anything, there is reason to suspect that the style and substance of populist foreign policy, including related to religion, resonated with Trump's strongest supporters. It should be noted that, because this survey was in the field after the Trump administration, it is not suitable for sorting out whether Trump tapped into preexisting patterns in America's religious politics or created them by his own initiative as the populist leader. It seems likely that both were true, to an extent. However, the data does show that, at this point, these relationships were robust, and therefore could attract future candidates seeking to build on Trump's populist successes.

With that said, the *non*-result related to clergy endorsement increasing support for Trump in the classified document investigation also bears noting. At least by 2022, it is not clear that Trump garnered any additional public support when endorsed by clergy than when backed by any anonymous devotee. What could this mean for the foreign policy of religion in a future administration, including one potentially led by Trump himself? If future benefits to the populist from clerical endorsement are fairly indistinct, it would stand to reason that future religious foreign policy concessions would only make sense if they came at fairly low cost to the populist leader. Foreign policy, as we have seen, contains many low cost, largely symbolic opportunities to deliver for loyalists, from ambassadorial appointments to convening initiatives like Pompeo's Commission on Unalienable Rights. Results would seem to point to more of this in future, right-wing populist administrations.

The most lasting, and perhaps unexpected, effects of blessing America First may, however, be on American religion rather than American politics. Clerical endorsement for Trump in the classified documents investigation sharply decreased support for clergy speaking out in public life among Trump's non-supporters. Further research could probe how lasting this effect will be. For instance, does blessing America First cause Americans to react negatively even to relatively less partisan religious interventions in foreign policy, like engaging religious groups in combatting HIV/AIDS abroad? The current design does not directly address this question. However, it does add another weighty piece of evidence to the list of findings that conservative religious mobilization in the past quarter century has generated significant blowback from portions of the American religious landscape, what Putnam and Campbell call a "second aftershock," tracing all the way back to the contentious 1960s.[45] Others have shown that conservative religious mobilization has played a part in the rise of the religiously unaffiliated in recent decades, and evidence here suggests that blessing America First could shift religious-political norms among non-Trump supporters. Normatively, it seems troubling that clergy endorsement also increased extremity in views on religious politics. While figure 7.1 shows that, in the absence of blessing America First, the modal response of Americans was in the middle of the clergy politics scale, that mode becomes strongly centered on the more extreme responses in the treatment condition.

To return to the core focus of this book, these findings suggest a tough path back to the relatively bipartisan consensus over the place of religion in the foreign policy bureaucracy that existed in summer 2016. What Gregorio Bettiza termed the "regime complex" of religion across the State Department, USAID, National Security Council, and other foreign policy centers developed slowly, over the course of roughly a quarter century, during Democratic and Republican administrations. As chapter 6 showed, much of this bureaucratization reflected discretion on the part of presidents and high-level political appointees, seen clearly, for instance, in Secretary Kerry's unique role in the creation of the Religion and Global Affairs office. In the wake of Trump's 2020 defeat, would that old equilibrium return? That question will be taken up in more depth in this book's conclusion. At the very least, these quantitative findings suggest that Democrats, (after the Trump presidency) draw on supporters who have reacted strongly against the involvement of religion in populist politics. Democratic presidents are likely to be aware of these domestic dynamics, and perhaps have less incentive to venture onto uncertain religious ground in the foreign policy bureaucracy.

PART IV

EFFECTS BEYOND THE POPULIST

8

FAITHFUL PARTNERS

Religious Populism and International Ties

I n May 2017, Vice President Mike Pence met with Metropolitan Hilarion Alfeyev, then the Russian Orthodox Church's top cleric for external affairs, on the margins of a religious freedom summit hosted by evangelist Franklin Graham. The Graham family has ties to Russia that stretch back decades, including Billy Graham's controversial 1982 visit to the former Soviet Union. Franklin, the most public inheritor of Billy Graham's ministry, built on this foundation in developing ties to post-Soviet Russia that culminated in a 2015 meeting with President Vladimir Putin. Thus, the ties between certain American evangelicals and Putin's Russia were not the result of Trump's 2016 election. However, with Trump in office, a new set of religious leaders suddenly enjoyed influence over the structure and priorities of religion in U.S. foreign policy.

As already demonstrated in chapters 3 and 4, Trump's populism impacted the internal workings of the foreign policy bureaucracy. This chapter now turns outward to probe the implications of religious populism for international ties. In short, Trump's populism facilitated international ties that served populism's twin goals: constructing thin ideological boundaries and deploying a personalist structure of rule. This global network of religious populists contrasted with the international experts grounding the pre-Trump equilibrium in religion and U.S. foreign policy. Considering populism's international ties is appropriate at this late stage in *Blessing America First* because they provide a channel through which populism's effects endure, even after the individual populist leaves the political stage. In the end, Trump's 2020 election defeat (at least temporarily) removed the American advocates of blessing America First from the levers of U.S. diplomacy. However, relationships persist, and ties among the global populist right could easily shape U.S. foreign policy again in future years.

In more theoretical terms, this chapter turns from the domestic effects of populism to its impact on international networks. The rise of populism in religious foreign policy provided a kind of "soft power" that facilitated new international bonds.[1] Highlighting these bonds is consistent with Peter Henne's call to adopt a "relational turn" in religion and international relations.[2] Populism's rise provided a political opportunity to a new set of actors, who pursued cooperation abroad, intended to further populism's two dimensions: thin ideological boundaries and a personalist political logic rejecting institutional constraint and privileging charismatic stylistic performance. Where international actors provided targets of convenience to meet either of these goals, domestic populist allies took blessing America First to the global stage.

These ties cannot be reduced to simple ideological rallying within "civilizational" blocs described in Samuel Huntington's work. While Trump administration religious allies encouraged far-right Christian nationalists in Europe, their work extended more broadly, observable in engagement with actors as diverse as the Russian Orthodox Church, anti-Islamist authoritarians across the Middle East, and Hindu nationalists in India.[3] At times, in service to populist ends, Trump's allies even overlooked international petitions from groups seeking to make ideological appeals based on shared Christian identity, precisely because populism's ideological thinness renders such appeals uncompelling. The claim here is not that populists necessarily cooperate with other populists, in a carnival mirror image of democratic peace theory. Populists can easily be drawn into conflict with one another, as was the case between Trump and some of Latin America's left populists in places like Venezuela. However, where international actors share an overlapping consensus regarding ideological boundaries or personalist rule, populist allies are likely to take advantage of the opportunity.

This chapter traces the changing international ties associated with religion and U.S. foreign policy, in four parts. First, it documents the extent to which the pre-Trump religion "regime complex" in U.S. foreign policy had international coalitional effects. By late 2016, an observable international network of expertise in religious diplomacy emerged, especially between the U.S. and traditional European allies, that fit the general model of a transnational "epistemic community."[4] Next, I turn to the changes under populist leadership when populist allies, in and out of government, pursued international ties reinforcing identity boundaries and personalist rule. I begin by looking at what might be thought of as "easy" cases of cooperation: other conservative Christian populists, in Hungary, Poland, and Brazil. The analysis then turns to cases where international ties stretched across boundaries of civilization and regime type (Russia and India). I conclude by examining the extent to which these relationships have persisted beyond the Trump presidency, suggesting a latent force likely to challenge the liberal international order, should conservative populism come to control the levers of the American foreign policy bureaucracy again in the future.

EXPERT RELIGION ABROAD: INTERNATIONAL TIES AND THE PRE-TRUMP EQUILIBRIUM

Before turning to populist effects on international ties, a return to the pre-Trump equilibrium of mid-2016 is helpful to establish a baseline against which we can observe populism's impact. Chapter 2 described the internal workings of Gregorio Bettiza's regime complex at that point in history, with particular attention to the model represented in the Office of Religion and Global Affairs (RGA). As Elizabeth Shakman Hurd has observed, this pattern of bureaucratization provided political opportunities to a particular set of agents, what she describes as representatives of "expert religion," across government, university research centers, think tanks, and other corners of the foreign policy community. In this world, "white papers abound."[5] Bettiza argues that this constituted an epistemic community in the U.S. context, "producing policy-relevant knowledge about religion in world affairs" that shapes U.S. foreign policy.[6] The concept of an epistemic community draws on a long tradition of studying "networks of knowledge-based experts," largely in constructivist international relations scholarship, who use control of knowledge and information to constitute the understanding of state interests and influence policy decision-making.[7]

The actors empowered to speak on behalf of expert religion built a network, not only within the D.C. Beltway, but more broadly with foreign governments sympathetic to this bureaucratizing approach. Scholars of epistemic communities and policy diffusion have long recognized that such networks may have the ability to shape transnational politics through agenda setting and framing.[8] Similar effects took place across portions of religion and the foreign policy bureaucracy in the pre-Trump period. As Bettiza demonstrates, such international effects operated in two ways: diffusion from the United States abroad, and "knowledge circulation and mutual learning between the United States and other parties."[9]

The United States's focus on promotion of international religious freedom, especially after the International Religious Freedom (IRF) Act, institutionalized its presence within the State Department and empowered a set of actors with clear-cut international effects. The State Department's IRF office formed transnational ties with offices tied to traditional American allies like the Canadian foreign ministry's Office of Religious Freedom, established in 2013 under the leadership of Andrew Bennett. Such initiatives emerged in regional organizations as well, most prominently via the European Union's "Guidelines on the promotion and protection of freedom of religion or belief" (FoRB), adopted in 2013, and institutionalized within its diplomatic bureaucracy through the creation of a special envoy on FoRB. Similar positions emerged in several EU member states during this time. While differences exist among these actors, as reflected in the tendency of EU partners to adopt the framing of Freedom of Religion or Belief, the similarity is apparent. Related bureaucratization existed at the UN as well, with a longstanding commitment through its Commission on Human Rights to a Special Rapporteur on issues of religious freedom.[10] The existence of ties between U.S. IRF offices and multilateral organizations like the EU and the UN is no accident. It reflects the extent to which the elite actors leading these offices were deeply enmeshed in the mainstream national and multinational organizations of the post-World War II liberal international order.

Similar affinities existed between other portions of the U.S. religion regime complex and international partners. In the development sphere,

USAID was hardly alone in seeing a place for religion in foreign assistance programming. The World Bank's World Faiths Development Dialogue grew under the leadership of Katherine Marshall in roughly the same period as expanded faith-based partnerships in U.S. development work, and international funders like Germany's Gesellschaft für Internationale Zusammenarbeit (GiZ) developed religion-oriented foreign assistance programs that contributed to mutual learning with the U.S. faith-based foreign assistance bureaucracy. In terms of network construction, the GiZ-supported International Partnership on Religion and Sustainable Development exists to "convene governments, multilateral entities, civil society organizations . . . and research or academic institutions."[11] Again, member governments reflect traditional Western European allies of the liberal international order like Canada, Finland, and Denmark, along with international funders like the Global Fund to Fight AIDS, Tuberculosis and Malaria.

RGA similarly contributed to international ties cultivated by practitioners of expert religion, especially among traditional American allies and supporters of the liberal international order. RGA's founding director Shaun Casey remarked in late 2016, "In three short years, we have engaged literally thousands of actors all across the globe," and core partners in those engagements began to form a transnational network of diplomats, academics, and practitioners refining the religious engagement approach.[12] As Bettiza points out, some of these initiatives predated RGA's creation in 2013, for instance among the foreign ministries of France and Italy.[13] The Transatlantic Policy Network on Religion and Diplomacy (TPNRD) was founded, in large part, to coordinate RGA-like efforts among Western allies, "a forum of diplomats from Europe and North America who are the designated point people on issues of religion and diplomacy within their respective foreign ministries. Founded in 2015 by officials from the European External Action Service and the U.S. State Department, the network aims to equip participants to more effectively analyze religious dynamics and engage religious actors in the pursuit of shared policy objectives."[14] RGA leaders encouraged the growth of such offices in allied foreign ministries while in government service, and former RGA staff like Peter Mandaville remained engaged in TPNRD leadership after leaving active government. TPNRD's director, Judd Birdsall, formerly served in the State Department.

These international networks occasionally took on more specific form, as well, in response to discrete policy challenges like diplomatic efforts to address climate change, implement public health programs designed to combat HIV/AIDS, and facilitate refugee resettlement. By 2016, in these areas and others, American diplomats regularly engaged with partners from sympathetic foreign governments, religious organizations, international organizations, and nongovernmental organizations. American efforts to combat anti-Semitism provide one concrete example of these international network effects in practice. The State Department's special envoy to monitor and combat antisemitism (SEAS) was deeply networked into international diplomatic efforts to address growing anti-Semitic incidents. Ira Forman, who held the SEAS position until the close of Obama's terms, worked especially closely with European governments, for instance, through the Organization for Security and Cooperation in Europe's work on the 10th Anniversary of the Berlin Conference on Antisemitism. At that convening, 495 participants from forty-two distinct countries gathered, including working-level diplomats and cabinet officials like Samantha Powers, then-U.S. permanent representative to the United Nations. The elite network involved in these efforts included high-level diplomatic representation from partner countries, but also a network of religious and civil society elites who had been involved in similar convenings for a decade prior. The American delegation included not only representatives from Jewish American organizations, but also Muslim and Sikh associations along with a range of prominent secular human and civil rights organizations.[15] Participants in this sort of elite network certainly do not cooperate in all policy particulars. The International Holocaust Remembrance Association's Working Definition of Antisemitism, for example, sometimes divides even those dedicated to combatting anti-Semitism because of its implication in the politics of the Israeli-Palestinian relationship.[16] But those differences took place within institutions that facilitated diplomatic exchange even in times of disagreement, much like the religion regime complex had done in U.S. foreign policy in the decades before the Trump presidency.

All told, the diverse regime complex around religion that had grown within the U.S. foreign policy bureaucracy by mid-2016 facilitated international ties that reflected those offices' missions, under the general umbrella of utilizing religion to promote U.S. interests and values. These international ties involved mutual learning, particularly among American diplomats and colleagues from foreign ministries of prominent Western allies and multilateral organizations. In this sense, religious diplomacy served as a reinforcement of general, bipartisan trends in American foreign policy, centered on strengthening security and economic cooperation with European allies, and (more broadly) promoting the post-World War II liberal international order.

INTERNATIONAL TIES AND POPULIST FOREIGN POLICY

As chapters 3 and 4 documented, the 2016 election brought substantial change to religion in the structure and content of U.S. foreign policy. What was apparent, even from the earliest days of the Trump administration, was that the new actors empowered by this populist moment would also draw on a very distinct set of international ties as they moved into formal and informal diplomatic work. On the whole, the Trump administration's religious loyalists found common ground with an array of international actors constituting a new, distinct international network of religious populism. These ties provided a resource akin to religious soft power in which shared cultural understandings promoted pursuit of national interests alongside more conventional forms of military and economic influence. Advocates of blessing America First pursued international ties that would reinforce populism's distinct characteristics: identity boundaries and personalist governance.

Populism's thin ideology, cementing "the people" as in-group while excluding constructed out-groups, should provide one primary axis of international cooperation under populist rule. Recall that ideological claims about populism are two-sided, with both an inclusionary and exclusionary dimension. On the inclusionary dimension, there is ample evidence that the Trump administration's broader turn to Christian nationalism to cement its domestic coalition facilitated ties with an array of traditionalist religious actors on the international stage. The content of this cooperation frequently centered on advocacy of traditional marriage and gender roles, as well as some religious freedom advocacy tied to the expansion of LGBTQ+ rights. The exclusionary aspect of populism's identity boundaries also shaped international interactions, especially in skepticism of Muslim actors and international institutions promoting LGBTQ+ rights and women's equality. Evidence of ties facilitated by populism's thin ideology was especially strong involving the Russian Orthodox Church and elements of right-wing European populism. It emerged, as well, in interactions with certain Muslim elites and right-wing Hindu movements.

Populism's personalist dimension, which rejects formal institutional constraint and deploys a charismatic, performative style, should also be expected to impact the nature of international religious ties. First, religious allies of the populist should find common cause with religious elites abroad who reject institutional constraint, both in their domestic politics and from international organizations. Such ties serve the domestic needs of the populist, reinforcing anti-institutional framing and sharing information on reducing the costs of international constraint. Second, personalism should drive international ties into more informal channels outside the reach of formal bureaucracies, where direct, transactional exchanges avoid public scrutiny and serve the interests of populist elites. Third, the distinctive populist style encourages ties to international actors with a similar affinity for charismatic performance. To make the point concrete, international ties should move from elites who operate through closed-door diplomatic processes to those comfortable in performative, informal nongovernmental convenings like the National Prayer Breakfast.

Before moving to consider evidence of this international cooperation, two points are worth clarifying regarding the relationship between international ties, populism, and civilizational rhetoric. Populist international cooperation may at times look civilizational in nature, but in practice this is misleading. First, civilizational rhetoric from actors around the Trump administration and its international partners did not reflect the internally coherent civilizational boundaries that Huntington proposed would structure post-Cold War conflict and cooperation. Rather, it reflected an opportunistic attempt to *construct* such boundaries. While Huntington's ideal-typical civilizations were unified blocs rooted in centuries of historical accumulation, the rhetoric of civilizationalists around Trump, instead, reflected a loss of cohesion. Religious populists willingly identified as internal minorities, a vanguard striking out against a predominant globalist order. Second, populism's international religious ties were not as consistent as implied by accounts of ideological civilizational boundaries. Huntington distinguished Orthodox civilization from others in the West, posited a unified Muslim world that would exist in particular tension with the West, and distinguished Hindu and Buddhist civilizations as well. Because populist cooperation seeks opportunities of convenience to reinforce populism's dimensions, it cuts across all of these more rigidly ideological categories, a point which comes up especially clearly in considering the Indian case discussed later.

CLOSE POPULIST KIN: THE RELIGIOUS-POPULIST ARC FROM LATIN AMERICA TO CENTRAL EUROPE

The most likely cases of international populist ties arose in contexts where local leaders most closely shared the Trump administration's thin ideology and personalism. As many have noted, Trump's election took place alongside several other cases of democratic backsliding tied to right-wing populist governments.[17] These governments, particularly in Hungary, Poland, and Brazil, shared many of the Trump administration's identity-based boundaries. and its personalist rejection of institutional constraint from either international organizations or domestic critics. The new network of religious elites around the Trump administration found ample ground for international cooperation with these types of governments. In short, evidence exists that religion-related initiatives facilitated ties with each of these populist fellow travelers.

Populists in this group closely aligned with Trump's in-group identification of the people. Perhaps the closest affinity between Trump's religious allies and an international populist movement was with Prime Minister Viktor Orbán in Hungary. He repeatedly tied a loosely defined idea of "Christian democracy" to his political rise, while insisting, "We want to preserve Hungary as a Hungarian country."[18] Orbán has emphasized that "Christian culture is the unifying force of the nation," and "the inner essence and meaning of the state."[19] Poland's Law and Justice party (PiS) is perhaps even more thickly tied to religious-nationalist ideology than Hungary. Even before the PiS's rise, post-Cold War populist parties in

Poland had merged "the traditional moral order of the Nation with a fundamental role for Christianity."[20] PiS would link itself to similar claims as it rose to power, for instance, in a document titled, "A Catholic Poland in a Christian Europe."[21] Similar identitarian ties shaped the U.S.-Brazil relationship during this period.[22] President Jair Bolsonaro's inaugural address centered on the mission to "unite the people . . . value the family, respect religions and our Judeo-Christian tradition, fight gender ideology, and preserve our values."[23] Bolsonaro's wife played a role in this religious-nationalist in-group definition, stating at one prayer rally during campaign season, "We will bring the presence of the Lord Jesus to the government and declare that this nation belongs to the Lord."[24] These diffuse utilizations of religion as a thin ideological category defining in-group membership share obvious affinities with Trumpism's populist appeals.

In terms of populism's exclusionary dimension, Orbán and his supporters shared significant ground with the Trump administration. He not only raised concerns with Muslim persecution of Christians in the Middle East, but specifically highlighted Muslim refugees in Europe as a threat to the continent's future. Even before Trump's election, Orbán railed in 2015, "We shouldn't forget that the people who are coming here grew up in a different religion and represent a completely different culture. Most are not Christian, but Muslim . . . Or is it not worrying that Europe's Christian culture is already barely able to maintain its own set of Christian values?"[25] Later, he would remark that Europe was "under invasion" from such refugees.[26] His exclusionary rhetoric also targeted supposedly disloyal global elites, including criticisms of prominent critic George Soros that invoked anti-Semitic tropes: "We are fighting an enemy that is different from us. Not open, but hiding; not straightforward but crafty; not honest but base; not national but international; does not believe in working but speculates with money; does not have its own homeland but feels it owns the whole world."[27] PiS in Poland went so far as to create "LGBT-free zones," making the rhetorical exclusion of gay and lesbian communities legal.[28] President Bolsonaro in Brazil proudly used homophobic slurs, and encouraged restrictions on gender and sexuality education in the country's schools.[29]

Leaders in each of these cases were also staunchly personalist, rejecting any institutional constraint on their exercise of power, whether from domestic courts or international organizations. Orbán in Hungary and PiS leaders in Poland regularly deployed attacks on the European Union and its associated bureaucracy, especially when such institutions threatened to constrain their domestic behavior. After his 2018 election, for instance, Orbán insisted, "The European Union must return to reality," in particular "changing its thinking on migration, mass population movement and immigration . . . We shall oppose the mandatory quotas, stand up for Christian culture, and fight to defend borders."[30] Hungary and Poland have consistently resisted potential accountability via the EU for their actions related to migration and maintaining democratic institutions. In Brazil, rejection of international constraint took a slightly different track, frequently tied to criticism of what Bolsonaro terms "radical environmentalism" domestically and from world leaders critical of his practices in the Amazon. The specific policy sphere may vary from country to country, but in each, a socially conservative in-group definition, exclusion of religious and moral outsiders, and rejection of institutional constraint had strong echoes of Trumpism in the United States.

In each case, religious allies of Trump drew on the foreign policy process to cultivate international ties. Nowhere was the diffusion of these personalistic gatherings more obvious than Hungary during the opening months of the Trump administration. High-profile Trump foreign policy advisor Sebastian Gorka had long-standing ties to the country's right-wing politics, even attracting criticism for appearing at a Trump inauguration ball with a family Hungarian medal allegedly tied anti-Semitism. In 2017, the country began to hold its own prayer breakfast event, hosted the World Congress of Families, and convened an International Consultation on Christian Persecution. At that last meeting, Orbán himself sounded populism's central refrain in remarks when he insisted, "What is at stake today is nothing less than the future of the European way of life, and of our identity."[31] The convening included not only Hungarian leaders and members of persecuted Christian communities in the Middle East, but also leading figures in the Russian Orthodox Church and American religious conservative leaders like Nina Shea. Shea explicitly used the event to criticize the "cold indifference" of the United Nations to Christian suffering in Iraq, and to call for the Trump administration to bring "the right political appointees [to] issue directives to his cabinet" that would direct financial resources to churches and their allies.[32]

Hungary's State Secretary for the Aid of Persecuted Christians Tristan Azbej, would claim that his country's approach to bypassing international organizations and funding churches directly was a "source of inspiration" for the Trump administration's eventual direction of USAID funds in a similar way through its Genocide Recovery and Persecution Response program.[33] Such cooperation extended to Poland as well, with, for example, a 2018 Memo of Understanding between USAID and Poland intended to "increase coordination on helping communities in the Middle East recover from genocide and persecution."[34] This cooperation constituted a "growing coalition of conservative governments and advocates who view direct support to persecuted Christians as part of a global contest over culture, rights and national borders."[35] This network's workings reflected the personalism of the Trump administration in honoring the Hungarian minister Azbej with an award presented at the former president's Mar-a-Lago Club.[36]

This web of personalistic relationships extended to Brazil, where Bolsonaro and his family were close political allies of Steve Bannon, the Trump advisor at the center of religious-populist agenda setting. Bannon endorsed Bolsonaro in advance of his 2018 election, with Bolsonaro's son boasting that he and Trump "share the same worldview . . . especially against cultural Marxism."[37] Trump evangelical advisory board member Michele Bachmann recorded a video urging Brazilian evangelicals to support Bolsonaro.[38] Bolsonaro loyalists imported the American brand of the Conservative Political Action Coalition (CPAC) for a regional conference of right-wing populists. American evangelist Ralph Drollinger reportedly integrated Brazilian pastors into his D.C.-based Capitol Ministries networks, famous for ties to Secretary of State Pompeo, Vice President Pence, and others in Trump's religious orbit.[39] Brazil's ties to the networks that plan the U.S. National Prayer Breakfast date to Cold War-era military dictatorship, and Bolsonaro's son Eduardo has ties to current Prayer Breakfast leadership in the U.S. and Brazil.[40] The Christian Broadcasting Network secured an extensive and glowing interview with Bolsonaro on the occasion of his White House meetings with President Trump in 2019 and Brazil volunteered to host the 2021 Ministerial to Advance Religious Freedom (following Poland in 2020). These ties, at times, bypass the United States entirely. For example, Bolsonaro's religious advisors engaged directly with Hungarian officials, and Orbán attended Bolsona-ro's inauguration.[41]

REDEFINING CIVILIZATIONAL BOUNDS? TRUMP'S RELIGIOUS ALLIES AND RUSSIA

Hungary, Poland, and Brazil might all appear to be easy cases for popu-list affinities in foreign policy, as each featured leaders who shared in-group definition, out-group exclusion, and personalist rejection of international institutional constraint. However, international elite ties linked to Trump's religious populism stretched beyond other right-wing populists. Some of the strongest evidence that Trump's religious popu-lism fueled international ties comes from relations between the former president's religious supporters and Russia, in particular ties to leading figures in the Russian Orthodox Church.

The presence of Metropolitan Hilarion at the Billy Graham Evangelis-tic Association Summit in the opening months of the Trump adminis-tration was just one, very visible indicator of these ties. Considering the ways in which Trump's populism strengthened these relationships pro-vides useful evidence nuancing the application of civilizational theories to explaining Trump foreign policy. It is indeed true that both Trump's religious loyalists and leaders of the Russian Orthodox Church frequently invoked civilizational rhetoric in explaining their cooperation. However, these claims cut across one of the primary civilizational boundaries in Huntington's original framework: the West and the Orthodox world. The actors promoting these ties prioritized constructing populism's in- and out-groups over the deep historical differences in politics and theology that had divided these civilizations. Trump's religious allies and Russian Orthodox Church leaders regularly promoted both dimensions of Trump's populist agenda: a thin ideology of inclusion and exclusion, along with a personalistic structure of rule that rejected institutional constraint, espe-cially from international organizations.

The appearance of Metropolitan Hilarion in Washington, D.C. in May 2017 built on a relationship that had strengthened for several decades before Trump's election.[42] In remarks from this period, the in-group definition around traditional values to the exclusion of liberals, human rights promoters, and those challenging traditional gender and sexuality norms stands out consistently. Franklin Graham, for example, met with Hilarion and Russian Orthodox Church Patriarch Kirill in 2015, where Kirill explicitly grounded their meeting in a need to preserve Western civilization in opposition to those who would divide that civilization internally against itself. He stated, "Radical changes in spiritual life have occurred in the West in the past few years. Western countries have stopped identifying themselves with the Christian tradition. On the basis of the fact that not only Christians now live in the West, they have gone to the idea of society in which Christian moral values should not dominate . . . Christians who defend the eternal significance of Christian moral values are subjected to all kinds of pressure."[43] In his Facebook posts about that meeting, Graham agreed that the exchange centered on "a secular culture [that] knows nothing of God and His love for them. I appreciate Patriarch Kirill's very clear moral voice on issues of marriage, family, and the sanctity of life."[44]

Graham and Kirill's 2015 meeting itself built on earlier engagements, notably Metropolitan Hilarion's remarks to a forum that Graham facilitated in 2014. In that speech, Hilarion lamented the fact that "liberalization of moral teaching . . . deviation from the ethical norms laid down by Holy Scripture of the New Testament" had led to "a serious crisis" in Russian Orthodox Church relationships with certain American Protestant churches.[45] Hilarion goes on to decry the Episcopal Church's consecration of Bishop Gene Robinson, an openly gay cleric, to criticize abortion, and to rail against "gay parades [that] have swept over European cities."[46] These internal targets of exclusion were paired with the "monstrous power of hatred and terror" facing Christians from terrorists in the Middle East.[47] In contrast to this exclusion, in that same speech Hilarion insisted, "The Russian Orthodox Church has remained open to contacts with the North American confessions which have stayed faithful to the traditions of our dialogue and which are firmly committed to biblical morality," and "is prepared for broad cooperation with these communities."[48] He continued, "Today we, Christians of various confessions, should unite around the very simple common human values which are subjected to mockery and profanation against the background of wild manifestation of all kinds of 'non-traditional' models of behaviour."[49]

Similar themes stood out in remarks from American evangelicals and Russian Orthodox Church officials at the May 2017 World Summit in Defense of Persecuted Christians held in Washington, D.C. Metropolitan Hilarion's keynote remarks at that gathering are an almost perfect distillation of the type of international tie that populism's thin ideology facilitated. The need for alliances to protect traditional family values stood out as a foundation theme: "It is with sadness and concern that we observe the growing process of the dechristianization of the public sphere of the Old and New worlds, which historically have always been important strongholds of Christian civilization. Churches and communities are consigned to being relics of the past and not an equal participant in social processes."[50] Similarly, he claimed that "[Christian] persecution has been particularly severe in those countries where the dominant religion is Islam . . . The scale of the persecution of Christians, meanwhile, is willfully passed over in silence by the mass media and by the international community."[51] This supposedly built on "centuries [when] Christians were subjected to a great variety of persecution from the Arabs, Turks, Mongols and various representatives of other peoples who were adherents of Islam."[52] And, in a regular theme of Trump's own rhetoric involving terrorism, Hilarion called on Christian leaders to "challenge Islamic leaders throughout the world to condemn terrorism as something that contradicts the teaching of the Koran, openly curse those who commit terrorist acts supposedly in the name of Allah."[53]

Remarks in these exchanges similarly prepared a moral justification for the Trump administration's personalistic strategy, particularly its rejection of institutional constraint tied to multilateral cooperation and international norms. In 2015, Hilarion sounded themes familiar to right-wing populists in Hungary, complaining, "The states that seek to enter the European Union are required today to hold gay parades as a permit for obtaining the status of candidate."[54] In May 2017, sounding themes that could have come from an American cleric blessing America First, Hilarion argued, "The Saviour emphasizes that the Christian mission bears within its origin the nature of conflict, and that this mission will be accomplished *in spite of the established laws* in both the Jewish and Gentile worlds, that it will evoke irritation, non-acceptance and aggression."[55] He went on to criticize the supposed failure of international organizations to address Christian persecution: "They attempt to pass the problem over in silence and redirect the subject matter towards a politically correct discussion on tolerance to various minorities, sexual and otherwise."[56] Putting this personalism into practice, convicted Russian agent Maria Butina utilized the opportunities provided by the National Prayer Breakfast to access D.C. power players without the formal vetting associated with State Department visits.[57]

POPULIST TIES BEYOND CHRISTIANITY? TRUMP AND HINDU NATIONALISM

Could international ties expand beyond the bounds of Christian elites? An analysis which only emphasizes the role of Christian nationalism in fueling Trumpism might be skeptical of such ties. However, because of the thinness of populism's ideology, there has been nothing so rigid as civilizational boundaries in the international ties facilitated by blessing America First. Instead, where affinities exist in either boundary construction or lending moral legitimacy to personalist politics, Trump and his religious allies proved willing to forge populist ties that went beyond the bounds of Christian nationalism. Nowhere is this more apparent than the working relationship between Trump allies and the Hindu nationalist government of India's Prime Minister Narendra Modi. Shared assumptions about out-groups, in this case Muslims, and hostility to constraint from international organizations provided Trump's allies opportunity to work with Modi and others in the Hindu nationalist orbit. This case is especially useful because these ties, at times, cut against the wishes of more consistently ideological actors, especially those prioritizing religious freedom claims for Christians in India. Because populism's ideological commitments are thin, not binding, these concerns proved no great barrier to ties with Modi and his allies.

As with the rise of right-wing populism in cases like Hungary and Poland, the Bharatiya Janata Party's (BJP) rise in India long predated Trump's election. While independence-era Indian state builders, particularly Prime Minister Jawaharlal Nehru, deployed a nuanced form of political secularism in the country, the past quarter century has seen the steady rise of openly-Hindu nationalist politics, first in certain regional centers and eventually on the national stage.[58] Hindu nationalists have engaged in communal violence involving the country's Muslim minority, most prominently in the destruction of the Babri Masjid. Much like Christian nationalists in the United States, Hindu nationalists engage in historical revisionism to reconstruct a (supposedly) religiously pure past in which Indian in-group membership is reserved for those of Hindu religious identity. Various other out-groups earned the ire of these religious populists, including, at times, the country's Christian minority, which has been subject to occasional communal violence.[59]

Like all populists, Modi and his allies have rejected institutional constraint and altered existing political checks in the process of securing power. Most controversially, Modi has altered India's citizenship law to reshape access to citizenship in confessional terms. The 2019 Citizenship Amendment Act instituted privileged access to citizenship for Hindus, Parsis, Sikhs, Buddhists, Jains, and Christians fleeing regional Muslim-majority countries, but denied similar protection to Muslims.[60] Not only did the law exclude Muslims in India from protection, it neglected to extend protection to those fleeing religious persecution in non-Muslim-majority regional countries like Sri Lanka and Myanmar.[61] The law launched nationwide protests, which led to further crackdowns on institutional freedoms, including limitations on internet access and freedom of assembly. While a Christian leader (and BJP party member) on the official National Commission for Minorities claimed that the law "is good for Christians and should be welcomed by all,"[62] protests extended to Mumbai's Catholic Cardinal Oswald Gracias, who called it "a cause of great anxiety for all citizens . . . there is a danger that there could be a polarization of our peoples along religious lines, which is very harmful for the country."[63]

Modi and Trump's supporters share significant affinities, particularly due to their exclusion of Muslims from the political community. Trump advisor Steve Bannon repeatedly expressed admiration for Modi's political rise in India, telling a gathering of conservative Catholics in the Vatican in 2014 that "Modi's great victory" was part of a "global revolt" that should be welcomed by the global Christian right.[64] These ties were not limited to the United States. Members of the European parliament from several far-right populist parties, including those of Poland, visited India's contentious Kashmir region in 2019, in the midst of the Modi government's coercive lockdown of the Muslim-majority region.[65] European-Indian, right-wing relationships are not new, but build on a historical legacy of ties between Hindu nationalist leaders and European fascists in the interwar period.[66]

Affinities extend to a preference for personalism, with its emphasis on direct ties and bombastic populist style. Bannon and Newt Gingrich, whose wife Calista served as the Trump administration's ambassador to the Holy See, acted as honorary cochairs of the Republican Hindu Coalition (RHC). At an RHC event, Bannon crowed that, "If it weren't for you and your outreach to Hindu-American voters, then we would not have a President Trump right now."[67] The RHC offered "full-throated support" for the Trump administration's Muslim Ban,[68] and the RHC vice chair/president joined President Trump's "Namaste Trump" delegation to India in the closing year of his presidency.[69] Trump himself appeared with the Indian leader at a massive event in Houston, typifying the populist style: a "Howdy, Modi" rally before 50,000 at NRG Stadium, where Trump praised India for sharing the United States's "great faith and a fierce devotion to our national independence" and pledged that the two countries would work together "to protect innocent civilians from the threat of radical Islamic terrorism."[70] Characteristic of populist personalism, these ties were largely unmediated by official bureaucratic institutions, instead relying on direct personal communication including voicing RHC disapproval of a potential appointment of Mitt Romney as secretary of state.[71]

India presents an intriguing case for international populist ties because it seems to, in some ways, cut against Trump's in-group definition of political community. Modi's time in national office has seen significant spikes in anti-Christian persecution, from church attacks to anti-conversion legislation that impacts Christian communities. International Religious Freedom advocates expressed concern: "The United States should always lead with its values, and instead of welcoming Mr. Modi to the United States in Houston at the Howdy Modi event, [leaders] should use the opportunity to protest Modi and his regime's policies and to publicly condemn his and his party's hate-filled rhetoric."[72] Another Christian religious freedom advocate summed things up similarly around the Modi visit: "Other top Christian leaders in America . . . have ministry interests in India, and each is very close to President Trump today—many serve as personal advisors. It would not take much to create a united front to demand an end to this growing persecution."[73]

And yet, those core advisors generally toed the line in this area. Franklin Graham claimed the situation for Christians in India to be "very troubling," but then rationalized Trump support for Modi because "we can do more by building a relationship . . . We've got to believe God can change his heart."[74] Political commentator Dinesh D'Souza, despite clearing his throat by noting that he is "not an unqualified fan of Narendra Modi," went on to claim that "his reelection in India is another affirmation of the triumph of Trumpian nationalism."[75] Why didn't the administration's supposed advocacy of Christian interests get in the way of this cooperation?

In short, populism's ideological thinness does not require any consistent commitments beyond that to the leader's rule. As documented earlier in chapters 3 and 4, the Trump administration did place rhetorical emphasis on the IRF bureaucracy, even launching "ministerial" meetings marked by the populist style. The 2018 State Department International Religious Freedom Report, which was released in summer 2019, raised concerns about violence targeting religious minorities in India. In the closing year of the Trump administration, the United States Commission on International Religious Freedom (USCIRF) even recommended designating India as a Country of Particular Concern (CPC), which would bring some diplomatic consequences to the bilateral relationship.

However, Trump and his senior officials simply permitted India to sidestep these concerns in favor of furthering populist ties. India did not send an official delegation to the 2018 International Religious Freedom Ministerial and engaged in multiple contentious exchanges with portions of the religious freedom bureaucracy. Secretary Pompeo was on message by the time he visited India in the week after the 2018 IRF report criticized the country, using a policy speech to extoll India for "protect[ing] unalienable rights" and Trump and Modi as "two leaders who aren't afraid to blaze new trails," while only obliquely mentioning a call to "stand up together in defense of religious freedom for all."[76] Trump's State Department simply overruled the USCIRF recommendation regarding India's CPC status, instead keeping India in a lower tier of concern.

U.S.-India ties shed useful light on the operation of religious soft power in a populist environment. There has been significant cooperation between populist elites in each case, especially in exclusionary rhetoric and rejection of institutional constraint on populist power, in spite of the impacts of Modi's leadership on local Christian populations. Sumit Ganguly argued, "Sectarian tensions at home may limit the capacity of India's new emphasis on religious soft power to pay dividends on the global stage."[77] This may be true in some political environments. However, evidence from Trump's term in office seems to indicate that such tensions may be comfortably bracketed when populist elites sense political advantage in cooperation.

EFFECTS AND ENDURANCE OF INTERNATIONAL POPULIST BONDS

It is reasonable to ask, as with many claims about soft power, whether these shared rhetorical patterns and personal ties corresponded to actual foreign policy change.[78] The actors involved certainly intended their initiatives to impact the broader strategic relationship between the countries. As Russian agent Maria Butina remarked to an unnamed American contact after the 2017 National Prayer Breakfast, "A new relationship between two countries always begins better when it begins in faith."[79] Similarly, in the aftermath of their May 2017 appearance at the World Summit in Defense of Persecuted Christians, "Metropolitan Hilarion and Reverend Graham stressed the importance of Russia and the United States setting aside their differences . . . In anticipation of the expected meeting between President Donald J. Trump and President Vladimir Putin, the leaders of the two nations, Reverend Graham and Metropolitan Hilarion call upon Christians and churches worldwide to pray for this important meeting."[80] However, with Trump eventually facing impeachment on matters related to the U.S.-Russia relationship, and Butina herself convicted of acting as a foreign agent, it would be too much to claim that a broad reorientation of the U.S.-Russia relationship took place because of religious soft power. One could similarly argue that the Trump administration's approach to India policy primarily resulted from America's growing strategic rivalry with China and economic concerns tied to the trade relationship with India, with religious soft power ties largely epiphenomenal to bilateral material interests. Especially with many of these transnational ties existing outside of the career foreign policy bureaucracy, how much do they really matter to understanding the substance of international order?

Blessing America First's broader claim, that it was the Trump administration's *populism* that mattered to changing religion's place in U.S. foreign policy, points to a reorientation of this question of how these ties "mattered." The political logic of populism is fundamentally domestic, not international. Populists use foreign policy as they do other policy spheres: an instrumental means of maintaining personal power, via constructing ideological boundaries and justifying a personalistic structure of rule. The international religious populist affinities that emerged in these cases (and others) during the Trump administration mattered because they provided a resource for the short-term political success of populist leaders. In this regard, while difficult to quantify, these international ties likely had significant effect. Cementing transnational ties in opposition to gay rights and Muslim immigration, for example, likely reinforced Trump's standing in domestic, white evangelical communities that formed the core of his electoral support. It is plausible that some of Trump's improved electoral performance among Hispanic Protestants in the United States rested on his warm ties with regional hardliners like Bolsonaro. Effects on Indian American voting are less clear-cut, with one study finding that the demographic remained staunchly pro-Biden in 2020 vote intention, at least, in part, because of perceived Christian favoritism on the part of the Trump administration.[81] That study did find Trump support significantly stronger among Indian American Christians, perhaps suggesting that the limitations on cooperation provoked by civilizational differences are also detectable in mass public opinion data.

Beyond this short-term, essentially domestic importance, transnational ties deserve attention because, like any epistemic community, they have the potential to form a reserve of relationships, specialized knowledge, and shared understandings that can outlive the term in office of a given populist leader. With Trump's electoral defeat in 2020, one might have wondered whether the international ties documented in here would quickly wither away. However, there is ample evidence that global ties between right-wing Christian populists have persisted beyond the Trump administration, and these seem likely to return to policy relevance should religious populists return to the White House. It is certainly true that, with the transition of power, populist political appointees mostly left official postings at the State Department and National Security Council, replaced by actors with very distinct priorities. However, the religious populist ties nurtured during the Trump administration have shown staying power. There is no sign of diminished enthusiasm between Hungary's Viktor Orbán and American conservatives—quite the contrary. He addressed the 2022 CPAC conference just weeks after he generated international head- lines for a speech decrying "mixed-race" countries in Europe. CPAC held another Latin American convening in Brazil in summer 2022, and core Trump populists Steve Bannon and Stephen Miller reportedly advised Brazil's Jair Bolsonaro on responding to his 2022 electoral defeat.[82]

However, a tougher test is whether these ties can persist in a period of higher-stakes international crisis, without the person of the populist in power. In the context of Trump's religious loyalists, this challenge has been most apparent in the sudden crisis in international order brought on by the 2022 Russian invasion of Ukraine. The Russian invasion of Ukraine has revealed significant division within these networks. Franklin Graham did tweet in the days before the invasion, calling on his followers to "Pray for President Putin,"[83] but later clarified, "I don't support war and I don't know of any Christian that supports war. We pray for peace, not war. I don't support this at all."[84] Liberty University reportedly lit up a campus building in the colors of the Ukrainian flag.[85] Not all voices among Trump's religious loyalists were so critical. Talk show host Eric Metaxas claimed that the "American Deep State" was ultimately responsible for Putin's invasion,[86] while Trump himself characterized Putin as a "genius" and "pretty smart" for launching the attack on the Ukraine. A guest on Steve Bannon's War Room podcast explicitly used the Ukraine invasion to justify his view that "civilizations and national interests and realism actually did win the day," while self-described Christian nationalist Rep- resentative Marjorie Taylor Greene insisted that American funding for Ukraine's war effort come to an end.[87] Early survey evidence reflects these tensions, with one study finding white evangelicals in the pews were no more favorable to Putin than Americans as a whole, but another arguing that Christian nationalism is a particularly strong source of Putin support.[88]

As the war in Ukraine moves beyond opening stages, it is too early to tell how this conflict will intersect with the religious foreign policy dynam- ics associated with Trump's populist movement. Some of Trump's religious allies have expressed vocal opposition to Russia's invasion, while others have kept a lower profile or, even in some cases, demonstrated sympathy for Putin and Russian leaders. One clear prediction would be this: the outcome of these internal divisions will be tied to the domestic political interests of Trump and his populist allies. As former Republican Senate candidate Lauren Witzke remarked on February 24, 2022, seamlessly transitioning from religious identity into political interests, "I identify more with Putin's Christian values than I do with Joe Biden."[89]

CONCLUSION

Religion and Foreign Policy After Populism

I n mid-February 2021, as the Biden administration settled into office, it issued Executive Order 14015, "Establishment of the White House Office of Faith-Based and Neighborhood Partnerships." At the stroke of a pen, it revoked the Trump administration's Executive Order 13831, which was used to establish its own White House Faith and Opportunity Initiative in May 2018. The Biden administration simultaneously announced the appointment of Melissa Rogers as executive director of the White House Faith-Based Office and senior director of Faith and Public Policy in the White House Domestic Policy Council. Rogers served in a similar capacity in the second term of the Obama administration. It appeared that, one month into office, institutions related to religion and U.S. foreign policy might be returning to their prepopulist equilibrium. These rapid moves certainly contrasted with the Trump administration's emphasis on personal ties at a similar point during its term.

The symbolism of the early Biden administration in many ways reinforced this restorationist impression. Biden's 2021 inauguration featured an invocation and benediction from longtime clerical colleagues, Catholic priest Fr. Leo O'Donovan, SJ and African Methodist Episcopal Rev. Dr. Silvester Beaman. Biden's address drew on his own Catholic faith in ways that were obvious, quoting scripture and the writings of St. Augustine, and more subtle, emphasizing the harmony between faith and reason. Within the year, Biden had met with Pope Francis in the Vatican.

And yet, in these early stages, questions emerged about the populist legacy that the Biden administration faced. Even relative optimists about American institutions among scholars of populism acknowledged that "Trump may well do serious damage in policy areas where the president has a great deal of decision-making latitude, such as environmental and foreign policy."[1]

Could a new president undo the combination of identity-based exclusion and personalistic structure of rule that had reshaped religion in U.S. foreign policy? Could something like Gregorio Bettiza's fairly bipartisan "regime complex" across agencies like the State Department, USAID, and the National Security Council reemerge from the populist turmoil documented earlier in this book? And how might those changes in foreign policy interact with the broader challenge of reinforcing America's democratic institutions in the wake of the Trump administration and the God-haunted violence of January 6, 2021?

This conclusion briefly takes up each of these questions. Its conclusions are necessarily tentative, highlighting areas in which a new administration has restored institutions, and others where populist legacies seem more lasting. Trump's most lasting legacy may be the deepening of American polarization over the place of religion in our politics, suggesting an uncertain role for religion in the future of American diplomacy.

EFFORTS TO RESTORE
THE PREPOPULIST EQUILIBRIUM

The foundation for recalibrating religion's place in the foreign policy bureaucracy emerged before President Biden's November 2020 election. The most visible sign of these efforts was a report from the nonpartisan, establishment-minded Brookings Institution entitled *A Time to Heal, A Time to Build*. Under the authorship of Melissa Rogers and E. J. Dionne Jr., the report drew on dozens of interviews with veterans of religion in the federal bureaucracy to offer "recommendations for the next administration on respecting religious freedom and pluralism, forging civil society partnerships, and navigating faith's role in foreign policy."[2]

These authors, and the broader network interviewed as a part of their report, represent precisely the type of epistemic community that provides a potential path of institutional restoration after populist rule. Interviewees included previous appointees in Democratic and Republican administrations. Indicating its basically restorationist goals, the report insisted, "The next administration must repair this damage without retreating from the conversation about religion's intersection with foreign policy. The temptation to do so will be enormous."[3]

What indications exist that this goal was put into practice? As an initial indicator, several high-profile political appointments related to religion and diplomacy took place in the opening months of the Biden administration. In summer 2021, the administration announced its intent to nominate an ambassador-at-large for International Religious Freedom, a special envoy to monitor and combat antisemitism (SEAS), and appointees to the United States Commission for International Religious Freedom.[4] Politically-appointed leadership similarly arrived in the first months of the administration at USAID offices related to religion and development assistance, via its traditional Faith-Based and Neighborhood Partnerships office and the more novel Local, Faith, and Transformative Partnerships Hub.

Other more subtle steps indicated a return to more working-level bureaucratization of religion. For instance, USAID provided a public opportunity to comment on draft language on "Building Bridges in Development: A Policy on Engaging Faith-Based and Community Partners."[5] In mid-2021, the Office of International Religious Freedom (IRF) announced an open grant competition for "Promoting and Defending Religious Freedom Inclusive of Atheist, Humanist, Non-Practicing, and Non-Affiliated Individuals."[6] Beyond State and USAID, the Department of Homeland Security "reinvigorated" its Faith-Based Security Advisory Council in mid-2022, via the type of public declaration of an interfaith board that would have been at home in the Bush or Obama administrations.[7]

These steps should be understood as reacting to the personalism of populist rule. Recall that, in its first months in office, the Trump administration insisted that formal bureaucratic appointments mattered less than prayer sessions in the White House. Trump's eventual executive order establishing a formal, faith-based office took eighteen months to arrive— Biden's dropped a month into office. These steps show the double-edged nature of executive dominance in foreign policy: it facilitated populist change, but also provided ample political opportunity to undo those changes once the populist left office.

Regarding the substance of religion and foreign policy, the Biden administration can also point to efforts to reverse initiatives marked by the Trump administration's identity-based populist exclusions. Most visibly, in January 2021, Biden issued a "Proclamation on Ending Discriminatory Bans on Entry to the United States" that was explicitly intended to overturn the Trump administration "Muslim Ban," which it judged "a stain on our national conscience" and "inconsistent with our long history of welcoming people of all faiths and no faith at all."[8] After some delay, the Biden team subsequently raised the number of refugees authorized for resettlement in fiscal year 2022 to 125,000.[9] White House statements point to substantive faith-based foreign policy engagements related to combatting trafficking in persons, refugee resettlement, and broadening international access to COVID-19 vaccines, and explicitly frame these steps as intended "to demonstrate the administration's recommitment to multilateral engagement."[10] In contrast to the populist style of charismatic performance, these initiatives primarily consisted of the working-level, substantive policy engagement more characteristic of the prepopulist equilibrium in religion and foreign policy.

THE AMBIGUOUS FUTURE
OF RELIGIOUS ENGAGEMENT

Of the diverse components of Bettiza's regime complex of religion, the Office of Religion and Global Affairs (RGA) was the most clear-cut casualty of Trump's religious populism. As a relatively new part of the bureaucracy, it faced an uncertain future under any new administration, but the Trump administration effectively shuttered the office, radically shrinking staff size, relocating it under the Office of International Religious Freedom, and rebranding it as the Strategic Religious Engagement team. Would the election of Biden and the appointment of Secretary of State Antony Blinken, who served as deputy secretary of state in RGA's heyday, mean a quick return to the office's 2016 name, size, and visibility?

In short, not immediately. "Religious engagement" functions remained housed within IRF, which described its own mission in December 2021 documents as "Lead[ing] the Department's strategic engagement of–and partnership with–religious actors, organizations, and institutions as part of equal and broader civil society outreach to achieve U.S. foreign policy objectives."[11] Rogers herself argued, in the October 2020 Brookings report, "Reestablishing an office that is separate from the religious freedom office along the lines of the Office of Religion and Global Affairs is the better approach. Directing the secretary to do so via executive order will help ensure that the office's mission is understood and may make the office more durable."[12] And yet, entering the closing year of the Biden administration's initial term, change to this dimension of the religion regime complex was slow coming. In summer 2023, former RGA Senior Advisor Peter Mandaville, with his colleague Julia Schiwal at the U.S. Institute of Peace, wrote of the persistent need for "a refresh" in considering the future bureaucratic structure and policy substance of religious engagement.[13]

Any explanation of this outcome will require a longer time horizon. It may be the case that Roger's hypothetical executive action regarding religious engagement appears in time. However, the delay in its appearance, up to this writing in summer 2023, is noteworthy for this book's conclusions. Restoring institutions after populist neglect will not happen without determined agency on the part of new occupants of relevant departments. Even populist legacies can take on a path-dependent character. Overcoming this may be easiest in areas linked to prominent congressional sponsors or external interest groups. RGA, in contrast, rested on a fairly elite epistemic community of scholars and policy practitioners, not a legislative mandate or mass mobilization organization. Without this and given the inevitable international crises that face new administrations, the future of RGA as an office remains unresolved.

With that said, a funny thing happened in spite of this delayed resolution: the language of religious engagement began to appear outside of the formal State Department unit previously tasked with this function. In October 2020, USAID hosted an "evidence summit on strategic religious engagement," which included "nearly 300 individuals from the NGO community, the U.S. Government, universities, and other institutions from around the world."[14] The updated USAID office subsequently circulated draft policy guidance on "engaging faith-based and community partners," which was finalized in late 2023. The term pops up outside of government as well. The United States Institute of Peace issued a report on "Strategic Religious Engagement in Peace Processes," and the policy-relevant *Review of Faith in International Affairs* issued a special issue on strategic religious engagement in 2021. It may be that the relatively elite epistemic community that initially grounded the RGA office has, through journals, think tanks, and academic research centers, preserved some of the function of RGA's work without the formality of a 7th floor office.

Would anything meaningful be lost in that exchange? There are several ways in which much of the recent religious engagement talk is distinct from the pre-Trump approach that RGA developed. First, it is more heavily centered on questions of development programming, with potential application to diverse areas such as public health assistance and disaster response. There is no doubt that there is ample room for an engagement approach to play a part in these areas. Partnerships in development assistance have a long pedigree. The USAID faith-based office traces its history to the early days of the George W. Bush administration's "faith-based initiative," and substantial partnerships have developed over decades through programs like the President's Emergency Plan for AIDS Relief (PEPFAR). Refining these relationships, for instance, by issuing new guidance on programmatic partnerships with faith-based groups, is quite important work, delivering pragmatic progress and serving American values. Notwithstanding the utility of this work, refining development partnerships is distinct from the assessment and advising on more diverse diplomatic priorities that was RGA's remit at the peak of its capacity.

Moreover, this leaves the question of religious engagement's bureaucratic place within the State Department itself unresolved. A series of pragmatic, prudential judgments needed to be made in late 2016 about RGA's future. Should its future leadership be a senior career Foreign Service Officer, or a political appointee? Should it remain in the secretary's suite of offices, or be moved to the Undersecretariat for Civilian Security and Global Affairs, the cluster of State Department offices that focuses on topics like governance and conflict stabilization where RGA had much of its most substantive success?[15] Should the RGA office exist as a singular unit, or should career staff with religious engagement briefs instead be embedded within the front offices of the State Department's regional bureaus, which are often seen as the true working core of the department?

And what sorts of established processes, from formalized assessment frameworks to routinized training modules, might eventually mean that RGA, as an office, was no longer necessary because its approach had been successfully embedded within the department as a whole? These questions are distinct from those answered by religious engagement's appearance in development work and require answers if the pre-Trump regime complex is to truly be reinvigorated.

DOMESTIC POLARIZATION AND THE UNCERTAIN FUTURE OF RELIGION AND U.S. FOREIGN POLICY

The days of religion as a "missing dimension statecraft," as Doug Johnston and Cynthia Sampson provocatively wrote in 1994, seem long gone.[16] Religion appears regularly in public analysis geopolitics, from Russia's invasion of Ukraine to the Israeli-Palestinian conflict, and various corners of the U.S. foreign policy bureaucracy attempt to account for religion in American diplomacy. Whether in the USAID faith-based office, the Office of International Religious Freedom, the SEAS, or the Foreign Service Institute's training efforts tied to religion and foreign policy, elements of what Bettiza termed a regime complex on religion in foreign policy persist.

And yet, the future of the work in agencies like the State Department, USAID, and the National Security Council remains tenuous. In the end, the greatest single legacy of the Trump administration in religion and foreign policy may turn out to be that it brought domestic polarization over religion into the foreign policy bureaucracy. This was, of course, by design, as it served the short-term populist need of Trump and his loyalists to define domestic identity boundaries and deploy personalist governance. Future Republican administrations may be less populist in nature, but there is no clarity on this point. Indeed, elements of conservative Christian ideology remain among the strongest predictors of Republican electoral support, and links between Christianity, conspiracy politics, and racialized grievance were deeply implicated in the violence of January 6, 2021.[17]

The Trump administration's polarizing legacy may be felt as strongly on the left as on the right. It was striking that the survey evidence presented in chapter 7 pointed to the strongest effects of "blessing America First" as impacting *non*-Trump voters, in a negative direction. A decade of evidence has tied conservative religious mobilization to declining religious affiliation in the general public, and similar blowback might exist on the part of elites, especially Democrats.[18] As Mandaville shrewdly observed in the late-2020 Brookings report, "The highly partisan resonance of religion, religious freedom, and perceived religious activism in the current political environment may give rise to a widespread reluctance on the part of any new administration . . . to appreciate the ongoing importance of religion to advancing U.S. priorities both at home and abroad." President Biden's personal faith commitments may have alleviated this force in the short-term, but it is difficult to see polarization over religious issues fading when he departs office.

The domestic reality of this polarization makes it even more essential to rebuild as much of the nonpartisan, career staff-led religious capacity within the foreign policy bureaucracy as possible. As chapter 5 demonstrated, it is not reasonable to expect career Foreign Service Officers and civil servants to act as "deep state" resistance to maneuverings like those that the Trump administration brought to the State Department. Cultural norms work against overt resistance, and significant official authority rests with duly elected presidents and their political appointees. Career bureaucrats will be most successful in stabilizing religious and U.S. foreign policy where mandates and legal authority are most clear-cut. This consideration may point toward future leadership of religion-related offices from career Foreign Service Officers or those with extended records of nonpartisan government service, rather than political appointees, should an office like RGA be reestablished on a truly independent basis.

The Office of Religion and Global Affairs, like many other offices tasked with religion in the foreign policy bureaucracy, came into being because of the event-driven, pragmatic need for enhanced diplomatic capacity to address religion as it impacts U.S. foreign policy priorities. Nothing has happened to diminish that need. Across the globe, American diplomats strive to understand religious dynamics and develop strategic responses to those realities in ways that best serve American interests and ideals. The greatest obstacles to meeting this need will be America's domestic politics, not forces beyond its borders.

One crucial advantage American institutions enjoy is a working civic history of cooperation across religious and partisan boundaries in service to the common good. Trump's Muslim Bans touched off protests, not only from non-Christian communities in the United States, but also the U.S. Conference of Catholic Bishops, the Southern Baptist Convention, and the National Association of Evangelicals. Sikhs, Jews, Muslims, and members of the Secular Coalition for America contributed to the Brookings *A Time to Heal, A Time to Build* report of late 2020, as did both Democrats and Republicans. The norms and information flows cultivated in these networks could prove crucial as American institutions navigate this current period of democratic uncertainty.

APPENDIX

T his appendix presents detailed quantitative models referenced or presented graphically in chapter 7. See text of chapter 7 for references linking those graphs to individual models in these tables.

TABLE A.1 Religion and Correlates of Deep State Threat

	(1)	(2)	(3)
Christian Nationalism	0.39***	0.32***	0.28***
	(0.02)	(0.02)	(0.02)
Religious Attendance	−0.02	−0.04**	−0.05**
	(0.01)	(0.01)	(0.02)
Evangelical ID	0.00	0.03	0.03
	(0.06)	(0.05)	(0.06)
Demographic Controls?		Y	Y
Political Controls?			Y
Constant	1.92***	1.72***	1.53***
	(0.06)	(0.13)	(0.14)
r2	0.19	0.25	0.28
N	1758	1755	1566

* $p < 0.05$, ** $p < 0.01$, *** $p < 0.001$

Note: OLS models; standard errors in parentheses. Models correspond to graphics in figure 7.3.

TABLE A.2 Thin Ideology and 2020 Trump Support

	(1)	(2)	(3)	(4)	(5)	(6)
Muslim Feeling Thermometer	−0.01*** (0.00)	−0.01** (0.00)	−0.01** (0.00)			
UN Feeling Thermometer				−0.02*** (0.00)	−0.01*** (0.00)	−0.01*** (0.00)
Demographic Controls?	Y	Y	Y	Y	Y	Y
Political Controls?		Y	Y		Y	Y
Religious Controls?			Y			Y
Constant	1.09* (0.44)	−4.31*** (0.74)	−5.81*** (0.81)	1.38** (0.45)	−3.91*** (0.75)	−5.31*** (0.81)
N	1294	1229	1229	1294	1229	1229

* $p < 0.05$, ** $p < 0.01$, *** $p < 0.001$

Note: Logit models; standard errors in parentheses. Models correspond to graphs presented in figure 7.4.

TABLE A.3 Rejecting Institutional Constraint and 2020 Trump Support

	(1)	(2)	(3)	(4)	(5)	(6)
Deep State Index	1.07*** (0.08)	0.87*** (0.12)	0.72*** (0.12)			
Government Employ Feeling Thermometer				−0.01*** (0.00)	−0.01* (0.00)	−0.01** (0.00)
Demographic Controls?	Y	Y	Y	Y	Y	Y
Political Controls?		Y	Y		Y	Y
Religious Controls?			Y			Y
Constant	−3.27*** (0.53)	−7.36*** (0.83)	−7.94*** (0.86)	1.18** (0.45)	−4.40*** (0.75)	−5.76*** (0.81)
N	1292	1227	1227	1294	1229	1229

* $p < 0.05$, ** $p < 0.01$, *** $p < 0.001$

Note: Logit models; standard errors in parentheses. Models correspond to graphs presented in figure 7.4.

TABLE A.4 Conditional Effects of Religious Leader Endorsement

	(1) Trump Support	(2) Clergy Moral Authority
Treatment (Clergy Endorsement)	0.12 (0.22)	−0.57* (0.23)
Trump Voter 2020	5.51*** (0.24)	1.32*** (0.25)
Treatment* Trump Voter	−0.10 (0.34)	1.03** (0.35)
Constant	2.08*** (0.16)	3.63*** (0.16)
r2	0.45	0.08
N	1306	1306

$^* p < 0.05,\ ^{**} p < 0.01,\ ^{***} p < 0.001$

Note: OLS models; standard errors in parentheses

NOTES

INTRODUCTION: SEEKING DIVINE INTERVENTION

1. Benjamin Wittes, Susan Hennessey, and Quinta Jurecic, "Full Text of Draft Dissent Channel Memo on Trump Refugee and Visa Order," *Lawfare*, January 20, 2017, https://lawfareblog.com/full-text-draft-dissent-channel-memo-trump-refugee-and-visa-order.

2. Eric Katz, "Trump Has Slashed Jobs at Nearly Every Federal Agency; Biden Promises a Reversal," *GovExec.com*, November 19, 2020, https://www.govexec.com/workforce/2020/11/trump-has-slashed-jobs-nearly-every-federal-agency-biden-promises-reversal/170203/.

3. John L. Campbell, *Institutions Under Siege: Donald Trump's Attack on the Deep State* (Cambridge: Cambridge University Press, 2022), 144.

4. Elizabeth Byers, "How the State Department Workforce Changed Under the Trump Administration," *Partnership for Public Service*, January 20, 2022, https://ourpublicservice.org/blog/how-the-state-department-workforce-changed-under-the-trump-administration/.

5. Eliot Cohen, "The Worst Secretary of State in Living Memory," *The Atlantic*, December 1, 2017, https://www.theatlantic.com/politics/archive/2017/12/rexit/547295/.

6. Jason Zengerle, "Rex Tillerson and the Unraveling of the State Department," *New York Times*, October 17, 2017.

7. Katie Zavadski, "Zionist Gala Toasts Donald Trump's 'Divine' Election Victory," *Daily Beast*, July 12, 2017, https://www.thedailybeast.com/zionist-gala-toasts-donald-trumps-divine-election-victory.

8. David Graham, "Donald Trump's Excellent Abrahamic Adventure," *The Atlantic*, May 4, 2017, https://www.theatlantic.com/international/archive/2017/05/donald-trumps-excellent-abrahamic-adventure/525429/.

9. Daniel W. Drezner, "The Angry Populist as Foreign Policy Leader: Real Change or Just Hot Air," *Fletcher F. World Affairs* 41, no. 2 (2017): 27.

10. Nadia Marzouki, Duncan McDonnell, and Olivier Roy, *Saving the People: How Populists Hijack Religion* (Oxford: Oxford University Press, 2016).

11. Kurt Weyland, "A Political-Strategic Approach," in *The Oxford Handbook of Populism*, eds. Cristóbal Kaltwasser et al. (Oxford: Oxford University Press, 2017), 48–72.

12. Gregorio Bettiza, *Finding Faith in Foreign Policy: U.S. Foreign Policy in a Post-Secular World* (Oxford: Oxford University Press, 2019).

13. The USAID office's precise name tends to change slightly from administration to administration, but its core functions remain fairly constant.

14. Robert C. Lieberman et al., "The Trump Presidency and American Democracy: A Historical and Comparative Analysis," *Perspectives on Politics* (2018): 470.

15. Douglas Johnston and Cynthia Sampson, *Religion, the Missing Dimension of Statecraft* (New York: Oxford University Press, 1994).

16. Alexander L. George and Andrew Bennett, *Case Studies and Theory Development in the Social Sciences* (Cambridge, MA: MIT Press, 2005), 241.

17. David Dessler, "Beyond Correlations: Toward a Causal Theory of War," *International Studies Quarterly* 35, no. 3 (1991): 343.

18. Shaun Casey, *Chasing the Devil at Foggy Bottom: The Future of Religion in American Diplomacy* (Grand Rapids, MI: William B. Eerdmans, 2023).

19. Anna Grzymała-Busse, *Nations Under God: How Churches Use Moral Authority to Influence Policy* (Princeton, NJ: Princeton University Press, 2015), 12; David T. Buckley, "Demanding the Divine? Explaining Cross-National Support for Clerical Control of Politics," *Comparative Political Studies* 49, no. 3 (2016): 357–90.

20. Jeffrey Haynes, *From Huntington to Trump: Thirty Years of the Clash of Civilizations* (Washington, D.C.: Rowman & Littlefield, 2019); M. Arsalan Suleman, "Return of the Clash: Operationalizing a Tainted Worldview," *Washington Quarterly* 40, no. 4 (2017): 49–70.

1. WHAT DOES POPULISM HAVE TO DO WITH RELIGION AND FOREIGN POLICY?

1. Douglas Johnston and Cynthia Sampson, *Religion, the Missing Dimension of Statecraft* (New York: Oxford University Press, 1994).

2. RGA's founding leader, Shaun Casey, has published the most comprehensive account of that particular office's founding and early development. Shaun Casey, *Chasing the Devil at Foggy Bottom: The Future of Religion in American Diplomacy* (Grand Rapids, MI: William B. Eerdmans, 2023).

3. John L. Campbell, *Institutions Under Siege: Donald Trump's Attack on the Deep State* (Cambridge: Cambridge University Press, 2022), 2.

4. See for example, Jack L. Snyder, *Religion and International Relations Theory* (New York: Columbia University Press, 2011); Timothy Samuel Shah, Alfred C. Stepan, and

Monica Duffy Toft, *Rethinking Religion and World Affairs* (New York: Oxford University Press, 2012). Diplomatic historians have long studied the ways in which religious actors have shaped the historical development of U.S. foreign policy. See for example, Walter A. McDougall, *Promised Land, Crusader State: The American Encounter with the World Since 1776* (Boston: Houghton Mifflin, 1997); Andrew Preston, *Sword of the Spirit, Shield of Faith: Religion in American War and Diplomacy* (New York: Alfred A. Knopf, 2012); Walter Russell Mead, *God and Gold: Britain, America, and the Making of the Modern World* (New York: Alfred A. Knopf, 2007); and William Inboden, *Religion and American Foreign Policy, 1945–1960: The Soul of Containment* (Cambridge: Cambridge University Press, 2008).

5.   Carolyn M. Warner and Stephen G. Walker, "Thinking About the Role of Religion in Foreign Policy: A Framework for Analysis," *Foreign Policy Analysis* 7, no. 1 (2011): 113–35; Jeffrey Haynes, "Religion and Foreign Policy Making in the USA, India and Iran: Towards a Research Agenda," *Third World Quarterly* 29, no. 1 (2008): 143–65; Nukhet A. Sandal and Jonathan Fox, *Religion in International Relations Theory: Interactions and Possibilities* (New York: Routledge, 2013); Snyder, *Religion and International Relations Theory*.

6.   Timothy A. Byrnes, *Reverse Mission: Transnational Religious Communities and the Making of US Foreign Policy* (Washington, D.C.: Georgetown University Press, 2011).

7.   Mark R. Amstutz, *Evangelicals and American Foreign Policy* (Oxford: Oxford University Press, 2014); Melani McAlister, *The Kingdom of God Has No Borders: A Global History of American Evangelicals* (New York: Oxford University Press, 2018).

8.   Samuel Goldman, *God's Country: Christian Zionism in America* (Philadelphia: University of Pennsylvania Press, 2018).

9.   Peter Henne, *Islamic Politics, Muslim States, and Counterterrorism Tensions* (New York: Cambridge University Press, 2016).

10.   S. P. Huntington, "The Clash of Civilizations," *Foreign Affairs* 72, no. 3 (Summer 1993): 22–49.

11.   Jonathan Fox, "Paradigm Lost: Huntington's Unfulfilled Clash of Civilizations Prediction in the 21st Century," *International Politics* 42, no. 4 (December 2005): 428–57; Giacomo Chiozza, "Is There a Clash of Civilizations? Evidence from Patterns of International Conflict Involvement, 1946–97," *Journal of Peace Research* 39, no. 6 (November 1, 2002): 711-34.

12.   Jeffrey Haynes, "Donald Trump, 'Judeo-Christian Values,' and the 'Clash of Civilizations,' " *Review of Faith & International Affairs* 15, no. 3 (2017): 66–75; M. Arsalan Suleman, "Return of the Clash: Operationalizing a Tainted Worldview," *Washington Quarterly* 40, no. 4 (2017): 49-70; Rogers Brubaker, "Between Nationalism and Civilizationism: The European Populist Moment in Comparative Perspective," *Ethnic and Racial Studies* 40, no. 8 (2017): 1191–1226.

13.   Elizabeth Shakman Hurd, *Beyond Religious Freedom: The New Global Politics of Religion* (Princeton, NJ: Princeton University Press, 2015); Winnifred Fallers Sullivan et al., *Politics of Religious Freedom* (Chicago: University of Chicago Press, 2015).

14. Robert M. Bosco, *Securing the Sacred Religion, National Security, and the Western State* (Ann Arbor: University of Michigan Press, 2014); Jocelyne Cesari, *Muslims in the West After 9/11: Religion, Politics, and Law* (New York: Routledge, 2010); Talal Asad, *Formations of the Secular: Christianity, Islam, Modernity* (Stanford, CA: Stanford University Press, 2003); Peter Mandaville, "Designating Muslims: Islam in the Western Policy Imagination," *Review of Faith & International Affairs* 15, no. 3 (2017): 54–65.

15. It is telling that in an online symposium hosted in 2013 by the Social Science Research Council on the establishment of the State Department's Office of Religion and Global Affairs, which was intentionally left outside of the religious freedom-oriented portions of the foreign policy bureaucracy, a significant portion of the contributions highlighted concerns about the office's involvement in the promotion of international religious freedom. See "Engaging Religion at the Department of State," Social Science Research Council, September 26, 2019, https://tif.ssrc.org/2013/07/30/engaging-religion-at-the-department-of-state/.

16. Johnston and Sampson, *Religion, the Missing Dimension of Statecraft*; Douglas Johnston, *Faith-Based Diplomacy: Trumping Realpolitik* (Oxford: Oxford University Press, 2003); Dennis Hoover and Douglas Johnston, *Religion and Foreign Affairs: Essential Readings* (Waco, TX: Baylor University Press, 2012).

17. Gregorio Bettiza, *Finding Faith in Foreign Policy: U.S. Foreign Policy in a Post-Secular World* (Oxford: Oxford University Press, 2019).

18. Sara Silvestri, "Islam and Religion in the EU Political System," *West European Politics* 32, no. 6 (2009): 1212–39.

19. Joseph S. Nye, "Soft Power," *Foreign Policy*, no. 80 (1990): 164, and *Soft Power: The Means to Success in World Politics* (New York: Public Affairs, 2004).

20. Haynes, "Religion and Foreign Policy Making in the USA, India and Iran."

21. Peter Mandaville and Shadi Hamid, "Islam as Statecraft: How Governments Use Religion in Foreign Policy" (Washington, D.C.: Brookings Institution, 2018), https://www.brookings.edu/articles/islam-as-statecraft-how-governments-use-religion-in-foreign-policy/; Gregorio Bettiza, "States, Religions, and Power: Highlighting the Role of Sacred Capital in World Politics" (Washington, D.C.: Berkley Center for Religion, Peace and World Affairs, 2020), https://berkleycenter.georgetown.edu/publications/states-religions-and-power-highlighting-the-role-of-sacred-capital-in-world-politics; Peter Henne, "The Geopolitics of Faith: Religious Soft Power in Russian and U.S. Foreign Policy" (Washington, D.C.: Berkley Center for Religion, Peace and World Affairs, 2019), https://berkleycenter.georgetown.edu/posts/the-geopolitics-of-faith-religious-soft-power-in-russian-and-u-s-foreign-policy.

22. Bettiza, "States, Religions, and Power."

23. Mohammad Ayatollahi Tabaar, *Religious Statecraft: The Politics of Islam in Iran* (New York: Columbia University Press, 2018), 28.

24. Haynes, "Religion and Foreign Policy Making in the USA, India and Iran," 144.

25. Jocelyne Cesari, *We God's People: Christianity, Islam and Hinduism in the World of Nations* (Cambridge: Cambridge University Press, 2021), 359.

26. Tabaar, *Religious Statecraft*, 2.

27. Bettiza, *Finding Faith in Foreign Policy*, 22.
28. Robert R. Kaufman and Stephan Haggard, "Democratic Decline in the United States: What Can We Learn from Middle-Income Backsliding?," *Perspectives on Politics* 17, no. 2 (2018): 422.
29. Angelos Chryssogelos, "Populism in Foreign Policy," in *Oxford Research Encyclopedia of Politics*, 2017, 1.
30. Kurt Weyland, "A Political-Strategic Approach," in *The Oxford Handbook of Populism*, eds. Cristóbal Kaltwasser et al. (Oxford: Oxford University Press, 2017), 48.
31. Cas Mudde and Cristóbal Rovira Kaltwasser, *Populism: A Very Short Introduction* (Oxford: Oxford University Press, 2017); Daniele Albertazzi and Duncan McDonnell, *Populists in Power* (London: Routledge, 2015), 5.
32. Kurt Weyland, "Clarifying a Contested Concept: Populism in the Study of Latin American Politics," *Comparative Politics* 34, no. 1 (2001): 14.
33. Weyland, "A Political-Strategic Approach," 54.
34. Weyland, "A Political-Strategic Approach," 54.
35. Bertjan Verbeek and Andrej Zaslove, "Populism and Foreign Policy," in *The Oxford Handbook of Populism*, 384–405; Chryssogelos, "Populism in Foreign Policy."
36. Jose Pedro Zúquete, "Populism and Religion," in *The Oxford Handbook of Populism*, 445-66; Bilge Yabanci and Dane Taleski, "Co-Opting Religion: How Ruling Populists in Turkey and Macedonia Sacralise the Majority," *Religion, State & Society* 46, no. 3 (2018): 283–304.
37. Andrew Arato and Jean L. Cohen, "Civil Society, Populism, and Religion," *Routledge Handbook of Global Populism*, ed. Carlos de la Torre (New York: Routledge, 2019), 290.
38. José Casanova, *Public Religions in the Modern World* (Chicago: University of Chicago Press, 1994).
39. Mudde and Kaltwasser, *Populism*.
40. Nadia Marzouki, Duncan McDonnell, and Olivier Roy, *Saving the People: How Populists Hijack Religion* (Oxford: Oxford University Press, 2016).
41. David Buckley, Steven Brooke, and Bryce Kleinsteuber, "How Populists Engage Religion: Mechanisms and Evidence from the Philippines," *Democratization*, 29, no. 8 (2022): 1455–75.
42. Nadia Urbinati, *Me the People: How Populism Transforms Democracy* (Cambridge, MA: Harvard University Press, 2019).
43. Brubaker, "Between Nationalism and Civilizationism," 1191–1226.
44. Nadia Marzouki and Duncan McDonnell, "Populism and Religion," in *Saving the People*, 2.
45. Brubaker, "Between Nationalism and Civilizationism," 1210.
46. Tobias Cremer, *The Godless Crusade* (Cambridge: Cambridge University Press, 2023).
47. Olivier Roy, "Beyond Populism: The Conservative Right, the Courts, the Churches, and the Concept of a Christian Europe," in *Saving the People*, 201.
48. Zoltán Ádám and András Bozóki, " 'The God of Hungarians': Religion and Right Wing Populism in Hungary," in *Saving the People*, 133.

49. Buckley, Brooke, and Kleinsteuber, "How Populists Engage Religion"; Nicole Curato, "Politics of Anxiety, Politics of Hope: Penal Populism and Duterte's Rise to Power," *Journal of Current Southeast Asian Affairs* 35, no. 3 (2016): 91–109.
50. Andrew L. Whitehead and Samuel L. Perry, *Taking America Back for God: Christian Nationalism in the United States* (Oxford: Oxford University Press, 2020).
51. Jeffrey Haynes, "Donald Trump, 'Judeo-Christian Values,' and the 'Clash of Civilizations,'" *Review of Faith & International Affairs* 15, no. 3 (2017): 66–75.
52. Clifford Bob, *The Global Right Wing and the Clash of World Politics* (New York: Cambridge University Press, 2012).
53. John Otis, "Hugo Chavez and the Vatican," *PRI: The World*, March 14, 2013.
54. Elizabeth Shakman Hurd and Winnifred Fallers Sullivan, *At Home and Abroad: The Politics of American Religion* (New York: Columbia University Press, 2021), 3.
55. Cesari, *We God's People*, 15.
56. Weyland, "A Political-Strategic Approach," 54.
57. Weyland, "A Political-Strategic Approach," 50.
58. For more on the complex material interests of religious actors and their political implications, see rationalist scholarship including Guillermo Trejo, "Religious Competition and Ethnic Mobilization in Latin America: Why the Catholic Church Promotes Indigenous Movements in Mexico," *American Political Science Review* 103, no. 3 (2009): 323–42; Anthony James Gill, *Rendering Unto Caesar: The Catholic Church and the State in Latin America* (Chicago: University of Chicago Press, 1998).
59. Bettiza, *Finding Faith in Foreign Policy*.
60. Weyland, "A Political-Strategic Approach," 58.
61. Jon D. Michaels, "The American Deep State Symposium: Administrative Lawmaking in the Twenty-First Century," *Notre Dame Law Review* 93, no. 4 (2017): 1653.
62. Stephen Skowronek, John A Dearborn, and Desmond King, *Phantoms of a Beleaguered Republic: The Deep State and the Unitary Executive* (Oxford: Oxford University Press, 2021), 3.
63. Kirk A. Hawkins, "Is Chávez Populist? Measuring Populist Discourse in Comparative Perspective," *Comparative Political Studies* 42, no. 8 (2009): 1040-67; Margaret Canovan, "Trust the People! Populism and the Two Faces of Democracy." *Political Studies* 47, no. 1 (1999): 2–16.
64. Daniel W. Drezner, *The Toddler in Chief: What Donald Trump Teaches Us About the Modern Presidency* (Chicago: University of Chicago Press, 2020).
65. William G. Howell and Terry M. Moe, *Presidents, Populism, and the Crisis of Democracy* (Chicago: University of Chicago Press, 2020), 106.
66. Rufus E. Miles, "The Origin and Meaning of Miles' Law," *Public Administration Review* 38, no. 5 (1978): 399–403; Graham T. Allison and Philip Zelikow, *Essence of Decision: Explaining the Cuban Missile Crisis* (Boston: Little, Brown, 1971).
67. Daniel Drezner, "Ideas, Bureaucratic Politics, and the Crafting of Foreign Policy," *American Journal of Political Science* 44, no. 4 (2000): 733–49.
68. Robert Mickey, Steven Levitsky, and Lucan Ahmad Way, "Is America Still Safe for Democracy," *Foreign Affairs* (May/June 2017): 28.

69. David E. Lewis, *The Politics of Presidential Appointments: Political Control and Bureaucratic Performance* (Princeton, NJ: Princeton University Press, 2010).
70. Drezner, "Ideas, Bureaucratic Politics, and the Crafting of Foreign Policy."
71. Drezner, "Ideas, Bureaucratic Politics, and the Crafting of Foreign Policy."
72. Kurt Weyland, "Populism's Threat to Democracy: Comparative Lessons for the United States," *Perspectives on Politics* 18, no. 2 (2020): 389.
73. Alfred Stepan, "Religion, Democracy, and the 'Twin Tolerations,'" *Journal of Democracy* 11, no. 4 (2000): 37–57; Jeremy Menchik, "Soft Separation Democracy," *Politics and Religion* 11, no. 4 (2018): 863–83; David T. Buckley, *Faithful to Secularism: The Religious Politics of Democracy in Ireland, Senegal, and the Philippines* (New York: Columbia University Press, 2017).
74. Noah Feldman, *Divided by God: America's Church-State Problem—and What We Should Do About It* (New York: Farrar, Straus and Giroux, 2005); Kent Greenawalt, *Religion and the Constitution. Vol. 2: Establishment and Fairness* (Princeton, NJ: Princeton University Press, 2009); Winnifred Fallers Sullivan, *The Impossibility of Religious Freedom* (Princeton, NJ: Princeton University Press, 2005).
75. Hurd and Sullivan, *At Home and Abroad: The Politics of American Religion*, 4.
76. Mickey, Levitsky, and Way, "Is America Still Safe for Democracy," 28.
77. Stephen R. Weissman, *A Culture of Deference: Congress' Failure of Leadership in Foreign Policy* (New York: Basic Books, 1996); David Mitchell, *Making Foreign Policy: Presidential Management of the Decision-Making Process* (Burlington, VT: Ashgate, 2005).
78. Kurt Weyland and Raúl L. Madrid, *When Democracy Trumps Populism: European and Latin American Lessons for the United States* (Cambridge: Cambridge University Press, 2019), 4.
79. See for probably the most prominent example, Robert D. Putnam and David E. Campbell, *American Grace: How Religion Divides and Unites Us* (New York: Simon & Schuster, 2010).
80. See for example, the extensive recent scholarship on Christian nationalism from Perry and Whitehead along with Eric L. McDaniel, Irfan Nooruddin, and Allyson F. Shortle, *The Everyday Crusade: Christian Nationalism in American Politics* (Cambridge: Cambridge University Press, 2022).
81. Joshua D. Kertzer et al., "Moral Support: How Moral Values Shape Foreign Policy Attitudes," *Journal of Politics* 76, no. 3 (2014): 825–40.
82. James L. Guth, "The Religious Roots of Foreign Policy Exceptionalism," *Review of Faith & International Affairs* 10, no. 2 (2012): 77–85, and "Religion and American Public Opinion: Foreign Policy Issues," in *Oxford Handbook of Religion and American Politics*, eds. Corwin Smidt et al. (New York: Oxford University Press, 2017), 243–65.
83. Motti Inbari, Kirill M. Bumin, and M. Gordon Byrd, "Why Do Evangelicals Support Israel?," *Politics and Religion* 14, no. 1 (2021): 1–36.
84. Stephen Chaudoin, David Thomas Smith, and Johannes Urpelainen, "American Evangelicals and Domestic Versus International Climate Policy," *Review of International Organizations* 9, no. 4 (2014): 441–69.
85. See Hurd, *Beyond Religious Freedom*.

86. Valerie M. Hudson and Benjamin S. Day, *Foreign Policy Analysis: Classic and Contemporary Theory* (Lanham, MD: Rowman & Littlefield, 2019); Kenneth Neal Waltz, *Theory of International Politics* (Reading, MA: Addison-Wesley, 1979).

87. Alexander Cooley and Daniel Nexon, *Exit from Hegemony: The Unraveling of the American Global Order* (New York: Oxford University Press, 2020); Walter Russell Mead, "The Jacksonian Revolt: American Populism and the Liberal Order," *Foreign Affairs* 96, no. 2 (2017): 2–7.

88. Verbeek and Zaslove, "Populism and Foreign Policy"; Johannes Plagemann and Sandra Destradi, "Populism and Foreign Policy: The Case of India," *Foreign Policy Analysis* 15, no. 2 (2019): 283–301.

2. THE BLOB GETS RELIGION: RGA AND THE PREPOPULIST EQUILIBRIUM

1. Shaun Casey, "Remarks at 'Religion and Diplomacy Conference,' " Remarks, U.S. Department of State, Washington, D.C., September 26–27, 2016.

2. In the interest of space, I do not offer a similarly detailed baseline for the other offices concerned with religion at State and USAID. Bettiza's *Finding Faith* provides a sure foundation in this regard, particularly as the other offices in the bureaucracy were more firmly established at the time of his research and writing.

3. Shaun Casey, *Chasing the Devil in Foggy Bottom: The Future of Religion in American Diplomacy* (Grand Rapids, MI: William B. Eerdmans, 2023).

4. Gregorio Bettiza, *Finding Faith in Foreign Policy: U.S. Foreign Policy in a Post-Secular World* (Oxford: Oxford University Press, 2019).

5. In borrowing Bettiza's general categorization scheme, I leave largely unaddressed questions related to the presence of religion within the defense and intelligence communities, which feature heavily in nearly all areas of U.S. foreign policy. While RGA staff interacted with colleagues at other agencies, the analysis here will remain largely focused on work internal to the State Department and USAID.

6. Religion and Foreign Policy Working Group, "Ensuring the Opportunity for Mutual Counsel and Collaboration," U.S. Department of State, October 16, 2012.

7. Office of Religion and Global Affairs, "U.S. Strategy on Religious Leader and Faith Community Engagement," U.S. Department of State, https://2009-2017.state.gov/s/rga/strategy/index.htm.

8. Executive Order No. 13559. 75 Federal Register 71319. November 17, 2010.

9. John Kerry, "Remarks at the Launch of the Office of Faith-Based Community Initiatives," Remarks, Washington, D.C., August 7, 2013, https://2009-2017.state.gov/secretary/remarks/2013/08/212781.htm.

10. Kerry, "Remarks at the Launch of the Office of Faith-Based Community Initiatives."

11. Secretary's Office of Religion and Global Affairs, "U.S. Strategy on Religious Leader and Faith Community Engagement."

12. A one-pager summarizing RGA's structure and strategy in late 2016, https://2009-2017 .state.gov/s/rga/262375.htm.

13. See, for example, Casey, "Remarks at 'Religion and Diplomacy Conference.' "

14. Casey, "Remarks at 'Religion and Diplomacy Conference.' "

15. For a more extended discussion of rightsizing, see Peter Mandaville, "Right-Sizing Religion and Religious Engagement in Diplomacy and Development," *Review of Faith & International Affairs* 19 (2021): 92–97.

16. While Hurd uses the term "expert religion" with a critical edge, empirically it is undeniably true that RGA involved an array of individuals with advanced humanities and social sciences training in the study of religion, who drew on that expertise to, in theory, make American diplomats more effective in their engagements with religion in policy work.

17. Office of Religion and Global Affairs, "Religion and Diplomacy: A Practical Handbook," United States Department of State (2017), 3.

18. Office of Religion and Global Affairs, "Religion and Diplomacy: A Practical Handbook," 4.

19. Robert A. Orsi, "Is the Study of Lived Religion Irrelevant to the World We Live In? Special Presidential Plenary Address, Society for the Scientific Study of Religion, Salt Lake City, November 2, 2002," *Journal for the Scientific Study of Religion* 42, no. 2 (2003): 169–74.

20. Office of Religion and Global Affairs, "Religion and Diplomacy: A Practical Handbook," 3. Given the contrast drawn between "expert religion" and lived religion in works like Hurd's *Beyond Religious Freedom,* it is worth noting that Special Representative Casey titled his own opening remarks at the 2016 RaDCon, "A Lived Religion Approach."

21. Office of Religion and Global Affairs, "Religion and Diplomacy: A Practical Handbook," 4.

22. Office of Religion and Global Affairs, "Religion and Diplomacy: A Practical Handbook," 7.

23. Frank R. Wolf International Religious Freedom Act, Public Law No. 114-281, 130 Stat. 1426 (2016).

24. Office of Religion and Global Affairs, "Religion and Diplomacy: A Practical Handbook," 10.

25. Office of Religion and Global Affairs, "Religion and Diplomacy: A Practical Handbook," 10.

26. Office of Religion and Global Affairs, "Religion and Diplomacy: A Practical Handbook," 11.

27. Office of Religion and Global Affairs, "Religion and Diplomacy: A Practical Handbook," 14.

28. Office of Religion and Global Affairs, "Religion and Diplomacy: A Practical Handbook," 13.

29. Office of Religion and Global Affairs, "Religion and Diplomacy: A Practical Handbook," 13.

30.   Office of Religion and Global Affairs, "Religion and Diplomacy: A Practical Handbook," 14.

31.   Elizabeth Shakman Hurd, *Beyond Religious Freedom: The New Global Politics of Religion* (Princeton, NJ: Princeton University Press, 2015), 18.

32.   Hurd, *Beyond Religious Freedom*, 73.

33.   Bettiza, *Finding Faith*, 48.

34.   Transparency International, "Corruption Perceptions Index-Nigeria," 2021, https://www.transparency.org/en/cpi/2021/index/nga.

35.   "Nigerian Church Collapses Kills at Least 160 Worshippers-Reports," Associated Press, December 10, 2016.

36.   Leena Koni Hoffman and Raj Navanit Patel, "Collective Action on Corruption in Nigeria: The Role of Religion" (London: Chatham House, 2021), https://www.chathamhouse.org/2021/03/collective-action-corruption-nigeria/summary.

37.   For analysis of this initial convening, see Katherine Marshall, "Nigeria: Faith Against Corruption," Berkley Center for Religion, Peace and World Affairs, February 1, 2016, https://berkleycenter.georgetown.edu/posts/nigeria-faith-against-corruption.

38.   Ben Ezeamalu, "U.S. Partners Religious Leaders, BudgIT to Launch Anti-Corruption Website," *Premium Times,* July 12, 2017.

39.   Ezeamalu, "U.S. Partners Religious Leaders."

40.   U.S. Mission Nigeria, "U.S. Consulate, Religious Leaders Launch Anti-Corruption Website," United States Department of State, January 31, 2022, https://ng.usembassy.gov/u-s-consulate-religious-leaders-launch-anti-corruption-website/.

41.   Indeed, there may be reason to suspect that certain religious messages have unintended effects on attitudes and behavior regarding corruption. Nic Cheeseman and Caryn Peiffer, "The Curse of Good Intentions: Why Anticorruption Messaging Can Encourage Bribery," *American Political Science Review* 116, no. 3 (2022): 1081–95.

42.   For an overview of the current state of U.S. CWT diplomacy, see: Bureau of Oceans and International Environmental and Scientific Affairs, "2021 END Wildlife Trafficking Strategic Review," United States Department of State, November 4, 2021, https://www.state.gov/2021-end-wildlife-trafficking-strategic-review/.

43.   Bureau of Oceans and International Environmental and Scientific Affairs, "2021 END Wildlife Trafficking Strategic Review."

44.   World Wildlife Fund, "African Religious Leaders Join Forces to Help Stop Illegal Wildlife Trade," September 21, 2012, https://wwf.panda.org/wwf_news/?206250/African-religious-leaders-join-forces-to-help-stop-illegal-wildlife-trade.

45.   Jeremy Hance, "Sri Lanka to Give Poached Ivory to Buddhist Temple, Flouting International Agreements," *Mongabay News,* February 5, 2013; Bryan Christy, "In Global First, Philippines to Destroy Its Ivory Stock," *National Geographic,* May 3, 2021.

46.   See details on the "Furs for Life" program at: https://panthera.org/furs-life.

47.   "Secure, Empowered, Connected Communities," Catholic Relief Services, https://www.crs.org/our-work-overseas/program-areas/justice-and-peacebuilding/secure-empowered-connected-communities.

48. Office of Religion and Global Affairs, "U.S. Strategy on Religious Leader and Faith Community Engagement."

49. Kerry, "Remarks at the Launch of the Office of Faith-Based Community Initiatives."

50. This is not to say that expert religion is without criticism, as Elizabeth Shakman Hurd's *Beyond Religious Freedom* develops at great length. But this approach is conceptually distinct from the unchecked individual discretion analyzed by scholars of populist personalism.

51. R. Scott Appleby, Richard Cizik, and Thomas Wright, *Engaging Religious Communities Abroad: A New Imperative for U.S. Foreign Policy* (Chicago: Chicago Council on Global Affairs, 2010).

52. Casey, "Remarks at 'Religion and Diplomacy Conference.' "

53. Peter Mandaville, "The Future of Religion and U.S. Foreign Policy under Trump" (Washington, D.C.: Brookings Institution, 2017), https://www.brookings.edu/articles /the-future-of-religion-and-u-s-foreign-policy-under-trump/.

54. Shaun Casey, "How the State Department Has Sidelined Religion's Role in Democracy," *Religion & Politics*, September 5, 2017, https://religionandpolitics.org/2017/09/05/how -the-state-department-has-sidelined-religions-role-in-diplomacy/.

55. This distinction is often lost on critics of State Department efforts related to religion. It is telling, for instance, how many authors in the Social Science Research Council's online roundtable on RGA conflated its work with that of religious freedom promotion or exclusively focus on politics of Muslim-majority countries.

56. Judd Birdsall, "Keep the Faith: How American Diplomacy Got Religion, and How to Keep It," *Review of Faith & International Affairs* 14, no. 2 (2016): 110–115.

3. "THE FAITH OF THE ADMINISTRATION": POPULIST IDEOLOGY, RELIGION, AND FOREIGN POLICY

1. Sarah Huckabee Sanders, "Press Briefing by Press Secretary Sarah Sanders," White House, February 27, 2018, https://trumpwhitehouse.archives.gov/briefings-statements /press-briefing-press-secretary-sarah-sanders-022718/.

2. Sanders, "Press Briefing."

3. Gregorio Bettiza, *Finding Faith in Foreign Policy: U.S. Foreign Policy in a Post-Secular World* (Oxford: Oxford University Press, 2019), 22.

4. Cas Mudde and Cristóbal Rovira Kaltwasser, *Populism: A Very Short Introduction* (Oxford: Oxford University Press, 2017).

5. Mudde and Kaltwasser, *Populsim*.

6. Kurt Weyland, "A Political-Strategic Approach," in *The Oxford Handbook of Populism*, eds. Cristóbal Kaltwasser et al. (Oxford: Oxford University Press, 2017), 50.

7. Nadia Marzouki, Duncan McDonnell, and Olivier Roy, *Saving the People: How Populists Hijack Religion* (Oxford: Oxford University Press, 2016); Rogers Brubaker, "Between Nationalism and Civilizationism: The European Populist Moment in Comparative Perspective," *Ethnic and Racial Studies* 40, no. 8 (2017): 1191–1226; Philip Gorski, "Why

Evangelicals Voted for Trump: A Critical Cultural Sociology," in *Politics of Meaning/Meaning of Politics* (New York: Springer, 2019): 165–83.

8.   Margaret Canovan, *The People* (Cambridge, MA: Polity Press, 2005), 75.

9.   Mudde and Kaltwasser, *Populsim.*

10. Ben Stanley, "The Thin Ideology of Populism," *Journal of Political Ideologies* 13, no. 1 (2008): 96.

11. Stanley, "The Thin Ideology of Populism," 101.

12. Daniele Albertazzi and Duncan McDonnell, *Populists in Power* (London: Routledge, 2015).

13. Jan-Werner Müller, "Parsing Populism: Who Is and Who Is Not a Populist These Days?," *Juncture* 22, no. 2 (2015): 83.

14. Mudde and Kaltwasser, *Populism,* 9.

15. Cas Mudde and Cristóbal Rovira Kaltwasser, "Studying Populism in Comparative Perspective: Reflections on the Contemporary and Future Research Agenda," *Comparative Political Studies* 51, no. 13 (2018): 1670.

16. Stanley, "The Thin Ideology of Populism," 105.

17. Mudde and Kaltwasser, *Populism,* 12.

18. Canovan, *The People,* 3.

19. Jon D. Michaels, "The American Deep State," *Notre Dame Law Review* 93, no. 4 (2017): 1653.

20. Jan-Werner Müller, *What is Populism* (Philadelphia: University of Pennsylvania Press, 2016), 2.

21. Marzouki and McDonnell, "Populism and Religion," in *Saving the People: How Populists Hijack Religion,* 5.

22. Weyland, "A Political Strategic Approach," 58.

23. Marzouki and McDonnell, "Populism and Religion," 5.

24. William G. Howell and Terry M. Moe, *Presidents, Populism, and the Crisis of Democracy* (Chicago: University of Chicago Press, 2020), 65.

25. David T. Buckley, Steven Brooke, and Bryce Kleinsteuber, "How Populists Engage Religion: Mechanisms and Evidence from the Philippines," *Democratization* 29, no. 8 (2022): 1455–75.

26. Valerie M. Hudson and Benjamin S. Day, *Foreign Policy Analysis: Classic and Contemporary Theory* (Lanham, MD: Rowman & Littlefield, 2019).

27. Brian C. Rathbun, *Partisan Interventions: European Party Politics and Peace Enforcement in the Balkans* (Ithaca, NY: Cornell University Press, 2004).

28. Peter Henne, *Islamic Politics, Muslim States, and Counterterrorism Tensions* (New York: Cambridge University Press, 2016).

29. Thorsten Wojczewski, "Trump, Populism, and American Foreign Policy," *Foreign Policy Analysis* 16, no. 3 (2020): 293.

30. "Trump Promises Tariffs on Companies That Leave U.S. to Create Jobs Overseas," Reuters, August 28, 2020.

31. Bertjan Verbeek and Andrej Zaslove, "Populism and Foreign Policy," in *The Oxford Handbook of Populism,* 384–405.

32. Corina Lacatus, "Populism and President Trump's Approach to Foreign Policy: An Analysis of Tweets and Rally Speeches," *Politics* 41, no. 1 (2021): 31–47.

33. David L. Rousseau and Rocio Garcia-Retamero, "Identity, Power, and Threat Perception: A Cross-National Experimental Study," *Journal of Conflict Resolution* 51, no. 5 (2007): 744–71; Zoltán I. Búzás, "The Color of Threat: Race, Threat Perception, and the Demise of the Anglo-Japanese Alliance (1902–1923)," *Security Studies* 22, no. 4 (October 1, 2013): 573–606.

34. Angelos Chryssogelos, "Populism in Foreign Policy," *Oxford Research Encyclopedia of Politics*, 2017, 7; Rogers Brubaker, "Between Nationalism and Civilizationism, the European Populist Movement in Comparative Perspective," argues that populists in parts of Northern Europe were more preoccupied with the internal threat of Islam, while Trump adopted more external/security-focused concerns. This would make Islam even more relevant to Trump administration foreign policy, rather than domestic governance.

35. Jonny Hall, "In Search of Enemies: Donald Trump's Populist Foreign Policy Rhetoric," *Politics* 41, no. 1 (2021): 48–63.

36. Stanley, "The Thin Ideology of Populism," 107.

37. Weyland, "A Political-Strategic Approach," 53.

38. Walter Russell Mead, "The Jacksonian Revolt: American Populism and the Liberal Order," *Foreign Affairs* 96, no. 2 (2017): 2–7.

39. Donald Trump, "Remarks by President Trump at Values Voter Summit," Remarks, Washington, D.C., October 12, 2019, https://trumpwhitehouse.archives.gov/briefings -statements/remarks-president-trump-values-voter-summit/.

40. Brubaker, "Between Nationalism and Civilizationism."

41. Trump, "Remarks by President Trump at Values Voter Summit."

42. Andrew L. Whitehead and Samuel L. Perry, *Taking America Back for God: Christian Nationalism in the United States* (New York: Oxford University Press, 2020).

43. This is generally consistent with analysis from analysts like Haynes and Suleman, who point to a similar dynamic in identifying civilizational ideology as bounding "the people" and shaping Trump foreign policy. Jeffrey Haynes, *From Huntington to Trump: Thirty Years of the Clash of Civilizations* (Lanham, MD: Rowman & Littlefield, 2019); M. Arsalan Suleman, "Return of the Clash: Operationalizing a Tainted Worldview," *Washington Quarterly* 40, no. 4 (2017): 49–70.

44. Mike Pence, "Remarks by Vice President Pence at Ministerial to Advance Religious Freedom," Remarks, Washington, D.C., July 26, 2018, https://trumpwhitehouse.archives .gov/briefings-statements/remarks-vice-president-pence-ministerial-advance -religious-freedom/.

45. Mark Silk, "Mike Pompeo Claims the Judeo-Christian Tradition for His Agenda," *Religion News Service*, August 5, 2020.

46. J. Lester Feder, "This is How Steve Bannon Sees the Entire World," *Buzzfeed News*, November 16, 2016.

47. Donald Trump, "Remarks by President Trump at the 68th Annual National Prayer Breakfast," Remarks, Washington, D.C., February 6, 2020, https://trumpwhitehouse

.archives.gov/briefings-statements/remarks-president-trump-68th-annual-national
-prayer-breakfast/.

48. Donald Trump, "Remarks on Signing of an Executive Order Combating Anti-Semitism
at a Hanukkah Reception," Remarks, Washington, D.C., December 11, 2019, https://
www.govinfo.gov/content/pkg/DCPD-201900858/pdf/DCPD-201900858.pdf.

49. Donald Trump, "Remarks by President Trump Before White House Iftar Dinner,"
Remarks, Washington, D.C., June 6, 2018, https://trumpwhitehouse.archives.gov
/briefings-statements/remarks-president-trump-white-house-iftar-dinner/.

50. Donald Trump, "President Trump's Speech to the Arab Islamic American Summit,"
Remarks, Saudi Arabia, May 21, 2017, https://trumpwhitehouse.archives.gov/briefings
-statements/president-trumps-speech-arab-islamic-american-summit/.

51. Hamza Yavuz and Mehmet Akif Okur, "Reactions of the American Jews to Trump's
Jerusalem Embassy Move: Continuation of the Historical Pattern?," *Alternatives: Global,
Local, Political* 43, no. 4 (2018): 207–21.

52. Donald Trump, "Statement by Former President Trump on Jerusalem," U.S. Embassy
in Israel, December 7, 2020, https://il.usembassy.gov/statement-by-president-trump-on
-jerusalem/.

53. Tasneem Nashrulla, "The White House Says It Has No Idea How the Controversial Religious Leaders Were Involved in The Jerusalem Embassy Opening," *BuzzFeed News*,
May 14, 2018.

54. Allison Kaplan Sommer, "Trump Says Moved Israel Embassy to Jerusalem 'for the
Evangelicals' - U.S. News," *Haaretz* (Israel), August 19, 2020.

55. Yasmeen Abutaleb and Joseph Tanfani, "As Trump Rewrites Public Health Rules, Pence
Sees Conservative Agenda Born Again," Reuters, May 30, 2019.

56. The "Mexico City" policy "restricted U.S. family planning assistance to foreign NGOs
engaged in voluntary abortion activities, even if such activities are conducted with
non-U.S. funds." For an overview of the Mexico City policy, see Luisa Blanchfield,
"Abortion and Family Planning-Related Provisions in U.S. Foreign Assistance
Law," *Congressional Research Service*, October 2019. For the Trump administration's
changes see, "Memorandum: The Mexico City Policy," 82 Federal Register 8495, January 25, 2017.

57. Michael Igoe, "Christians and the New Age of AIDS," *Devex*, July 23, 2018, https://www
.devex.com/news/christians-and-the-new-age-of-aids-93128; Adva Saldinger, "What
Happened with PEPFAR's Faith-Based Initiative?," *Devex*, October 14, 2020, https://
www.devex.com/news/what-happened-with-pepfar-s-faith-based-initiative-98295.

58. John Barsa, "Acting Administrator John Barsa Letter to UN Secretary General
Guterres," U.S. Agency for International Development, May 18, 2020, https://2017-2020
.usaid.gov/news-information/press-releases/may-18-2020-acting-administrator-john
-barsa-un-secretary-general-antonio-guterres.

59. For the official Global Magnitsky designations, see: https://www.treasury.gov/resource
-center/sanctions/OFAC-Enforcement/Pages/20200731.aspx.

60. Nahal Toosi and Gabby Orr, "White House Taps Pence Aide for Religious Freedom
Role," *Politico*, February 4, 2020.

61. Office of International Religious Freedom, "Declaration of Principles for the International Religious Freedom Alliance," U.S. Department of State, February 5, 2020. https://www.state.gov/declaration-of-principles-for-the-international-religious-freedom-alliance/.

62. Executive Order No. 13926, 85 Federal Register 34951, June 2, 2020.

63. For one example, see Shaun Casey, "The Gap Between Trump's Record and Rhetoric on Religious Freedom," *Sojourners*, June 15, 2020.

64. Jeffrey Haynes, "Trump and the Politics of International Religious Freedom," *Religions* 11, no. 8 (2020): 385.

65. See Michael Pompeo, "Secretary of State Michael Pompeo Keynote Address at the Ministerial to Advance Religious Freedom," Remarks, Washington, D.C., July 18, 2019, https://2017-2021.state.gov/secretary-of-state-michael-r-pompeo-keynote-address-at-the-ministerial-to-advance-religious-freedom/.

66. Pence, "Remarks by Vice President Pence."

67. Mark Green, "USAID Administrator Mark Green Remarks at the Ministerial to Advance International Religious Freedom," Remarks, Washington, D.C., July 16, 2019, https://2017-2021.state.gov/usaid-administrator-mark-green-remarks-at-the-ministerial-to-advance-international-religious-freedom/.

68. Donald Trump, "Remarks by President Trump at Values Voter Summit."

69. Peter Montgomery, "Mike Pompeo Says Unalienable Rights Commission Will Return Human Rights Policy to 'Judeo-Christian Tradition on Which This Country Was Founded,'" *Right Wing Watch*, April 13, 2020, https://www.rightwingwatch.org/post/mike-pompeo-says-unalienable-rights-commission-will-return-human-rights-policy-to-judeo-christian-tradition-on-which-this-country-was-founded/.

70. "Mike Pompeo's Cairo Speech on Mideast Policy and Obama," *Haaretz* (Israel), January 10, 2019.

71. Mudde and Kaltwasser, *Populism*.

72. Albertazzi and McDonnell, *Populists in Power*, 6.

73. Brubaker argues that Trump's confrontation with Islam was more driven by security concerns than the questions of internal diversity that face many European populists. If anything, this may have made foreign policy an even more tempting target for constructing these out-group exclusions, since domestic issues tied to Muslims in the United States are generally lower salience. Brubaker, "Between Nationalism and Civilizationalism."

74. Donald Trump, "The Inaugural Address," Remarks, Washington, D.C., January 20, 2017, https://trumpwhitehouse.archives.gov/briefings-statements/the-inaugural-address/.

75. Trump, "Remarks by President Trump at Values Voter Summit."

76. William Barr, "Attorney General William B. Barr Delivers Remarks to the Law School and the de Nicola Center for Ethics and Culture at the University of Notre Dame," Remarks, University of Notre Dame, October 11, 2019, https://www.justice.gov/opa/speech/attorney-general-william-p-barr-delivers-remarks-law-school-and-de-nicola-center-ethics.

77. For a transcript of these remarks, see J. Lester Feder, "This is How Steve Bannon Sees the Entire World," *Buzzfeed News*, November 16, 2016.

78. Quoted in Joel Gehrke, "State Department Preparing for Clash of Civilizations with China," *Washington Examiner*, April 30, 2019.

79. Julia Edwards Ainsley et al., "Trump to Focus Counter-Extremism Program Solely on Islam—Sources," Reuters, February 1, 2017.

80. William McCants and Benjamin Wittes, "Should the Muslim Brotherhood be Designated a Terrorist Organization?," *Lawfare*, January 27, 2017, https://www.lawfareblog .com/should-muslim-brotherhood-be-designated-terrorist-organization.

81. Rex Tillerson, "Secretary of State Designate Rex Tillerson Senate Confirmation Hearing Opening Statement," Remarks, Washington, D.C., January 11, 2017, https:// www.foreign.senate.gov/imo/media/doc/011117_Tillerson_Opening_Statement .pdf.

82. Mehdi Hasan and Ryan Grim, "Leaked State Department Memo Advised Trump Administration to Push for 'Islamic Reformation,' " *The Intercept*, June 18, 2018.

83. *National Strategy for Counterterrorism of the United States of America*, October 2018.

84. Sarah Pulliam Bailey, "Trump's Statement on Ramadan Is Almost Entirely about Terrorism," *Washington Post*, October 27, 2021.

85. Jessica Taylor, "Trump Calls For 'Total and Complete Shutdown of Muslims Entering' U.S.," *NPR*, December 7, 2015.

86. The draft executive order is available at: https://assets.documentcloud.org/documents /3415943/Read-the-draft-of-the-executive-order-on.pdf.

87. The populist manipulation of "the Muslim world" may be novel, but its roots are much deeper in relationships between European and American powers and countries with significant Muslim populations. See Cemil Aydin, *The Idea of the Muslim World: A Global Intellectual History* (Cambridge, MA: Harvard University Press, 2017).

88. Trump, "Speech to the US-Arab Islamic Meeting."

89. Pranshu Verma, "Trump Appointee with History of Anti-L.G.B.T.Q. Remarks Leaves Aid Agency," *New York Times*, August 3, 2020.

90. See, for example, Trump's reference to "arrests of church leaders" in justifying his confrontation with Venezuela's regime: Donald Trump, "Remarks at the 68th Annual National Prayer Breakfast," Remarks, Washington, D.C., February 6, 2020, https:// trumpwhitehouse.archives.gov/briefings-statements/remarks-president-trump-68th -annual-national-prayer-breakfast/

91. Pence, "Ministerial to Advance Religious Freedom."

92. "U.S. Envoy for Religious Freedom Slams China during Hong Kong Visit," Reuters, March 8, 2019.

93. Donald Trump, "Remarks at the UN Event on Religious Freedom."

94. Michael Pompeo, "Remarks at the Release of 2018 Annual Report on International Religious Freedom," Remarks, Washington, D.C., June 21, 2019, https://br.usembassy.gov /secretary-of-states-remarks-at-the-release-of-the-2018-annual-report-on -international-religious-freedom/.

95. Michael Pompeo, "Secretary Pompeo Addresses Values Voter Summit," Remarks, Washington, D.C., September 21, 2018, https://www.c-span.org/video/?c4750549/secretary-pompeo-addresses-values-voter-summit.

96. Samuel Smith, "Pompeo Faces Criticism for Giving Speech on Being a 'Christian Leader,'" *Christian Post*, October 15, 2019.

97. Michael Pompeo, Speech on "Unalienable Rights and the Securing of Freedom," Remarks, Philadelphia, July 16, 2020, https://2017-2021.state.gov/unalienable-rights-and-the-securing-of-freedom/index.html.

98. Executive Order No. 13899, 84 Federal Register 68779, December 11, 2019.

99. Carol Morello and Steve Hendrix, "Pompeo Sets Off Debate on Boycott of Israel, Calling It an Anti-Semitic 'Cancer,'" *Washington Post*, November 19, 2020.

100. Jeffrey Haynes, "Donald Trump, 'Judeo-Christian Values,' and the 'Clash of Civilizations,'" *Review of Faith & International Affairs* 15, no. 3 (2017): 66. Haynes rightly ties this glocalization process to populist politics, although the implications of populism for the foreign policy process are not his primary concern.

101. Trump, "Speech to the US-Arab Islamic Meeting."

102. Hurd, *Beyond Religious Freedom*, 9.

4. WHO NEEDS AN OFFICE? POPULIST PERSONALISM AND RELIGION IN THE BUREAUCRACY

1. Sarah Huckabee Sanders, "Press Briefing by Press Secretary Sarah Sanders," Remarks, White House, February 27, 2018, https://trumpwhitehouse.archives.gov/briefings-statements/press-briefing-press-secretary-sarah-sanders-022718/.

2. Kurt Weyland, "Populism: A Political-Strategic Approach," in *The Oxford Handbook of Populism*, eds. Cristóbal Kaltwasser et al. (Oxford: Oxford University Press, 2017), 48–72.

3. Weyland, "Populism: A Political-Strategic Approach," 55.

4. Weyland, "Populism: A Political-Strategic Approach," 56.

5. Matthew Rhodes-Purdy and Raúl L. Madrid, "The Perils of Personalism," *Democratization* 27, no. 2 (2020): 322.

6. Nadia Urbinati, *Me the People: How Populism Transforms Democracy* (Cambridge, MA: Harvard University Press, 2019), 132.

7. Murat Somer, "Turkey: The Slippery Slope from Reformist to Revolutionary Polarization and Democratic Breakdown," *The ANNALS of the American Academy of Political and Social Science* 681, no. 1 (2018): 42–61.

8. Ronald A. Pernia, "Human Rights in a Time of Populism: Philippines Under Rodrigo Duterte," *Asia-Pacific Social Science Review* 19, no. 3 (2019): 56–71.

9. Robert Csehi and Edit Zgut, " 'We Won't Let Brussels Dictate Us': Eurosceptic Populism in Hungary and Poland," *European Politics and Society* 22, no. 1 (2021): 53–68.

10. Takis S. Pappas, "Populism Emergent: A Framework for Analyzing Its Contexts, Mechanics, and Outcomes," *RSCAS Working Papers* (2012), 14.

11. Jan-Werner Müller, *What is Populism?* (London: Penguin Books UK, 2017), 5.

12. Forest Colburn and Arturo Cruz, "Personalism and Populism in Nicaragua," *Journal of Democracy* 23, no. 2 (2012): 107.

13. Robert R. Barr, "Populists, Outsiders and Anti-Establishment Politics," *Party Politics* 15, no. 1 (2009): 40.

14. Tatiana Kostadinova and Barry Levitt, "Toward a Theory of Personalist Parties: Concept Formation and Theory Building," *Politics & Policy* 42, no. 4 (August 2014): 501.

15. Kirk A. Hawkins, "Is Chávez Populist? Measuring Populist Discourse in Comparative Perspective," *Comparative Political Studies* 42, no. 8 (2009): 1040–1067; Benjamin Moffitt, *The Global Rise of Populism: Performance, Political Style, and Representation* (Stanford, CA: Stanford University Press, 2016): 30.

16. Hawkins, "Is Chávez Populist?"

17. Moffitt, *The Global Rise of Populism*, 39.

18. Noam Gidron and Bart Bonikowski, "Varieties of Populism: Literature Review and Research Agenda," *Weatherhead Working Paper Series* no. 13-0004 (2013): 9.

19. Kirk Hawkins, "Populism in Venezuela: The Rise of Chavismo," *Third World Quarterly* 24, no. 6 (2003): 1137.

20. Margaret Canovan, "Trust the People! Populism and the Two Faces of Democracy," *Political Studies* 47, no. 1 (1999): 6.

21. Moffitt, *The Global Rise of Populism*, 51.

22. Canovan, "Trust the People!" 6.

23. Urbinati, *Me the People*, 127.

24. Angelos Chryssogelos, "Populism in Foreign Policy," *Oxford Research Encyclopedia of Politics* (2017), 11.

25. Johannes Plagemann and Sandra Destradi, "Populism and Foreign Policy: The Case of India," *Foreign Policy Analysis* 15, no. 2 (2019): 283.

26. Stephen Skowronek, John A. Dearborn, and Desmond King, *Phantoms of a Beleaguered Republic: The Deep State and the Unitary Executive* (New York: Oxford University Press, 2021), 3.

27. Jack Goldsmith, "The Trump Onslaught on International Law and Institutions," *Lawfare*, March 17, 2017.

28. For briefing slides from Secretary Tillerson to congressional authorities, see "Redesign Overview Capitol Hill Brief," U.S. Department of State and U.S. Agency for International Development, September 2017, https://www.politico.com/f/?id=0000015e-86a6-d7ac-a3fe-f7a714110000.

29. Yeganeh Torbati and Lesley Wroughton, "U.S. State Dept Keeps Hiring Freeze as Tillerson Looks to Downsize," Reuters, April 13, 2017; Gardiner Harris, "State Dept. Restores Job Offers to Students after Diplomat Outcry," *New York Times*, July 1, 2017.

30. Even after Tillerson's tumultuous tenure unceremoniously ended, multiple bureaus and offices saw significant attacks on "politicized and other improper personnel practices" from political appointees interested in vetting the loyalty of career officials to the Trump administration. See for example the State Department's Office of Inspector

General, related to management practices in the Bureau of International Organization. "Review of Allegations of Politicized and Other Improper Personnel Practices in the Bureau of International Organization Affairs," U.S. Department of State, August 2019, https://www.stateoig.gov/report/esp-19-05.

31. Daniel W. Drezner, *The Toddler in Chief: What Donald Trump Teaches Us About the Modern Presidency* (Chicago: University of Chicago Press, 2020), 151.

32. Ginger Gibson and Mark Hosenball, "Whistleblower Says Ivanka, Jared Got Security Clearance over Experts' Advice," Reuters, April 2, 2019.

33. Nick Wadhams and Erik Schatzker, "Kushner Is Said to Have Not Kept Tillerson Informed About Middle East Talks," *Boston Globe*, December 2, 2017.

34. Ilya Marritz, "Let's Recall What Exactly Paul Manafort and Rudy Giuliani Were Doing in Ukraine," *ProPublica*, June 23, 2022.

35. Maya Yang, "Trump 'Admired' Putin's Ability to 'Kill Whoever,' Says Stephanie Grisham," *The Guardian* (UK), March 9, 2022.

36. Chris Cillizza and Brenna Williams, "15 Times Donald Trump Praised Authoritarian Rulers," *CNN*, July 2, 2019.

37. Zack Budryk, "North Korea: We Won't 'Gift' Trump with Summit Before Concessions," *The Hill*, November 18, 2019.

38. BBC News, "Trump Tells Pentagon 'to Top' France Military Parade," *BBC News*, February 7, 2018.

39. See for example, Caleb Parke, "Pastors Praise Trump for Skipping UN Panel on 'Imaginary' Climate Crisis," *Fox News*, September 23, 2019.

40. Peter Mandaville, "The Future of Religion and U.S. Foreign Policy Under Trump," Brookings Institution, March 7, 2017, https://www.brookings.edu/articles/the-future-of-religion-and-u-s-foreign-policy-under-trump/; Judd Birdsall, "Keep the Faith: How American Diplomacy Got Religion, and How to Keep It," *The Review of Faith & International Affairs* 14, no. 2 (2016): 110–115.

41. This letter, from approximately forty religious and civil society organizations, https://maryknollogc.org/sites/default/files/article/attachment/S-RGA.let_.pdf.

42. Rex Tillerson, "Letter to the Honorable Bob Corker Regarding Special Envoys and Special Representatives," Updated August 29, 2017, https://www.politico.com/f/?id=0000015e-2b43-db52-a75e-ff7b3bfa0001.

43. Elizabeth Shakman Hurd, *Beyond Religious Freedom: The New Global Politics of Religion* (Princeton, NJ: Princeton University Press, 2015).

44. Samuel Smith, "Would Eliminating State Dept. Office of Religion and Global Affairs Be a Big Deal?," *Christian Post*, June 16, 2017.

45. Stav Ziv, "Rex Tillerson: Anti-Semitism Could Get Worse with a State Department Special Envoy," *Newsweek*, June 15, 2017. The Trump Administration did eventually appoint Special Envoy to Monitor and Combat Antisemitism Elan Carr, after the position sat vacant for two years.

46. Ziv, "Rex Tillerson."

47. Shaun Casey, *Chasing the Devil at Foggy Bottom: The Future of Religion in American Diplomacy* (Grand Rapids, MI: William B. Eerdmans, 2023), 297.

48. Smith, "Would Eliminating State Dept. Office of Religion and Global Affairs Be a Big Deal?"

49. John J. DiIulio, *Godly Republic: A Centrist Blueprint for America's Faith-Based Future: A Former White House Official Explodes Ten Polarizing Myths About Religion and Government in America Today* (Oakland, CA: University of California Press, 2007).

50. David T. Buckley, Steven Brooke, and Bryce Kleinsteuber, "How Populists Engage Religion: Mechanisms and Evidence from the Philippines," *Democratization* 29, no. 8: 1455–75.

51. "Iraq Prelate Backs Preference for Minority Religious Fleeing Genocide," *Crux*, February 2, 2017.

52. Mike Pence, "Remarks by the Vice President at the 'In Defense of Christians' Solidarity Dinner," Remarks, Washington, D.C., October 25, 2017, https://www.presidency.ucsb.edu/documents/remarks-the-vice-president-the-defense-christians-solidarity-dinner.

53. Donald Trump, "Remarks by President Trump at Values Voter Summit," Remarks, Washington, D.C., October 12, 2019, https://trumpwhitehouse.archives.gov/briefings-statements/remarks-president-trump-values-voter-summit/.

54. See the Genocide Recovery and Persecution Response Initiative homepage, https://2017-2020.usaid.gov/iraq/genocide-recovery-and-persecution-response.

55. See discussion related to USAID and funding of religious charities in Gregorio Bettiza, *Finding Faith in Foreign Policy: Religion and American Diplomacy in a Postsecular World* (Oxford: Oxford University Press, 2019), 111.

56. Yeganeh Torbati, "How Mike Pence's Office Meddled in Foreign Aid to Reroute Money to Favored Christian Groups," *ProPublica*, November 6, 2019.

57. Stephen Rasche, "Testimony to the Subcommittee on Africa, Global Health, Global Human Rights, and International Organizations," U.S. House of Representatives, October 3, 2017.

58. Mark Green, "Help is On the Way for Middle Eastern Christians," *Wall Street Journal*, June 13, 2018.

59. "ADS Chapter 303 Grants and Cooperative Agreements to Non-Governmental Organizations," U.S. Agency for International Development, December 23, 2019, https://www.usaid.gov/sites/default/agency-policy/303.pdf.

60. For reporting on this personnel change, see Emily Tamkin, "Here's What Happened to a USAID Official Who Ran Afoul of Mike Pence," *Buzz Feed News*, September 18, 2018.

61. Torbati, "How Mike Pence's Office Meddled."

62. Pence, "Remarks by the Vice President at the 'In Defense of Christians' Solidarity Dinner."

63. Jessica Donati and Nicholas Peter, "Pence Takes on Big Role in Foreign Policy—Vice President's Efforts are Backed by Evangelicals, a Key Trump Constituency," *Wall Street Journal*, February 20, 2018.

64. Max Primorac, "U.S. Agency for International Development Special Representative for Minority Assistance Programs in Iraq Max Primorac Interview with EWTN,"

Interview, Washington, D.C., November 8, 2018, https://2017-2020.usaid.gov/news -information/press-releases/nov-9-2018-special-representative-minority-assistance -iraq-interview-ewtn.

65. John Hudson, "Ex-Palin Aid Lands Job at Trump's State Department," *Foreign Policy*, February 9, 2017.

66. Adelle Banks, "Still No Sign of Leader for White House Faith Partnership Office," *Religion News Service*, March 31, 2017.

67. Art Moore, "Trump Faith Adviser: We're in 'Heart' of Policy Conversations," *WND*, February 27, 2018.

68. Moore, "Trump Faith Adviser."

69. Lori Johnston, "Trump's Evangelical Advisory Board Violates the Law, Advocacy Group Argues in New Filing," *Washington Post*, August 30, 2018.

70. Executive Order No. 13831. 85 Federal Register 2889. May 3, 2018.

71. Chris Mitchell, "Egyptian President Meeting with US Evangelicals 'Prophetic' and 'Historic,' " *Christian Broadcasting Network*, November 3, 2017.

72. Michelle Boorstein, "Trump's Evangelical Advisers Meet with Saudi Crown Prince and Discuss Jamal Khashoggi's Murder, 'Human Rights,' Spokesman Says," *Washington Post*, November 2, 2018.

73. Matthias Schwartz, "Acts of the Apostle," *New York Times Magazine*, November 3, 2019. These activities explicitly feed into the personalistic interests of the religious elites empowered by the populist leader. Ralph Drollinger has two dozen international scripture study groups mirroring his effort in the United States, with "most of them established since Trump's election." Similarly, the evangelical diplomatic initiatives to Egypt and Saudi Arabia involved open discussions of expanding evangelical access to those religiously restricted societies.

74. Samuel Smith, "US Evangelical Leaders Met, Prayed with Brazil's Conservative President Bolsonaro," *Christian Post*, March 22, 2019.

75. Matt Korade, Kevin Bohn, and Daniel Burke, "Controversial US Pastors Take Part in Jerusalem Embassy Opening," *CNN*, May 14, 2018.

76. Barak Ravid, "White House Working to Reassure Evangelicals on Middle East Peace Plan," *AXIOS*, March 9, 2019.

77. Michelle Kosinski and Jennifer Hansler, "State Department Bars Press Corps from Pompeo Briefing, Won't Release List of Attendees," *CNN*, March 20, 2019.

78. Kathryn Joyce, "The Christianization of U.S. Foreign Policy," *The New Republic*, September 28, 2023.

79. Some growth in IRF's capacity was owed to congressional action that predated Trump's populism, such as the Wolf International Religious Freedom Act of 2016's provisions related to IRF training by State Department staff. Even in the realm of training, however, the Trump administration took action to expand capacity, such as funding directives under Executive Order No. 13926. 85 Federal Register 34951. June 2, 2020.

80. See Pompeo's remarks, Michael Pompeo, "Secretary of State Michael R. Pompeo at the Release of the 2018 Annual Report on International Religious Freedom," Remarks, United States Department of State, December 1, 2020, https://2017-2021.state.gov

/secretary-of-state-michael-r-pompeo-at-the-release-of-the-2018-annual-report-on
-international-religious-freedom/.

81. Pompeo, "Secretary of State Michael R. Pompeo at the Release of the 2018 Annual
Report on International Religious Freedom."

82. Donald Trump, "Remarks by President Trump at the United Nations Event on Religious Freedom," Remarks, UN Headquarters, New York, September 23, 2019, https://
trumpwhitehouse.archives.gov/briefings-statements/remarks-president-trump
-united-nations-event-religious-freedom-new-york-ny/.

83. Noah Bookbinder, "Re: Enforcement of the Hatch Act Against Presidential Appointees," *Citizens for Responsibility and Ethics in Washington*, August 23, 2019, https://www
.citizensforethics.org/wp-content/uploads/legacy/2019/08/OSC-Hatch-Act
-enforcement-MSPB-8-23-19-FINAL.pdf; Yeganeh Torbati, "It's Illegal for Federal Officials to Campaign at Work. A Trump Official Just Did So," *ProPublica*, March 2, 2020.

84. Dan Friedman, "How Jay Sekulow Got Involved in US Foreign Policy," *Mother Jones*,
October 24, 2019.

85. Video of the exchange can be found here, Stavros Agorakis, "Donald Trump Asks
Andrew Brunson and His Wife Who They Voted For," *Vox*, October 13, 2018.

86. Notice 10777, 84 Federal Register 25109, May 30, 2019.

87. Rebecca Hamilton, "Draft Charter of Pompeo's 'Commission on Unalienable Rights'
Hides Anti-Human Rights Agenda," *Just Security*, March 12, 2020.

88. Hamilton, "Draft Charter."

89. Michael Pompeo, "Secretary of State Michael R. Pompeo Remarks to the Press,"
Remarks, Washington, D.C., Department of State, July 8, 2019, https://2017-2021
-translations.state.gov/2019/07/08/secretary-of-state-michael-r-pompeo-remarks-to
-the-press-7/.

90. Robert Menendez et al., "Letter to Secretary Michael Pompeo," United States Senate,
July 23, 2019, https://www.foreign.senate.gov/imo/media/doc/07-23-19%20Dems%20
letter%20re%20Commission%20on%20Unalienable%20Rights.pdf.

91. Menendez et al., "Letter to Secretary Michael Pompeo."

92. Jayne Huckerby and Sarah Knuckey, "Pompeo's 'Rights Commission' is Worse Than
Feared: Part 1," *Just Security*, March 13, 2020.

93. Commission on Unalienable Rights, "Draft Report of the Commission on Unalienable
Rights," U.S. Department of State, July 2020, https://www.state.gov/wp-content/uploads
/2020/07/Draft-Report-of-the-Commission-on-Unalienable-Rights.pdf.

94. Commission on Unalienable Rights, "Draft Report of the Commission on Unalienable
Rights," 49.

95. Kirk A. Hawkins, "Is Chávez Populist? Measuring Populist Discourse in Comparative
Perspective," *Comparative Political Studies* 42, no. 8 (2009): 1040–1067; Margaret Canovan, "Trust the People!" 2–16; Benjamin Moffitt and Simon Tormey, "Rethinking Populism: Politics, Mediatisation and Political Style," *Political Studies* 62, no. 2 (2014): 381–97.

96. Moffitt and Tormey, "Rethinking Populism," 392.

97. Hurd, *Beyond Religious Freedom*, 8; Bettiza, *Finding Faith in Foreign Policy*, 22.

98. Donald Trump, "President Trump's Speech to the Arab Islamic American Summit," Remarks, Saudi Arabia, May 21, 2017, https://trumpwhitehouse.archives.gov/briefings -statements/president-trumps-speech-arab-islamic-american-summit/.

99. Office of International Religious Freedom, "2019 Ministerial to Advance Religious Freedom," U.S. Department of State, December 1, 2020, https://2017-2021.state.gov/2019 -ministerial-to-advance-religious-freedom/index.html.

100. Office of International Religious Freedom, "2019 Ministerial to Advance Religious Freedom."

101. "President Donald J. Trump Signs H.R. 390-Iraq and Syria Genocide Relief and Accountability Act," December 12, 2018, https://www.flickr.com/photos/whitehouse45 /45565832834/in/photostream/.

102. Canovan, "Trust the People!," 6.

103. Hurd, *Beyond Religious Freedom*, 8.

104. Bettiza, *Finding Faith in Foreign Policy*, 34.

105. Hurd, *Beyond Religious Freedom*, 8.

106. See for example, James R. Edwards Jr., "Religious Agencies and Refugee Resettlement," *Center for Immigration Studies*, March 16, 2012, https://cis.org/Religious-Agencies-and -Refugee-Resettlement.

5. FAITH IN A DEEP STATE? BUREAUCRATIC PRESERVATION IN A POPULIST TRANSITION

1. See for example, Jean-Pierre Filiu, *From Deep State to Islamic State: The Arab Counter-Revolution and Its Jihadi Legacy* (New York: Oxford University Press, 2015).

2. Daniel W. Drezner, "Ideas, Bureaucratic Politics, and the Crafting of Foreign Policy," *American Journal of Political Science* 44, no. 4 (2000): 736.

3. Jon D. Michaels, "Trump and the Deep State: The Government Strikes Back," *Foreign Affairs* 96, no. 5 (2017): 52–56.

4. Abby Phillip, "Spicer: Diplomats Opposed to Immigrations Ban Should 'Either Get with the Program or They Can Go,'" *Washington Post*, November 26, 2021.

5. See Jon D. Michaels, "The American Deep State Symposium: Administrative Lawmaking in the Twenty-First Century," *Notre Dame Law Review* 93, no. 4 (2017): 1653–70, for a more extended discussion of the inconsistencies between the American bureaucracy and true deep states.

6. The bureaucratic politics literature is vast, including classics of international relations and foreign policy analysis. A full review is beyond the scope of this work, but for a classic treatment see Graham T. Allison and Morton H. Halperin, "Bureaucratic Politics: A Paradigm and Some Policy Implications," *World Politics: A Quarterly Journal of International Relations* 24, no. 2 (1972): 40–79.

7. Drezner, "Ideas, Bureaucratic Politics," 735.

8. Drezner, "Ideas, Bureaucratic Politics," 735.

9. Albert O. Hirschman, *Exit, Voice, and Loyalty: Responses to Decline in Firms, Organizations, and States* (Cambridge, MA: Harvard University Press, 1970).

10. Marissa Martino Golden, *What Motivates Bureaucrats? Politics and Administration During the Reagan Years* (New York: Columbia University Press, 2000), 17.

11. Golden, *What Motivates Bureaucrats?* 17.

12. Golden, *What Motivates Bureaucrats?* 18.

13. Drezner, "Ideas, Bureaucratic Politics," 738.

14. For a journalistic summary of exit in offices related to combatting climate change, for example, see Jean Chemnick, "Depleted Climate Staff 'in Limbo' as Agency Reshuffles," *Politico*, December 10, 2021.

15. Niyi Bello, "When Nigeria's Anti-Graft War Gets U.S. Support," *The Guardian* (Nigeria), July 18, 2017.

16. While not a partisan event, or one focused solely on foreign policy, the National Prayer Breakfast has a long history of ties to elite evangelical circles and draws a large international attendance, thus raising its salience for foreign policy. President Trump personally addressed the 2017 breakfast in the opening weeks of his administration and used the address to raise several concerns about international religious freedom as well as typical campaign-style remarks about terrorism and migration. See the text of those remarks at: Donald Trump, "Remarks by President Trump at National Prayer Breakfast," Remarks, Washington, D.C., February 2, 2017, https://trumpwhitehouse.archives .gov/briefings-statements/remarks-president-trump-national-prayer-breakfast/.

17. See for instance, this 2013 reporting on the role of faith-based organizations in combatting trafficking in Cambodia, https://berkleycenter.georgetown.edu/events/faith -efforts-against-human-trafficking-in-cambodia. It is worth noting that the report documents occasional controversies raised by the presence of faith-based organizations in this work.

18. "President Donald J. Trump is Working to End Human Trafficking," March 13, 2018, https://trumpwhitehouse.archives.gov/briefings-statements/president-donald-j -trump-working-end-human-trafficking/.

19. "IOM to Expand Counter Trafficking Ties with Indonesian Muslim Women's Group," *International Organization for Migration*, November 13, 2006, https://www.iom.int /news/iom-expand-counter-trafficking-ties-indonesian-muslim-womens-group; Lauren Seibert, "These Children Don't Belong in the Streets," *Human Rights Watch*, March 28, 2023, https://www.hrw.org/report/2019/12/16/these-children-dont-belong -streets/roadmap-ending-exploitation-abuse-talibes.

20. "US-Ghana Partnership to Tackle Child Slavery," *Anglican Communion News Service*, August 24, 2016.

21. "U.S. State Department Honors Nun as Anti-Trafficking 'Hero,' " *Our Sunday Visitor*, May 18, 2022.

22. Samuel Smith, "Would Eliminating State Dept. Office of Religion and Global Affairs Be a Big Deal?," *Christian Post*, June 16, 2017.

23. Elizabeth Shakman Hurd. *Beyond Religious Freedom: The New Global Politics of Religion* (Princeton, NJ: Princeton University Press, 2015).

24. Executive Order No. 13769, 82 Federal Register 8977, January 27, 2017.

25. Jessica Taylor, "Trump Calls For 'Total and Complete Shutdown of Muslims Entering' U.S.," *NPR*, December 7, 2015.

26. See the detailed chapter on RGA's early work related to refugee resettlement in Shaun Casey, *Chasing the Devil at Foggy Bottom: The Future of Religion in American Diplomacy* (Grand Rapids, MI: William B. Eerdmans, 2023), chapter 6.

27. United States Department of State, "Alternatives to Closing Doors in Order to Secure Our Borders," Dissent Channel, https://s3.documentcloud.org/documents/3438487/Dissent-Memo.pdf.

28. Shakira Dale, "HIAS v. Trump–Why We're Suing," *HIAS*, December 6, 2022, https://www.hias.org/blog/hias-v-trump-why-were-suing.

29. Daniel Burke, "100 Evangelical Leaders Sign Ad Denouncing Trump's Refugee Ban," *CNN*, February 8, 2017.

30. Rhina Guidos, "Tillerson Meets with Bishop Cantu to Discuss Immigration, Middle East and Africa," *America*, March 24, 2017.

31. Yeganeh Torbati, "Exclusive: Tillerson Declines to Host Ramadan Event at State Department," Reuters, May 26, 2017.

32. Callum Borchers and Amber Phillips, "Transcript: President Trump's Remarks on Leaving the Paris Climate Deal, Annotated," *Washington Post,* November 25, 2021.

33. John Kerry, "Remarks at the Launch of the Office of Faith-Based Community Initiatives," Remarks, Washington, D.C., August 7, 2013. https://2009-2017.state.gov/secretary/remarks/2013/08/212781.htm.

34. Perhaps surprisingly, a network of faith-based organizations was very active in the formation of U.S. involvement in the Green Climate Fund, particularly in Capitol Hill lobbying on the issue. https://www.devex.com/news/how-faith-based-groups-secured-global-climate-funds-91904.

35. Robert Jeffress: "The president is brilliant for deciding to skip attending a session on an imaginary crisis—climate change—and instead he chose to lead his own conference on a very real problem, global religious persecution," Twitter post, September 24, 2019, 8:31 p.m., https://twitter.com/robertjeffress/status/1176655397958115329.

36. Nahal Toosi, "White House Slap at Dissenting Diplomats Sparks Fear of Reprisal," *Politico*, January 30, 2017.

37. Drezner, "Ideas, Bureaucratic Politics," 736.

38. Peter Mandaville and Chris Seiple, "Advancing Global Peace and Security Through Religious Engagement: Lessons to Improve U.S. Policy" (Washington, D.C.: United States Institute of Peace, 2021), https://www.usip.org/publications/2021/11/advancing-global-peace-and-security-through-religious-engagement-lessons.

6. SALVATION IN INSTITUTIONS? AMERICAN SECULARISM, EXECUTIVE POWER, AND POPULIST CHANGE

1. Kurt Weyland and Raúl L Madrid, *When Democracy Trumps Populism: European and Latin American Lessons for the United States* (New York: Cambridge University Press, 2019), 2–3.

2. James Mahoney and Kathleen Thelen, *Explaining Institutional Change: Ambiguity, Agency, and Power* (New York: Cambridge University Press, 2010), 14.

3. Michael W. McConnell, "Accommodation of Religion," *The Supreme Court Review* 1985 (1985): 1–59.

4 Weyland and Madrid, *When Democracy Trumps Populism*, 154.

5. Mahoney and Thelen, *Explaining Institutional Change*, 19.

6. James Mahoney, "Path Dependence in Historical Sociology," *Theory and Society* 29, no. 4 (August 2000): 507–48.

7. Paul Pierson, "Increasing Returns, Path Dependence, and the Study of Politics," *American Political Science Review* 94, no. 2 (June 2000): 251–67.

8. Weyland and Madrid, *When Democracy Trumps Populism*, 154–55.

9. Robert R. Kaufman and Stephan Haggard, "Democratic Decline in the United States: What Can We Learn from Middle-Income Backsliding?," *Perspectives on Politics* 17, no. 2 (October 2018): 12.

10. Robert Mickey, Steven Levitsky, and Lucan Ahmad Way. "Is America Still Safe for Democracy: Why the United States Is in Danger of Backsliding," *Foreign Affairs* 96, no. 3 (2017): 29.

11. Robert C. Lieberman, Suzanne Mettler, Thomas B. Pepinsky, Kenneth M. Roberts, and Richard Valelly, "The Trump Presidency and American Democracy: A Historical Comparative Analysis." *Perspectives on Politics* 17, no. 2 (2018): 4.

12. Weyland and Madrid, *When Democracy Trumps Populism*, 158.

13. Jacob Hacker, "Privatizing Risk Without Privatizing the Welfare State: The Hidden Politics of Social Policy Retrenchment in the United States," *American Political Science Review* 98, no. 2 (2004): 243–60. Mahoney and Thelen, *Explaining Institutional Change*.

14. Ahmet T. Kuru, "Passive and Assertive Secularism," *World Politics* 59, no. 3 (2007): 568–94; Noah Feldman, *Divided by God: America's Church-State Problem—and What We Should Do About It* (New York: Farrar, Straus and Giroux, 2005).

15. Kent Greenawalt, *Religion and the Constitution, Vol. 2, Establishment and Fairness* (Princeton, NJ: Princeton University Press, 2009), 2.

16. Winnifred Fallers Sullivan, *The Impossibility of Religious Freedom* (Princeton, NJ: Princeton University Press, 2005).

17. Andrew R. Lewis, *The Rights Turn in Conservative Christian Politics: How Abortion Transformed the Culture Wars* (New York: Cambridge University Press, 2017).

18. James Goldgeier and Elizabeth N. Saunders, "The Unconstrained Presidency: Checks and Balances Eroded Long Before Trump Essays," *Foreign Affairs* 97, no. 5 (2018): 144–56. See also compelling evidence related to long-term limitations on both congressional and judicial oversight in Jasmine Farrier, *Constitutional Dysfunction on Trial: Congressional Lawsuits and the Separation of Powers* (Ithaca, NY: Cornell University Press, 2019).

19. Daniel W. Drezner. *The Toddler in Chief: What Donald Trump Teaches Us About the Modern Presidency* (Chicago: University of Chicago Press, 2020), 191.

20. Aaron Wildavsky, "The Two Presidencies," *Society* 35, no. 2 (1998): 23–31.

21. Paul E. Peterson, "The President's Dominance in Foreign Policy Making," *Political Science Quarterly* 109, no. 2 (1994): 215–34.

22. Linda L. Fowler, *Watchdogs on the Hill: The Decline of Congressional Oversight of U.S. Foreign Relations* (Princeton, NJ: Princeton University Press, 2015), 7.

23. Goldgeier and Saunders, "The Unconstrained Presidency," 151.

24. Kimi Lynn King and James Meernik, "The Supreme Court and the Powers of the Executive: The Adjudication of Foreign Policy," *Political Research Quarterly* 52, no. 4 (1999): 801.

25. Thomas M. Franck, "Courts and Foreign Policy," *Foreign Policy*, no. 83 (1991): 66–86.

26. For a more thoroughly typologized account, see Mahoney and Thelen, *Explaining Institutional Change*, 28–30.

27. Task Force on Religion and the Making of U.S. Foreign Policy, *Engaging Religious Communities Abroad: A New Imperative for U.S. Foreign Policy* (Chicago: Chicago Council on Global Affairs, 2010), 10.

28. Task Force on Religion and the Making of U.S. Foreign Policy, *Engaging Religious Communities Abroad*, 65.

29. Task Force on Religion and the Making of U.S. Foreign Policy, *Engaging Religious Communities Abroad*, 84.

30. Interagency Working Group on Faith-Based and Other Neighborhood Partnerships, "Report to the President: Recommendations of the Interagency Working Group on Faith-Based and Other Neighborhood Partnerships," April 2012, https://obamawhitehouse.archives.gov/sites/default/files/uploads/finalfaithbasedworkinggroupreport.pdf.

31. Religion and Foreign Policy Working Group, "Ensuring the Opportunity for Mutual Counsel and Collaboration," U.S. Department of State, October 16, 2012.

32. Office of Religion and Global Affairs, "U.S. Strategy on Religious Leader and Faith Community Engagement," U.S. Department of State, https://2009-2017.state.gov/s/rga/strategy/index.htm.

33. Executive Order No. 13559, 75 Federal Register 71319, November 17, 2010.

34. Melissa Rogers, "Remarks at the Launch of the Office of Faith-Based Community Initiatives," Remarks, Washington, D.C., August 7, 2013, https://2009-2017.state.gov/secretary/remarks/2013/08/212781.htm.

35. Rogers, "Remarks at the Launch of the Office of Faith-Based Community Initiatives."

36. John Kerry, "Remarks at the Launch of the Office of Faith-Based Community Initiatives," Remarks, Washington, D.C., August 7, 2013, https://2009-2017.state.gov/secretary/remarks/2013/08/212781.htm.

37. Office of Religion and Global Affairs, "Religion and Diplomacy: A Practical Handbook," U.S. Department of State (2017), 15.

38. The Supreme Court seems to have finally dispensed with *Lemon* entirely in its *Kennedy vs. Bremerton School District* decision in 2022.

39. Office of Religion and Global Affairs, "Religion and Diplomacy: A Practical Handbook," 15.

40. Donald Trump, "Donald Trump On Tim Kaine, Muslim Ban, Taxes, Roger Ailes," *Meet the Press*, NBC News, July 24, 2016, https://www.youtube.com/watch?v=YbvIeHC3ueU&t=452s.

41. Lori Johnston, "Trump's Evangelical Advisory Board Violates the Law, Advocacy Group Argues in New Filing," *Washington Post*, August 30, 2018.

42. Johnston, "Trump's Evangelical Advisory Board Violates the Law."

43. For ProPublica's extensive reporting on this episode, see Yeganah Torbati, "How Mike Pence's Office Meddled in Foreign Aid to Reroute Money to Favored Christian Groups," *ProPublica*, November 6, 2019.

44. Compare initial language in https://s3.documentcloud.org/documents/3416383/Trump-EO-Draft-on-Refugees.pdf with the eventual text of the executive order from January 27 at Executive Order No. 13769, 82 Federal Register 8977, January 27, 2017.

45. Executive Order No. 13769, 82 Federal Register 8977, January 27, 2017.

46. Rebecca Savransky, "Giuliani: Trump Asked Me How to do a Muslim Ban 'Legally,' " *The Hill*, January 29, 2017.

47. Aziz et al. v. Donald Trump, 234 F. Supp. 3d 724 (E.D. Va. 2017) at 13.

48. Aziz, 234 F. Supp. 3d at 15.

49. Aziz, 234 F. Supp. 3d at 17.

50. Aziz, 234 F. Supp. 3d at 21.

51. State of Washington v. Trump, 847 F.3d 1151 (9th Cir. 2017) at 18.

52. International Refugee Assistance Project v. Trump, 883 F. 3d 233 (4th Cir. 2018) at 28.

53. Sabrina Siddiqui, "Meet Stephen Miller, Architect of First Travel Ban, Whose Words May Haunt Him," *The Guardian* (UK), January 7, 2021.

54. Trump, President of the United States, v. Hawaii, 17 U.S. 965 (2018) at 2.

55. Trump v. Hawaii, 17-965 U.S. at 18.

56. "Transcript: Oral Argument in Trump v. Hawaii," U.S. Supreme Court, April 25, 2018, https://www.supremecourt.gov/oral_arguments/argument_transcripts/2017/17-965_l5gm.pdf.

57. "Transcript: Oral Argument in Trump v. Hawaii."

58. Trump v. Hawaii, 17-965 U.S. at 2.

59. Trump v. Hawaii, 17-965 U.S. at 3.

60. Trump v. Hawaii, 17-965 U.S. at 17.

61. Trump v. Hawaii, 17-965 U.S. at 29.

62. Trump v. Hawaii, 17-965 U.S. at 32.

63. Trump v. Hawaii, 17-965 U.S. at 7.

64. Trump v. Hawaii, 17-965 U.S. at 12.

65. Mahoney and Thelen, *Explaining Institutional Change*, 19.

66. "Global Anti-Semitism Review Act of 2004," Public Law No. 108-332, 118 Stat. 1282 (2004).

67. For the act's legislative history, see "Summary of S.2292 - Global Anti-Semitism Review Act of 2004," https://www.congress.gov/bill/108th-congress/senate-bill/2292.

68. Stav Ziv, "Rex Tillerson: Anti-Semitism Could Get Worse with a State Department Special Envoy," *Newsweek*, June 15, 2017.

69. Committee on Foreign Affairs, "Hearing on the FY 2018 Foreign Affairs Budget," U.S. House of Representatives, 115th Congress, June 14, 2017, https://www.govinfo.gov /content/pkg/CHRG-115hhrg25840/pdf/CHRG-115hhrg25840.pdf.

70. Robert Corker, "Corker Statement on State Department Special Envoy Changes," United States Senate Committee on Foreign Relations, August 28, 2017, https://www.foreign .senate.gov/press/rep/release/corker-statement-on-state-department-special-envoy -changes.

71. "Special Envoy to Monitor and Combat Anti-Semitism Act," Public Law No. 116-326, 134 Stat. 5095 (2021).

72. Mahoney and Thelen, *Explaining Institutional Change*, 25.

73. See for example Mark Hosenball, "Trump Administration Debates Designating Muslim Brotherhood as Terrorist Group," Reuters, January 29, 2017.

74. Committee on Foreign Relations, "Hearing Regarding Nomination of Rex Tillerson to be Secretary of State," United States Senate, January 11, 2017, https://www.congress.gov /event/115th-congress/senate-event/LC46421/text.

75. For one version of this legislation, which was introduced several times by Senator Ted Cruz, see "Muslim Brotherhood Terrorist Designation Act of 2017," S.B. 68, 115th Cong. (2017).

76. Peter Baker, "White House Weighs Terrorist Designation for Muslim Brotherhood," *New York Times*, February 7, 2017.

77. See People's Mojahedin Organization of Iran v. United States Department of State, 182 F.3d 17 (D.C. Cir. 1999) for one decision related to the PMOI's extensive legal contestation of the FTO designation.

78. For a detailed listing of the FTO designation standards and their ramifications, see "Designated Foreign Terrorist Organizations," Bureau of Counterterrorism, https:// www.state.gov/foreign-terrorist-organizations/.

79. William McCants and Benjamin Wittes, "Should the Muslim Brotherhood be Designated a Terrorist Organization," *Lawfare*, January 27, 2017.

80. See for example, the majority's decision in Holder v. Humanitarian Law Project, United States Supreme Court, 561U.S. 1 (2010).

81. Mahoney and Thelen, *Explaining Institutional Change*, 20.

7. A FAITHFUL AUDIENCE? PUBLIC OPINION AND TRUMP'S RELIGIOUS FOREIGN POLICY

1. Robert D. Putnam and David E. Campbell, *American Grace: How Religion Divides and Unites Us* (New York: Simon & Schuster, 2010).

2. José Casanova, *Public Religion in the Modern World* (Chicago: University of Chicago Press, 1994); Robert N. Bellah, "Civil Religion in America," *Daedalus* 134, no. 4 (2005): 40–55.

3. Michael Hout and Claude S. Fischer, "Why More Americans Have No Religious Preference: Politics and Generations," *American Sociological Review* 67, no. 2 (2002):

165–90; David E. Campbell, Geoffrey C. Layman, and John C. Green, *Secular Surge: A New Fault Line in American Politics* (New York: Cambridge University Press, 2020).

4. See for one example, Gabriel Almond, *The American People and Foreign Policy* (New York: Harcourt Brace, 1950).

5. Robert D. Putnam, "Diplomacy and Domestic Politics: The Logic of Two-Level Games," *International Organization* 42, no. 3 (1988): 427–60; Joshua D. Kertzer and Ryan Brutger, "Decomposing Audience Costs: Bringing the Audience Back Into Audience Cost Theory," *American Journal of Political Science* 60, no. 1 (2016): 234–49.

6. Adam J. Berinsky, "Assuming the Costs of War: Events, Elites, and American Public Support for Military Conflict," *Journal of Politics* 69, no. 4 (2007): 975–97.

7. Kurt Weyland, "Populism: A Political-Strategic Approach," in *The Oxford Handbook of Populism*, eds. Cristóbal Kaltwasser et al. (Oxford: Oxford University Press, 2017), 48–72.

8. Benjamin Moffitt, *The Global Rise of Populism: Performance, Political Style, and Representation* (Stanford, CA: Stanford University Press, 2016),

9. See for example, Putnam and Campbell, *American Grace*.

10. For a primer on Christian nationalism, see Philip S Gorski, Samuel L Perry, and Jemar Tisby, *The Flag and the Cross: White Christian Nationalism and the Threat to American Democracy* (New York: Oxford University Press, 2022). For studies of the quantitative relationship between Christian nationalism and Trump voting, see Andrew L. Whitehead, Samuel L. Perry, and Joseph O. Baker, "Make America Christian Again: Christian Nationalism and Voting for Donald Trump in the 2016 Presidential Election," *Sociology of Religion* 79, no. 2 (2018): 147–71.

11. "More Americans, Especially White Evangelicals, Now Say Personal Immorality Not Disqualifying for Elected Officials," *Public Religion Research Institute*, October 19, 2016, https://www.prri.org/research/prri-brookings-oct-19-poll-politics-election-clinton-double-digit-lead-trump/.

12. Joshua D. Kertzer et al., "Moral Support: How Moral Values Shape Foreign Policy Attitudes," *The Journal of Politics* 76, no. 3 (2014): 825–40.

13. James L. Guth, "The Religious Roots of Foreign Policy Exceptionalism," *The Review of Faith & International Affairs* 10, no. 2 (2012): 77–85, and "Religion and American Public Opinion: Foreign Policy Issues," in *Oxford Handbook of Religion and American Politics*, eds. Corwin Smidt et al. (New York: Oxford University Press, 2017), 243–65.

14. Motti Inbari, Kirill M. Bumin, and M. Gordon Byrd, "Why Do Evangelicals Support Israel?," *Politics and Religion* 14, no. 1 (2020): 1–36.

15. Stephen Chaudoin, David Thomas Smith, and Johannes Urpelainen, "American Evangelicals and Domestic Versus International Climate Policy," *The Review of International Organizations* 9, no. 4 (December 1 2014): 441–69.

16. James L. Guth, "Are White Evangelicals Populists? The View from the 2016 American National Election Study," *The Review of Faith & International Affairs* 17, no. 3 (2019): 20–35.

17. Allyson F. Shortle and Ronald Keith Gaddie, "Religious Nationalism and Perceptions of Muslims and Islam," *Politics and Religion* 8, no. 3 (2015): 435–57; Eric L. McDaniel,

Irfan Nooruddin, and Allyson F. Shortle, *The Everyday Crusade: Christian National-ism in American Politics* (New York: Cambridge University Press, 2022).

18.   Miles T. Armaly, David T. Buckley, and Adam M. Enders, "Christian Nationalism and Political Violence: Victimhood, Racial Identity, Conspiracy, and Support for the Capitol Attacks," *Political Behavior* 44, no. 2 (2022): 937–60.

19.   Joshua D. Kertzer and Thomas Zeitzoff, "A Bottom-Up Theory of Public Opinion About Foreign Policy," *American Journal of Political Science* 61, no. 3 (2017): 543–58.

20.   David E. Campbell, John C. Green, and Geoffrey C. Layman, "The Party Faithful: Par-tisan Images, Candidate Religion, and the Electoral Impact of Party Identification," *American Journal of Political Science* 55, no. 1 (2011): 42–58.

21.   Weyland, "A Political-Strategic Approach."

22.   Anna Grzymała-Busse, *Nations Under God: How Churches Use Moral Authority to Influence Policy* (Princeton, NJ: Princeton University Press, 2015).

23.   Tom Inglis, *Moral Monopoly: The Rise and Fall of the Catholic Church in Modern Ireland* (Dublin: University College Dublin Press, 1998).

24.   Inglis, *Moral Monopoly*, 39.

25.   David T. Buckley, "Demanding the Divine? Explaining Cross-National Support for Clerical Control of Politics," *Comparative Political Studies* 49, no. 3 (2016): 357–90.

26.   David T. Buckley, "Religious Elite Cues, Internal Division, and the Impact of Pope Francis' Laudato Si." *Politics and Religion* (2020): 1–33.

27.   Hout and Fischer, "Why More Americans Have No Religious Preference"; Campbell, Layman, and Green, *Secular Surge*.

28.   Michael Gerson, "Trump is Evangelicals' 'Dream President.' Here's Why." *Washington Post*, May 15, 2017.

29.   Ten minutes is also approximately the first decile mark.

30.   "2019 Pew Research Center American Trends Panel: Final Topline," Pew Research Group, February 2019, https://www.pewforum.org/wp-content/uploads/sites/7/2019/07/W44-Religious-Knowledge-TOPLINE-FOR-RELEASE-CHECK-COMPLETE.pdf.

31.   As a robustness check, the study also included a "feeling thermometer" for President Trump, from 0 (cold/negative) to 100 (warm/positive). Results described in the analy-sis section were entirely consistent irrespective of which indicator of Trump support was used as a dependent variable.

32.   See for example, "Lowest Opinion of Trump Among Voters in Seven Years, Quinnip-iac University National Poll Finds," *Quinnipiac University Poll*, December 14, 2022, https://poll.qu.edu/poll-release?releaseid=3863.

33.   Whitehead, Perry, and Baker, "Make America Christian Again"; Armaly, Buckley, and Enders, "Christian Nationalism and Political Violence."

34.   To be more specific, difference-of-means tests reveal no statistically significant differ-ences between treatment and control groups on the following covariates: sex, age, white-identification, Black-identification, Hispanic-identification, partisanship, political ideology, evangelical affiliation, religious attendance, or Christian nationalism.

35.   This is not just a hypothetical possibility. In the aftermath of FBI searches of Trump's Mar-a-Lago resort, several very high-profile Trump supporters in white evangelical

leadership positions rallied to his defense, including Franklin Graham, calling the search an indication that "As Americans, we are losing our freedoms," and another calling it "a federal abuse of power." See Michael Gryboski, " 'Deeply Disturbed': Conservative Evangelical Leaders Denounce FBI Raid on Trump Home," *Christian Post*, August 10, 2022.

36. See for example, Andrew Kohut et al., "More See 'Too Much' Religious Talk by Politicians" (Washington, D.C.: Pew Research Center, 2012), https://www.pewresearch.org/religion/2012/03/21/more-see-too-much-religious-talk-by-politicians/.

37. The statistical appendix contains more detailed regression results than summarized in the figures contained in this chapter. In this instance, Appendix Table 1 corresponds to the results visualized in figure 7.3.

38. Model 1 includes only the three religious covariates, while Model 2 adds standard demographic controls for sex, age, education, race and ethnicity, and region, and Model 3 adds political controls for party identification and political ideology.

39. See for example, Whitehead, Perry, and Baker, "Make America Christian Again." It is important to clarify that this is not to say that evangelical identification is not implicated in Trump's political base. Christian nationalism is highly correlated with white evangelical identification, so the ties between these variables and elements of Trump support, like hostility to government bureaucracy, are complex. For an overview of the links between Christian nationalism and various demographic measures including evangelical identification, see for one example Gorski, Perry, and Tisby, *The Flag and the Cross.*

40. This could also be seen as consistent with a study from the Democracy Study Group, which argued that more religious Trump voters were *less* enthusiastic supporters of some populist aspects of his presidency than less religious Trump voters. See Emily Ekins, "Religious Trump Voters: How Faith Moderates Attitudes about Immigration, Race, and Identity" (Washington, D.C.: Democracy and Voter Study Group, 2018), https://www.cato.org/public-opinion-brief/religious-trump-voters-how-faith-moderates-attitudes-about-immigration-race.

41. See Appendix Tables 2 and 3 for the quantitative models visualized in figure 7.4. For each independent variable of interest, Model 1 includes only the independent variable of interest with standard demographic controls, while Model 2 adds political controls, and Model 3 adds religious controls. Figure 7.4 presents Model 3 in each case.

42. To clarify, because of the direction of coding, a positive coefficient on the deep state index and a negative coefficient on the government employee feeling thermometer are substantively indicating the same relationship: increasing hostility to career government foreign policy institutions correlates to increased support for President Trump in 2020.

43. An interactive model, not shown, confirms a significant interaction between Trump voting and treatment on the extremity in clergy moral authority indicator ($p < .01$).

44. Armaly, Buckley, and Enders, "Christian Nationalism and Political Violence"; McDaniel, Nooruddin, and Shortle, *The Everyday Crusade.*

45. Putnam and Campbell, *American Grace.*

8. FAITHFUL PARTNERS: RELIGIOUS POPULISM AND INTERNATIONAL TIES

1. For extended treatment of the concept of religious soft power in contemporary global order, see especially the research of Peter Mandaville and other contributors to the *Geopolitics of Religious Soft Power* project, convened through Georgetown University's Berkley Center for Religion, Peace, and World Affairs, https://berkleycenter.georgetown.edu/projects/the-geopolitics-of-religious-soft-power.

2. Peter S. Henne, "Reassembling the Social in the Study of Religion and International Relations," *International Studies Review* 25, no. 3 (2023): 1–18.

3. This chapter presents systematic evidence involving ties with Hungary, Poland, Brazil, Russia, and India. This is not to imply that these are the only cases that could provide evidence of international right-wing religious populist cooperation. They have been chosen because a certain subset (Hungary, Poland, and Brazil) provides comparatively easy tests, or what researchers sometimes consider "most likely cases" for such ties, while others (Russia and India) may have, ex ante, been expected to pose more obstacles to such cooperation.

4. Peter M. Haas, "Introduction: Epistemic Communities and International Policy Coordination," *International Organization* 46, no. 1 (1992): 1–35.

5. Elizabeth Shakman Hurd, *Beyond Religious Freedom: The New Global Politics of Religion* (Princeton, NJ: Princeton University Press, 2015), 10.

6. Gregorio Bettiza, *Finding Faith in Foreign Policy: Religion and American Diplomacy in a Postsecular World* (New York: Oxford University Press, 2019), 7.

7. See for instance Haas, "Introduction," or Emanuel Adler, "The Emergence of Cooperation: National Epistemic Communities and the International Evolution of the Idea of Nuclear Arms Control," *International Organization* 46, no. 1 (1992): 101–45.

8. Margaret E. Keck and Kathryn Sikkink, *Activists Beyond Borders: Advocacy Networks in International Politics* (Ithaca, NY: Cornell University Press, 1998).

9. Bettiza, *Finding Faith*, 10.

10. The specific title within the bureaucracy has changed over time, but the core office mission remains fairly similar. See "Special Rapporteur on Freedom of Religion or Belief," https://www.ohchr.org/en/special-procedures/sr-religion-or-belief.

11. For information on International Partnership on Religion and Sustainable Development (PaRD), see https://www.partner-religion-development.org/members/overview.

12. Shaun Casey, "Remarks at 'Religion and Diplomacy Conference,' " Remarks, U.S. Department of State, Washington, D.C., September 26–27, 2016.

13. Bettiza, *Finding Faith*, 201.

14. "Religion and Diplomacy: About," Transatlantic Policy Network on Religion and Diplomacy, https://religionanddiplomacy.org/about/.

15. For a list of the civil society delegation's participants, see Ron Bigler, "American Civil Rights Delegation to Urge OSCE Nations for Greater Hate Crimes Protections at Berlin Anti-Semitism Conference," November 10, 2014, https://civilrights.org/2014/11/10

/american-civil-rights-delegation-to-urge-osce-nations-for-greater-hate-crimes
-protections-at-berlin-anti-semitism-conference/.

16. This debate continues even among those deeply dedicated to combatting anti-Semitism. See for example, Ari Hoffman and Joel Swanson, "Debate: Should the Biden Administration Adopt the IHRA Definition of Antisemitism?," *Forward*, April 4, 2022.

17. See for example, the many cases highlighted in Nadia Marzouki, Duncan McDonnell, and Olivier Roy, *Saving the People: How Populists Hijack Religion* (New York: Oxford University Press, 2016).

18. For a more extended discussion of this quote and the broader role of Christian identity in Orbán's populism, see Zoltán Ádám and András Bozóki, "'The God of Hungarians': Religion and Right Wing Populism in Hungary," in *Saving the People: How Populists Hijack Religion*, eds. Nadia Marzouki, Duncan McDonnell, and Olivier Roy (New York: Oxford University Press, 2016), 129–47.

19. Éva Balogh, "Viktor Orbán and the 'Christian-National Idea,'" *Hungarian Spectrum*, September 22, 2015.

20. Benjamin Stanley, "Defenders of the Cross: Populist Politics and Religion in Post-Communist Poland," in *Saving the People*, 109–28.

21. Stanley, "Defenders of the Cross."

22. As with other cases, this pattern of cooperation pre-dated Trump's election. See Benjamin A. Cowan, *Moral Majorities Across the Americas: Brazil, the United States, and the Creation of the Religious Right* (Chapel Hill, NC: University of North Carolina Press, 2021).

23. Raimundo Barreto and João Chaves, "Christian Nationalism is Thriving in Bolsonaro's Brazil," *Christian Century*, November 18, 2021.

24. David Biller, "Facing Electoral Defeat, Brazil's President Wages Campaign for Evangelical Vote," *Associated Press*, September 27, 2022.

25. Matthew Karnitschnig, "Orbán Says Migrants Threaten 'Christian' Europe," *Politico*, September 3, 2015.

26. Shaun Walker, "Hungarian Leader Says Europe is Now 'Under Invasion' by Migrants," *The Guardian* (UK), March 15, 2018.

27. Walker, "Hungarian Leader."

28. For example, see reporting from Rob Picheta and Ivana Kottasová, "'You Don't Belong Here': In Poland's 'LGBT-Free Zones,' Existing is an Act of Defiance," *CNN*, October 2020.

29. Cristian González Cabrera, "'I Became Scared, This Was Their Goal': Efforts to Ban Gender and Sexuality Education in Brazil," *Human Rights Watch*, May 12, 2022, https://www.hrw.org/report/2022/05/12/i-became-scared-was-their-goal/efforts-ban-gender-and-sexuality-education-brazil.

30. Viktor Orbán, "Viktor Orbán's Full Speech for the Beginning of his Fourth Mandate," *Visegrad Post*, May 12, 2018, https://visegradpost.com/en/2018/05/12/viktor-orbans-full-speech-for-the-beginning-of-his-fourth-mandate/.

31. Edward Pentin, "Hungary Hosts First Ever Government Conference for Persecuted Christians," *National Catholic Register*, October 14, 2017.

32. Pentin, "Hungary Hosts."

33. Michael Igoe, "To Direct More Funding to Christians, USAID Looks to Hungary," *Devex*, November 25, 2019.

34. U.S. Embassy and Consulate in Poland, "Signing of Memorandum of Understanding Between USAID and the Government of Poland," U.S. Department of State, November 30, 2018, https://pl.usembassy.gov/mou_usaid/.

35. Igoe, "To Direct More Funding."

36. David Fahrenthold, "Far-Right Group Warning of Islamist Infiltration to Hold Banquet at Trump's Mar-a-Lago Club," *Washington Post*, November 22, 2019.

37. "Steven Bannon Endorses Far-Right Brazilian Presidential Candidate," Reuters, October 26, 2018.

38. Peter Montgomery, "Religious Right Excited by White House Visit of Brazil's President Jair Bolsonaro, 'Trump of the Tropics,' " *Right Wing Watch*, March 19, 2019.

39. Barreto and Chaves, "Christian Nationalism."

40. See for example, this tweet by Eduardo Bolsonaro, https://twitter.com/bolsonarosp/status/1232753457150484481.

41. See for example, Raphael Tsavkko Garcia, "Bolsonaro and Brazil Court the Global Far Right," *NACLA Report on the Americas*, August 21, 2019.

42. For a more detailed treatment of the history of the conservative family movement, internationally, see for example Clifford Bob, *The Global Right Wing and the Clash of World Politics* (New York: Cambridge University Press, 2012); Doris Buss, *Globalizing Family Values: The Christian Right in International Politics* (Minneapolis: University of Minnesota Press, 2003); Kristina Stoeckl and Dmitry Uzlaner, *The Moralist International*, eds. Papanikolaou Aristotle and M. Purpura Ashley (New York: Fordham University Press, 2022).

43. " 'Western Countries Stop Identifying Themselves with Christian Tradition'—Patriarch Kirill," *Interfax News Agency*, October 29, 2015, https://web.archive.org/web/20151030105246/http://www.interfax-religion.com/?act=news&div=12448.

44. Franklin Graham, "This week I am in Moscow . . ." Facebook post, October 28, 2015, https://www.facebook.com/FranklinGraham/posts/1032519610137553.

45. Metropolitan Hilarion of Volokolamsk, "Speech by Metropolitan Hilarion of Volokolamsk at the Forum of Representatives of the Russia-USA Forum of Christian Leaders," Remarks, November 2014, https://mospat.ru/en/news/50935/.

46. Hilarion, "Speech at the Forum."

47. Hilarion, "Speech at the Forum."

48. Hilarion, "Speech at the Forum."

49. Hilarion, "Speech at the Forum."

50. Metropolitan Hilarion of Volokolamsk, "Presentation by the DECR Chairman Metropolitan Hilarion of Volokolamsk at the World Summit in Defense of Persecuted Christians," Remarks, Washington, D.C., May 2017, https://mospat.ru/en/news/48514/.

51. Hilarion, "Presentation at the World Summit."

52. Hilarion, "Presentation at the World Summit."

53. Hilarion, "Presentation at the World Summit."

54. Hilarion, "Presentation at the World Summit."

55. Hilarion, "Presentation at the World Summit."

56. Hilarion, "Presentation at the World Summit."

57. For details, see for example Katherine Stewart, "What Was Maria Butina Doing at the National Prayer Breakfast," *New York Times*, July 18, 2018.

58. For a more comprehensive overview of Indian secularism and the rise of Hindu nationalism, see for example Sumit Ganguly, "The Crisis of Indian Secularism," *Journal of Democracy* 14, no. 4 (2003): 11–25; Rajeev Bhargava, *Secularism and Its Critics* (New York: Oxford University Press, 1998).

59. See, for example, Krutika Pathi, "India's Modi Faces No-Confidence Vote in Parliament," *The Diplomat*, August 7, 2023.

60. For an overview of India's Citizenship Law, see Jhalak Kakkar, "India's New Citizenship Law and its Anti-Secular Implications," *Lawfare*, January 16, 2020.

61. The Indian Citizenship Act's focus on only offering protections to minorities fleeing Muslim-majority countries directly mirrors early versions of Trump's Muslim Ban executive orders that provided protections to those claiming religious persecution in Muslim countries *only* if they came from religious minority communities. There is no evidence that the provisions influenced one another, but the affinity is striking.

62. "Citizenship Amendment Act is Good for Christians, Says National Commission for Minorities Vice-Chairman," *The Hindu* (India), December 17, 2019.

63. Anto Akkara, "Indian Cardinal Says Religion Should Never be Basis for Citizenship," *National Catholic Reporter*, December 27, 2019.

64. J. Lester Feder, "This is How Steve Bannon Sees the Entire World," *BuzzFeed News*, November 16, 2016.

65. "Outrage Over Right-Wing Euro-MPs' Kashmir Visit," *BBC News*, October 30, 2019.

66. Marzia Casolari, "Hindutva's Foreign Tie-Up in the 1930s: Archival Evidence," *Economic and Political Weekly* 35, no. 4 (2000): 218–28.

67. "Steve Bannon–The First US Politician to Speak Out in Support of the Abrogation of Articles 370 and 35A," *Republican Hindu Coalition*, August 15, 2019, https://rhc-usa.org/2019/08/steve-bannon-the-first-us-politician-to-speak-out-in-support-of-the-abrogation-of-articles-370-and-35a/.

68. "Republican Hindu Coalition Announces Full-Throated Support for Trump Administration Executive Order on Immigration," *Republic Hindu Coalition*, January 29, 2017, https://rhc-usa.org/2017/01/republican-hindu-coalition-announces-full-throated-support-for-trump-administration-executive-order-on-immigration/.

69. "Republican Hindu Coalition (RHC) Vice Chair & President Haribhai Patel Recently Traveled to Ahmedabad, India with a Handful of Indian Americans as Part of Trump's Official 'Namaste Trump' Delegation on February 24th, 2020, Hosted by Prime Minister Modi," *Republican Hindu Coalition*, February 24, 2020, https://rhc-usa.org/2020/02/republican-hindu-coalition-rhc-vice-chair-president-haribhai-patel-recently-traveled-to-ahmedabad-india-with-a-handful-of-indian-americans-as-part-of-president-trumps-official-n/.

70. Donald Trump, "Remarks by President Trump and Prime Minister Modi of India at 'Howdy, Modi: Shared Dreams, Bright Futures' Event," Remarks, Houston, TX, September 22, 2019, https://trumpwhitehouse.archives.gov/briefings-statements/remarks-president-trump-prime-minister-modi-india-howdy-modi-shared-dreams-bright-futures-event/.

71. Asawin Suebsaeng, "Inside Steve Bannon's Failed Breitbart India Scheme," *Daily Beast*, April 10, 2017.

72. Matias Pettula, "Prime Minister Modi in Houston," *International Christian Concern*, September 12, 2019, https://www.persecution.org/2019/09/12/prime-minister-modi-houston/.

73. "Noted Peace Maker, Dr. K.A. Paul, and Indian Prime Minister Narendra Modi Will Both Face Serious Questions During President Trump's Meeting with the Indian PM Next Week in Washington, DC," *Newswire*, June 21, 2017.

74. David Brennan, "Christian Persecution in India is 'Very Troubling' Franklin Graham Says, But Backs Trump Friendship with Modi," *Newsweek*, September 24, 2019.

75. Dinesh D'Souza, "I'm not an unqualified fan of Narendra Modi but his re-election in India is another affirmation . . ." Twitter post, May 23, 2019, 11:40 a.m., https://twitter.com/dineshdsouza/status/1131585647620157441?lang=en.

76. Secretary of State Michael Pompeo, "Secretary Pompeo's on India US Policy June 26, 2019," Remarks, New Delhi, India, June 26, 2019, https://www.youtube.com/watch?v=TycsbmBXnoQ.

77. Sumit Ganguly, *The Possibilities and Limits of India's New Religous Soft Power* (Washington, D.C.: Berkley Center for Religion, Peace, and World Affairs, 2020).

78. For a more extended consideration from the point of view of international relations theory, see for example Peter S. Henne, *The Geopolitics of Faith: Religious Soft Power in Russian and U.S. Foreign Policy* (Washington, D.C.: Berkley Center for Religion, Peace, and World Affairs, 2019).

79. "In the Matter of an Application for Criminal Complaint for Mariia Butina, Also Known as Maria Butina," United States District Court for the District of Columbia, July 2018, https://www.justice.gov/opa/press-release/file/1080766/download.

80. Cody Morgan, "Joint Statement from Franklin Graham and Metropolitan Hilarion," Billy Graham Evangelistic Association, May 13, 2017, https://media.billygraham.org/joint-statement-from-franklin-graham-and-metropolitan-hilarion/.

81. Sumitra Badrinathan, Devesh Kapur, and Milan Vaishnav, *How Will Indian Americans Vote? Results From the 2020 Indian American Attitudes Survey* (Washington, D.C.: Carnegie Endowment for International Peace, 2020).

82. Elizabeth Dwoskin and Gabriela Sá Pessoa, "Trump Aides Bannon, Miller Advising the Bolsonaros on Next Steps," *Washington Post*, November 23, 2022.

83. Franklin Graham, "Pray for President Putin today. This may sound like a strange request, but we need to pray that God would work in his heart . . ." Twitter post, February 18, 2022, 5:10 p.m. https://twitter.com/Franklin_Graham/status/1494796401779351558.

84. Yonat Shimron, "Franklin Graham Sends Disaster Response Teams to Europe; Says He Opposes War," *Religion News Service*, February 26, 2022.

85. Molly Olmstead, "Can the Christian Right Quit Putin?," *Slate Magazine*, March 8, 2022.

86. Eric Metaxas, "The American Deep State is inherently UN-American—and their treatment of Russia since 1991 . . ." Twitter post, February 25, 2022, 11:00 a.m., https://twitter.com/ericmetaxas/status/1497240130071011330.

87. "Steven Bannon Praises Putin's Speech About Ukraine: 'You Wouldn't Hear an American Politician Except for Donald Trump Do That,'" *Media Matters for America*, February 22, 2022, https://www.mediamatters.org/jack-posobiec/steve-bannon-praises-putins-speech-about-ukraine-you-wouldnt-hear-american-politician.

88. Taylor Orth, "On Russia and Putin, Opinions of Evangelical Christians Resemble Those of Americans Overall," *YouGov*, March 15, 2022, https://today.yougov.com/topics/politics/articles-reports/2022/03/15/russia-and-putin-opinions-evangelical-christians; Samuel L. Perry et al., "The Religious Right and Russia: Christian Nationalism and Americans' Views on Russia and Vladimir Putin Before and After the Ukrainian Invasion," *Journal for the Scientific Study of Religion* 62, no. 2 (2023): 439–50.

89. Alex Henderson, "Republican QAnon Supporter Praises Putin's Decision," *Salon*, March 5, 2022.

CONCLUSION: RELIGION AND FOREIGN POLICY AFTER POPULISM

1. Kurt Weyland and Raúl L. Madrid, *When Democracy Trumps Populism: European and Latin American Lessons for the United States* (New York: Cambridge University Press, 2019), 3.

2. Melissa Rogers and E. J. Dionne Jr., *A Time to Heal, A Time to Build* (Washington, D.C.: Brookings Institution, October 2020), https://www.brookings.edu/wp-content/uploads/2020/10/A_Time_to_Heal_report.pdf.

3. Rogers and Dionne, *A Time to Heal*, 17.

4. Joe Biden, "President Biden Announces Intent to Nominate and Appoint Leaders to Serve in Key Religious Affairs Roles," Remarks, White House, July 30, 2021.

5. USAID officially launched the policy guidance based on this consultation period in fall 2023.

6. Office of International Religious Freedom, "DRL FY20 IRF Promoting and Defending Religious Freedom Inclusive of Atheist, Humanist, Non-Practicing and Non-Affiliated Individuals," United States Department of State, April 21, 2021, https://www.state.gov/statements-of-interest-requests-for-proposals-and-notices-of-funding-opportunity/drl-fy20-irf-promoting-and-defending-religious-freedom-inclusive-of-atheist-humanist-non-practicing-and-non-affiliated-individuals/.

7. "DHS Announces New Members of Faith-Based Security Advisory Council," Department of Homeland Security, September 19, 2022, https://www.dhs.gov/news/2022/09/19/dhs-announces-new-members-faith-based-security-advisory-council.

8. Proclamation No. 10141, 86 Federal Register 7005, January 25, 2021.

9. Presidential Determination No. 2022-02, 86 Federal Register 57527, October 18, 2021. This increase in the refugee admission cap was not the sole result of the humanitarian crisis that accompanied the Taliban's takeover of Afghanistan in late summer 2021, as Biden increased the cap across regions of the world.

10. "FACT SHEET: Biden-Harris Administration Celebrates First Anniversary of the Reestablishment of the White House Office of Faith-Based and Neighborhood Partnerships," White House Briefing Room, February 14, 2022, https://www.whitehouse.gov /briefing-room/statements-releases/2022/02/14/fact-sheet-biden-harris-administration -celebrates-first-anniversary-of-the-reestablishment-of-the-white-house-office-of-faith -based-and-neighborhood-partnerships/.

11. Office of International Religious Freedom, "Functional Bureau Strategy," U.S. Department of State, December 20, 2021, https://www.state.gov/wp-content/uploads/2022/02 /IRF_FBS_FINAL_Public-Version.pdf.

12. Rogers and Dionne, *A Time to Heal*, 19.

13. Peter Mandaville and Julia Schiwal, "The U.S. Strategy for International Religious Engagement: 10 Years On" (Washington, D.C.: United States Institute of Peace, 2023).

14. Office of Faith and Opportunity Initiatives, "2020 Evidence Summit on Strategic Religious Engagement," U.S. Agency for International Development, August 2020, https:// www.usaid.gov/faith-and-opportunity-initiatives/2020-evidence-summit-strategic -religious-engagement.

15. Peter Mandaville has made this recommendation on several occasions, from the early months of the Trump administration to the first year of the Biden administration. See for example, Peter Mandaville, "The Future of Religion and U.S. Foreign Policy Under Trump," Brookings Institution, March 2017, https://www.brookings.edu/articles/the -future-of-religion-and-u-s-foreign-policy-under-trump/.

16. Douglas Johnston and Cynthia Sampson, *Religion, The Missing Dimension of Statecraft* (New York: Oxford University Press, 1994).

17. Miles T. Armaly, David T. Buckley, and Adam M. Enders, "Christian Nationalism and Political Violence: Victimhood, Racial Identity, Conspiracy, and Support for the Capitol Attacks," *Political Behavior* 44, no. 2 (2022): 937–60.

18. Michael Hout and Claude S. Fischer, "Why More Americans Have No Religious Preference: Politics and Generations," *American Sociological Review* 67, no. 2 (April 2002): 165–90.

BIBLIOGRAPHY

Abutaleb, Yasmeen, and Joseph Tanfani. "As Trump Rewrites Public Health Rules, Pence Sees Conservative Agenda Born Again." *Reuters*, May 30, 2019.

Ádám, Zoltán, and András Bozóki. "'The God of Hungarians': Religion and Right-Wing Populism in Hungary." In *Saving the People: How Populists Hijack Religion*, ed. Nadia Marzouki, Duncan McDonnell, and Olivier Roy, 129–47. New York: Oxford University Press, 2016.

Adler, Emanuel. "The Emergence of Cooperation: National Epistemic Communities and the International Evolution of the Idea of Nuclear Arms Control." *International Organization* 46, no. 1 (1992): 101–45.

Agorakis, Stavros. "Donald Trump Asks Andrew Brunson and His Wife Who They Voted For." *Vox*. October 13, 2018.

Ainsley, Julia Edwards, Dustin Volz, and Kristina Cooke. "Trump to Focus Counter-Extremism Program Solely on Islam—Sources." *Reuters*, February 1, 2017.

Akkara, Anto. "Indian Cardinal Says Religion Should Never Be Basis for Citizenship." *National Catholic Reporter*, December 27, 2019.

Al-Rahim, Ahmed et al. "Engaging Religion at the Department of State." Social Science Research Council. September 26, 2019. https://tif.ssrc.org/2013/07/30/engaging-religion-at -the-department-of-state/.

Albertazzi, Daniele, and Duncan McDonnell. *Populists in Power.* London: Routledge, 2015.

Allison, Graham T., and Morton H. Halperin. "Bureaucratic Politics: A Paradigm and Some Policy Implications." *World Politics: A Quarterly Journal of International Relations* 24, no. 2 (1972): 40–79.

Allison, Graham T., and Philip Zelikow. *Essence of Decision: Explaining the Cuban Missile Crisis.* Boston: Little, Brown, 1971.

Almond, Gabriel Abraham. *The American People and Foreign Policy*. New York: Harcourt Brace, 1950.

Amstutz, Mark R. *Evangelicals and American Foreign Policy*. New York: Oxford University Press, 2014.

Appleby, R. Scott, Richard Cizik, and Thomas Wright. *Engaging Religious Communities Abroad: A New Imperative for U.S. Foreign Policy*. Chicago: Chicago Council on Global Affairs, 2010.

Arato, Andrew, and Jean L. Cohen. "Civil Society, Populism, and Religion." *Routledge Handbook of Global Populism*. New York: Routledge, 2018.

Arkin, Fatima. "How Faith-Based Groups Secured Global Climate Funds," *Devex*, May 25, 2020. https://www.devex.com/news/how-faith-based-groups-secured-global-climate-funds-91904.

Armaly, Miles T., David T. Buckley, and Adam M. Enders. "Christian Nationalism and Political Violence: Victimhood, Racial Identity, Conspiracy, and Support for the Capitol Attacks." *Political Behavior* 44, no. 2 (2022): 937–60.

Asad, Talal. *Formations of the Secular: Christianity, Islam, Modernity* (Cultural Memory in the Present). Stanford, CA: Stanford University Press, 2003.

Aydin, Cemil. *The Idea of the Muslim World: A Global Intellectual History*. Cambridge, MA: Harvard University Press, 2017.

Badrinathan, Sumitra, Devesh Kapur, and Milan Vaishnav. *How Will Indian Americans Vote? Results From the 2020 Indian American Attitudes Survey*. Washington, D.C.: Carnegie Endowment for International Peace. October 2020. https://carnegieendowment.org/files/2020-IAAS_full_final.pdf.

Bailey, Sarah Pulliam. "Trump's Statement on Ramadan Is Almost Entirely About Terrorism." *Washington Post*, October 27, 2021.

Balogh, Eva S. "Viktor Orbán and the 'Christian-National Idea.' " *Hungarian Spectrum*, September 22, 2015. https://web.archive.org/web/20150923091727/https://hungarianspectrum.org/2015/09/22/viktor-orban-and-the-christian-national-idea/.

Banks, Adelle. "Still No Sign of Leader for White House Faith Partnership Office." *Religion News Service*, March 31, 2017.

Barr, Robert R. "Populists, Outsiders and Anti-Establishment Politics." *Party Politics* 15, no. 1 (2009): 29–48.

Barr, William. "Remarks to the Law School and the de Nicola Center for Ethics and Culture." Lecture. University of Notre Dame. October 11, 2019.

Barreto, Raimundo, and João B. Chaves. "Christian Nationalism is Thriving in Bolsonaro's Brazil." *Christian Century*, November 18, 2021.

Barsa, John. "Acting Administrator John Barsa Letter to UN Secretary General Guterres." U.S. Agency for International Development. May 18, 2020. https://2017-2020.usaid.gov/news-information/press-releases/may-18-2020-acting-administrator-john-barsa-un-secretary-general-antonio-guterres.

Bellah, Robert N. "Civil Religion in America." *Daedalus* 134, no. 4 (2005): 40–55.

Bello, Niyi. "When Nigeria's Anti-Graft War Gets U.S. Support." *The Guardian* (Nigeria), July 18, 2017.

Berinsky, Adam J. "Assuming the Costs of War: Events, Elites, and American Public Support for Military Conflict." *Journal of Politics* 69, no. 4 (2007): 975–97.

Bettiza, Gregorio. *Finding Faith in Foreign Policy: Religion and American Diplomacy in a Post-secular World*. Oxford: Oxford University Press, 2019.

——. *States, Religions, and Power: Highlighting the Role of Sacred Capital in World Politics*. Washington, D.C.: Berkley Center for Religion, Peace & World Affairs, 2020. https://berkleycenter.georgetown.edu/publications/states-religions-and-power-highlighting-the-role-of-sacred-capital-in-world-politics.

Bhargava, Rajeev. *Secularism and Its Critics*. New York: Oxford University Press, 1998.

Biden, Joe. "President Biden Announces Intent to Nominate and Appoint Leaders to Serve in Key Religious Affairs Roles." Remarks, White House. July 30, 2021.

Bigler, Ron. "American Civil Rights Delegation to Urge OSCE Nations for Greater Hate Crimes Protections at Berlin Anti-Semitism Conference." Leadership Conference on Civil Rights. November 10, 2014. https://civilrights.org/2014/11/10/american-civil-rights-delegation-to-urge-osce-nations-for-greater-hate-crimes-protections-at-berlin-anti-semitism-conference/.

Biller, David. "Facing Electoral Defeat, Brazil's President Wages Campaign for Evangelical Vote." Associated Press, September 27, 2022.

Birdsall, Judd. "Keep the Faith: How American Diplomacy Got Religion, and How to Keep It." *Review of Faith & International Affairs* 14, no. 2 (2016): 110–115.

Blanchfield, Luisa. *Abortion and Family Planning-Related Provisions in U.S. Foreign Assistance Law*. Washington, D.C.: Congressional Research Service, October 2019.

Bob, Clifford. *The Global Right Wing and the Clash of World Politics*. New York: Cambridge University Press, 2012.

Bookbinder, Noah. "Re: Enforcement of the Hatch Act Against Presidential Appointees." Citizens for Responsibility and Ethics in Washington. August 23, 2019. https://www.citizensforethics.org/wp-content/uploads/legacy/2019/08/OSC-Hatch-Act-enforcement-MSPB-8-23-19-FINAL.pdf.

Boorstein, Michelle. "Trump's Evangelical Advisers Meet with Saudi Crown Prince and Discuss Jamal Khashoggi's Murder, 'Human Rights,' Spokesman Says." *Washington Post*, November 2, 2018.

Borchers, Callum, and Amber Phillips. "Transcript: President Trump's Remarks on Leaving the Paris Climate Deal, Annotated." *Washington Post*, November 25, 2021.

Bosco, Robert M. *Securing the Sacred Religion, National Security, and the Western State*. Ann Arbor: University of Michigan Press. 2014.

Brennan, David. "Christian Persecution in India is 'Very Troubling' Franklin Graham Says, But Backs Trump Friendship with Modi." *Newsweek*, September 24, 2019.

Brubaker, Rogers. "Between Nationalism and Civilizationism: The European Populist Moment in Comparative Perspective." *Ethnic and Racial Studies* 40, no. 8 (2017): 1191–226.

Buckley, David T. "Beyond the Secularism Trap: Religion, Political Institutions and Democratic Commitments." *Comparative Politics* 47, no. 4 (2015).

——. "Demanding the Divine? Explaining Cross-National Support for Clerical Control of Politics." *Comparative Political Studies* 49, no. 3 (2016): 357–90.

——. *Faithful to Secularism: The Religious Politics of Democracy in Ireland, Senegal, and the Philippines.* New York: Columbia University Press, 2017.

——. "Religious Elite Cues, Internal Division, and the Impact of Pope Francis' Laudato Si." *Politics and Religion* 15, no. 1 (2022): 1–33.

Buckley, David T., Steven Brooke, and Bryce Kleinsteuber. "How Populists Engage Religion: Mechanisms and Evidence from the Philippines." *Democratization* 29, no. 8 (2022): 1455–75.

Budryk, Zack. "North Korea: We Won't 'Gift' Trump with Summit Before Concessions." *The Hill,* November 18, 2019.

Buehler, Michael. *The Politics of Shari'a Law: Islamist Activists and the State in Democratizing Indonesia.* Cambridge: Cambridge University Press, 2016.

Bureau for the Middle East. "Genocide Recovery and Persecution Response." United States Agency for International Development. https://2017-2020.usaid.gov/iraq/genocide-recovery -and-persecution-response.

Bureau of Oceans and International Environmental and Scientific Affairs. "2021 END Wildlife Trafficking Strategic Review." United States Department of State. November 4, 2021. https://www.state.gov/2021-end-wildlife-trafficking-strategic-review/.

Burke, Daniel. "100 Evangelical Leaders Sign Ad Denouncing Trump's Refugee Ban." *CNN,* February 8, 2017.

Buss, Doris. *Globalizing Family Values: The Christian Right in International Politics.* Minneapolis: University of Minnesota Press, 2003.

Búzás, Zoltán I. "The Color of Threat: Race, Threat Perception, and the Demise of the Anglo-Japanese Alliance (1902–1923)." *Security Studies* 22, no. 4 (2013): 573–606.

Byers, Elizabeth. "How the State Department Workforce Changed Under the Trump Administration." Partnership for Public Service. January 20, 2022. https://ourpublicservice.org /blog/how-the-state-department-workforce-changed-under-the-trump-administration/.

Byrnes, Timothy A. *Reverse Mission: Transnational Religious Communities and the Making of US Foreign Policy.* Washington, D.C.: Georgetown University Press, 2011.

Cabrera, Cristian González. " 'I Became Scared, This Was Their Goal:' Efforts to Ban Gender and Sexuality Education in Brazil." Human Rights Watch. May 12, 2022. https://www.hrw .org/report/2022/05/12/i-became-scared-was-their-goal/efforts-ban-gender-and -sexuality-education-brazil.

Campbell, David E., John C. Green, and Geoffrey C. Layman. "The Party Faithful: Partisan Images, Candidate Religion, and the Electoral Impact of Party Identification." *American Journal of Political Science* 55, no. 1 (2011): 42–58.

Campbell, David E., Geoffrey C. Layman, and John C. Green. *Secular Surge: A New Fault Line in American Politics.* New York: Cambridge University Press, 2020.

Campbell, John L. *Institutions Under Siege: Donald Trump's Attack on the Deep State.* Cambridge: Cambridge University Press, 2022.

Canovan, Margaret. *The People.* Cambridge, MA: Polity Press, 2005.

——. "Trust the People! Populism and the Two Faces of Democracy." *Political Studies* 47, no. 1 (1999): 2–16.

Casanova, José. *Public Religions in the Modern World.* Chicago: University of Chicago Press, 1994.

Casey, Shaun. *Chasing the Devil at Foggy Bottom: The Future of Religion in American Diplomacy.* Grand Rapids, MI: William B. Eerdmans, 2023.

——. "How the State Department Has Sidelined Religion's Role in Democracy." *Religion & Politics,* September 5, 2017. https://religionandpolitics.org/2017/09/05/how-the-state-depart ment-has-sidelined-religions-role-in-diplomacy/.

——. "Remarks at 'Religion and Diplomacy Conference.' " Remarks. U.S. Department of State. Washington, D.C., September 26–27, 2016.

——. "The Gap Between Trump's Record and Rhetoric on Religious Freedom." *Sojourners,* June 15, 2020.

Casolari, Marzia. "Hindutva's Foreign Tie-Up in the 1930s: Archival Evidence." *Economic and Political Weekly* 35, no. 4 (2000): 218–28.

Cesari, Jocelyne. *Muslims in the West After 9/11: Religion, Politics, and Law.* New York: Rout ledge, 2010.

——. *We God's People: Christianity, Islam, and Hinduism in the World of Nations.* Cambridge: Cambridge University Press, 2021.

Chaudoin, Stephen, David Thomas Smith, and Johannes Urpelainen. "American Evangelicals and Domestic Versus International Climate Policy." *Review of International Organizations* 9, no. 4 (2014): 441–69.

Cheeseman, Nic, and Caryn Peiffer. "The Curse of Good Intentions: Why Anticorruption Messaging Can Encourage Bribery." *American Political Science Review* 116, no. 3 (2022): 1081–95.

Chemnick, Jean. "Depleted Climate Staff 'in Limbo' as Agency Reshuffles." *E&E News by Politico,* December 10, 2021.

Chiozza, Giacomo. "Is There a Clash of Civilizations? Evidence from Patterns of International Conflict Involvement, 1946–97." *Journal of Peace Research* 39, no. 6 (2002): 711–34.

Christy, Bryan. "In Global First, Philippines to Destroy Its Ivory Stock." *National Geographic,* May 3, 2021.

Chryssogelos, Angelos. "Populism in Foreign Policy." *Oxford Research Encyclopedia of Politics* (2017).

Cillizza, Chris, and Brenna Williams. "15 Times Donald Trump Praised Authoritarian Rulers." *CNN,* July 2, 2019.

"Citizenship Amendment Act is Good for Christians, Says National Commission for Minori ties Vice-Chairman." *The Hindu* (India), December 17, 2019.

Cohen, Eliot. "The Worst Secretary of State in Living Memory." *The Atlantic,* December 1, 2017.

Commission on Unalienable Rights. "Draft Report of the Commission on Unalienable Rights." U.S. Department of State. July 2020. https://www.state.gov/wp-content/uploads/2020/07 /Draft-Report-of-the-Commission-on-Unalienable-Rights.pdf.

Committee on Foreign Affairs. "Hearing on the FY 2018 Foreign Affairs Budget." U.S. House of Representatives. June 14, 2017. https://www.govinfo.gov/content/pkg/CHRG-115hhrg 25840/pdf/CHRG-115hhrg25840.pdf.

Committee on Foreign Relations. "Hearing Regarding Nomination of Rex Tillerson to be Secretary of State." United States Senate. January 11, 2017. https://www.congress.gov/event /115th-congress/senate-event/LC46421/text.

Cooley, Alexander, and Daniel Nexon. *Exit from Hegemony: The Unraveling of the American Global Order.* New York: Oxford University Press, 2020.

Corker, Robert. "Corker Statement on State Department Special Envoy Changes." United States Senate Committee on Foreign Relations. August 28, 2017. https://www.foreign.senate.gov /press/rep/release/corker-statement-on-state-department-special-envoy-changes.

Cowan, Benjamin A. *Moral Majorities Across the Americas: Brazil, the United States, and the Creation of the Religious Right.* Chapel Hill, NC: University of North Carolina Press, 2021.

Cremer, Tobias. *The Godless Crusade.* New York: Cambridge University Press, 2023.

Csehi, Robert and Edit Zgut. "'We Won't Let Brussels Dictate Us': Eurosceptic Populism in Hungary and Poland." *European Politics and Society* 22, no. 1 (2021): 53–68.

Curato, Nicole. "Politics of Anxiety, Politics of Hope: Penal Populism and Duterte's Rise to Power." *Journal of Current Southeast Asian Affairs* 35, no. 3 (2016): 91–109.

Dessler, David. "Beyond Correlations: Toward a Causal Theory of War." *International Studies Quarterly* 35, no. 3 (1991): 337–55.

DiIulio, John J. *Godly Republic: A Centrist Blueprint for America's Faith-Based Future: A Former White House Official Explodes Ten Polarizing Myths About Religion and Government in America Today.* Oakland, CA: University of California Press, 2007.

Donati, Jessica, and Nicholas Peter. "Pence Takes on Big Role in Foreign Policy—Vice President's Efforts Are Backed by Evangelicals, a Key Trump Constituency." *Wall Street Journal*, February 20, 2018.

Drezner, Daniel W. "The Angry Populist as Foreign Policy Leader: Real Change or Just Hot Air." *Fletcher Foreign World Affairs* 41, no. 2 (2017): 23–43.

——. "Ideas, Bureaucratic Politics, and the Crafting of Foreign Policy." *American Journal of Political Science* 44, no. 4 (2000): 733–49.

——. *The Toddler in Chief: What Donald Trump Teaches Us About the Modern Presidency.* Chicago: University of Chicago Press, 2020.

Dwoskin, Elizabeth, and Gabriela Sá Pessoa. "Trump Aides Bannon, Miller Advising the Bolsonaros on Next Steps." *Washington Post*, November 23, 2022.

Edwards, James R., Jr. "Religious Agencies and Refugee Resettlement." Center for Immigration Studies. March 16, 2012. https://cis.org/Religious-Agencies-and-Refugee-Resettlement.

Ekins, Emily. *Religious Trump Voters: How Faith Moderates Attitudes About Immigration, Race, and Identity.* Washington, D.C.: Democracy and Voter Study Group, 2018. https://www.cato .org/public-opinion-brief/religious-trump-voters-how-faith-moderates-attitudes-about -immigration-race.

Executive Order No. 13559. 75 Federal Register 71319. November 17, 2010.

Executive Order No. 13769. 82 Federal Register 8977. January 27, 2017.

Executive Order No. 13831. 85 Federal Register 2889. May 3, 2018.

Executive Order No. 13899. 84 Federal Register 68779. December 11, 2019.

Executive Order No. 13926. 85 Federal Register 34951. June 2, 2020.

Ezeamalu, Ben. "U.S. Partners Religious Leaders, BudgIT to Launch Anti-Corruption Website." *Premium Times* (Nigeria), July 12, 2017.

Fahrenthold, David. "Far-Right Group Warning of Islamist Infiltration to Hold Banquet at Trump's Mar-a-Lago Club." *Washington Post*, November 22, 2019.

Farr, Thomas F. *World of Faith and Freedom: Why International Religious Liberty is Vital to American National Security*. New York: Oxford University Press, 2008.

Farrier, Jasmine. *Constitutional Dysfunction on Trial: Congressional Lawsuits and the Separation of Powers*. Ithaca, NY: Cornell University Press, 2019.

Feder, J. Lester. "This is How Steve Bannon Sees the Entire World." *Buzzfeed News*, November 16, 2016.

Federal Agency Final Regulations Implementing Executive Order 13559. 81. Federal Register 19355. April 4, 2016.

Feldman, Noah. *Divided by God: America's Church-State Problem—and What We Should Do About It*. New York: Farrar, Straus and Giroux, 2005.

Filiu, Jean-Pierre. *From Deep State to Islamic State: The Arab Counter-Revolution and Its Jihadi Legacy*. New York: Oxford University Press, 2015.

Fowler, Linda L. *Watchdogs on the Hill: The Decline of Congressional Oversight of U.S. Foreign Relations*. Princeton, NJ: Princeton University Press, 2015.

Fox, Jonathan. "Paradigm Lost: Huntington's Unfulfilled Clash of Civilizations Prediction in the 21st Century." *International Politics* 42, no. 4 (2005): 428–57.

Franck, Thomas M. "Courts and Foreign Policy." *Foreign Policy*, no. 83 (1991): 66–86.

Frank R. Wolf International Religious Freedom Act. Public Law No. 114-281. 130 Stat. 1426 (2016).

Friedman, Dan. "How Jay Sekulow Got Involved in US Foreign Policy." *Mother Jones*, October 24, 2019.

Ganguly, Sumit. "The Crisis of Indian Secularism." *Journal of Democracy* 14, no. 4 (2003): 11–25.

——. "The Possibilities and Limits of India's New Religious Soft Power." Washington, D.C.: Berkley Center for Religion, Peace and World Affairs, 2020. https://berkleycenter .georgetown.edu/publications/the-possibilities-and-limits-of-india-s-new-religious-soft -power.

Garcia, Raphael Tsavkko. "Bolsonaro and Brazil Court the Global Far Right." *NACLA Report on the Americas*. August 21, 2019. https://nacla.org/news/2019/08/21/bolsonaro-and-brazil -court-global-far-right.

Gehrke, Joel. "State Department Preparing for Clash of Civilizations with China." *Washington Examiner*, April 30, 2019.

George, Alexander L., and Andrew Bennett. *Case Studies and Theory Development in the Social Sciences*. Cambridge, MA: MIT Press, 2005.

Gerson, Michael. "Trump Is Evangelicals' 'Dream President.' Here's Why." *Washington Post*, May 15, 2017.

Gibson, Ginger, and Mark Hosenball. "Whistleblower Says Ivanka, Jared Got Security Clearance over Experts' Advice." *Reuters*, April 2, 2019.

Gidron, Noam, and Bart Bonikowski. "Varieties of Populism: Literature Review and Research Agenda." *Weatherhead Working Paper Series* no. 13-0004 (2013).

Gill, Anthony James. *Rendering Unto Caesar: The Catholic Church and the State in Latin America.* Chicago: University of Chicago Press, 1998.

Global Anti-Semitism Review Act of 2004. Public Law No. 108-332. 118 Stat. 1282 (2004).

Golden, Marissa Martino. *What Motivates Bureaucrats? Politics and Administration During the Reagan Years.* New York: Columbia University Press, 2000.

Goldgeier, James, and Elizabeth N. Saunders. "The Unconstrained Presidency: Checks and Balances Eroded Long Before Trump." *Foreign Affairs* 97, no. 5 (2018): 144–56.

Goldman, Samuel. *God's Country: Christian Zionism in America.* Philadelphia: University of Pennsylvania Press, 2018.

Goldsmith, Jack. "The Trump Onslaught on International Law and Institutions." *Lawfare,* March 17, 2017. https://www.lawfaremedia.org/article/trump-onslaught-international-law-and-institutions.

Gorski, Philip. "Why Evangelicals Voted for Trump: A Critical Cultural Sociology." In *Politics of Meaning/Meaning of Politics: Cultural Sociology of the 2016 U.S. Presidential Election,* ed. Jason L. Mast and Jeffrey C. Alexander, 165–83. London: Palgrave Macmillan, 2019.

Gorski, Philip S., Samuel L. Perry, and Jemar Tisby. *The Flag and the Cross: White Christian Nationalism and the Threat to American Democracy.* New York: Oxford University Press, 2022.

Green, Mark. "Help Is on the Way for Middle Eastern Christians." *Wall Street Journal,* June 13, 2018.

——. "USAID Administrator Mark Green Remarks at the Ministerial to Advance Religious Freedom." Remarks. U.S. Department of State. Washington, D.C., July 16, 2019. https://2017-2021.state.gov/usaid-administrator-mark-green-remarks-at-the-ministerial-to-advance-international-religious-freedom/.

Greenawalt, Kent. *Religion and the Constitution. Vol. 2: Establishment and Fairness.* Princeton, NJ: Princeton University Press, 2009.

Gryboski, Michael. " 'Deeply Disturbed': Conservative Evangelical Leaders Denounce FBI Raid on Trump Home." *Christian Post,* August 10, 2022.

Grzymała-Busse, Anna. *Nations Under God: How Churches Use Moral Authority to Influence Policy.* Princeton, NJ: Princeton University Press, 2015.

Guidos, Rhina. "Tillerson Meets with Bishop Cantu to Discuss Immigration, Middle East and Africa." *America,* March 24, 2017.

Guth, James L. "Are White Evangelicals Populists? The View from the 2016 American National Election Study." *Review of Faith & International Affairs* 17, no. 3 (2019): 20–35.

——. "Religion and American Public Opinion: Foreign Policy Issues." In *Oxford Handbook of Religion and American Politics,* ed. Corwin Smidt et al., 243–65. New York: Oxford University Press, 2017.

——. "The Religious Roots of Foreign Policy Exceptionalism." *Review of Faith & International Affairs* 10, no. 2 (2012): 77–85.

Haas, Peter M. "Introduction: Epistemic Communities and International Policy Coordination." *International Organization* 46, no. 1 (1992): 1–35.

Hall, Jonny. "In Search of Enemies: Donald Trump's Populist Foreign Policy Rhetoric." *Politics* 41, no. 1 (2021): 48–63.

Hamilton, Rebecca. "EXCLUSIVE: Draft Charter of Pompeo's 'Commission on Unalienable Rights' Hides Anti-Human Rights Agenda." *Just Security*, March 12, 2020. https://www .justsecurity.org/64430/exclusive-draft-charter-of-pompeos-commission-on-unalienable -rights-hides-anti-human-rights-agenda/.

Hance, Jeremy. "Sri Lanka to Give Poached Ivory to Buddhist Temple, Flouting International Agreements." *Mongabay News* (Sri Lanka), February 5, 2013.

Harris, Gardiner. "State Dept. Restores Job Offers to Students After Diplomat Outcry." *New York Times*, July 1, 2017.

Hasan, Mehdi, and Ryan Grim. "Leaked State Department Memo Advised Trump Administration to Push for 'Islamic Reformation.'" *Intercept*, June 18, 2018.

Hassner, Ron E. "To Halve and to Hold: Conflicts Over Sacred Space and the Problem of Indivisibility." *Security Studies* 12, no. 4 (2003): 1–33.

Hawkins, Kirk A. "Is Chávez Populist? Measuring Populist Discourse in Comparative Perspective." *Comparative Political Studies* 42, no. 8 (2009): 1040–1067.

——. "Populism in Venezuela: The Rise of Chavismo." *Third World Quarterly* 24, no. 6 (2003): 1137–60.

Haynes, Jeffrey. "Donald Trump, 'Judeo-Christian Values,' and the 'Clash of Civilizations.'" *Review of Faith & International Affairs* 15, no. 3 (2017): 66–75.

——. *From Huntington to Trump: Thirty Years of the Clash of Civilizations.* Lanham, MD: Rowman & Littlefield, 2019.

——. "Religion and Foreign Policy Making in the USA, India and Iran: Towards a Research Agenda." *Third World Quarterly* 29, no. 1 (2008): 143–65.

——. "Trump and the Politics of International Religious Freedom." *Religions* 11, no. 8 (2020): 385–405.

Henderson, Alex. "Republican QAnon Supporter Praises Putin's Decision." *Salon*, March 5, 2022.

Henne, Peter. *Islamic Politics, Muslim States, and Counterterrorism Tensions.* New York: Cambridge University Press, 2016.

——. "The Geopolitics of Faith: Religious Soft Power in Russian and U.S. Foreign Policy." Washington, D.C.: Berkley Center for Religion, Peace and World Affairs. June 6, 2019. https://berkleycenter.georgetown.edu/posts/the-geopolitics-of-faith-religious-soft-power -in-russian-and-u-s-foreign-policy.

——. "Reassembling the Social in the Study of Religion and International Relations." *International Studies Review* 25, no. 3 (2023): 1–18.

Hetherington, Marc J., and Jonathan Daniel Weiler. *Authoritarianism and Polarization in American Politics.* New York: Cambridge University Press, 2009.

Hirschman, Albert O. *Exit, Voice, and Loyalty: Responses to Decline in Firms, Organizations, and States.* Cambridge, MA: Harvard University Press, 1970.

Hoffman, Ari, and Joel Swanson. "Debate: Should the Biden Administration Adopt the IHRA Definition of Antisemitism?" *Forward*, April 4, 2022.

Hoffman, Leena Koni, and Raj Navanit Patel. "Collective Action on Corruption in Nigeria: The Role of Religion." London: Chatham House, March 26, 2021. https://www.chatham house.org/2021/03/collective-action-corruption-nigeria/summary.

Hoover, Dennis, and Douglas Johnston. *Religion and Foreign Affairs: Essential Readings.* Waco, TX: Baylor University Press, 2012.

Hosenball, Mark. "Trump Administration Debates Designating Muslim Brotherhood as Terrorist Group." *Reuters*, January 29, 2017.

Hout, Michael, and Claude S. Fischer. "Why More Americans Have No Religious Preference: Politics and Generations." *American Sociological Review* 67, no. 2 (2002): 165–90.

Howell, William G., and Terry M. Moe. *Presidents, Populism, and the Crisis of Democracy.* Chicago: University of Chicago Press, 2020.

Huckerby, Jayne, and Sarah Knuckey. "Pompeo's 'Rights Commission' Is Worse Than Feared: Part 1." *Just Security*, March 13, 2020. https://www.justsecurity.org/69150/pompeos-rights -commission-is-worse-than-feared-part-i/.

Hudson, John. "Ex-Palin Aid Lands Job at Trump's State Department." *Foreign Policy*, February 9, 2017.

Hudson, Valerie M., and Benjamin S. Day. *Foreign Policy Analysis: Classic and Contemporary Theory.* Lanham, MD: Rowman & Littlefield, 2019.

Hunter, James Davison. *Culture Wars: The Struggle to Define America.* New York: Basic Books, 1991.

Huntington, Samuel P. "The Clash of Civilizations." *Foreign Affairs* 72, no. 3 (1993): 22–49.

Hurd, Elizabeth Shakman. *Beyond Religious Freedom: The New Global Politics of Religion.* Princeton, NJ: Princeton University Press, 2015.

Hurd, Elizabeth Shakman, and Winnifred Fallers Sullivan. *At Home and Abroad: The Politics of American Religion.* New York: Columbia University Press, 2021.

Igoe, Michael. "Christians and the New Age of AIDS." *Devex,* July 23, 2018. https://www.devex .com/news/christians-and-the-new-age-of-aids-93128.

——. "To Direct More Funding to Christians, USAID Looks to Hungary." *Devex*, November 25, 2019. https://www.devex.com/news/to-direct-more-funding-to-christians-usaid-looks-to -hungary-96055.

Inbari, Motti, Kirill M. Bumin, and M. Gordon Byrd. "Why Do Evangelicals Support Israel?" *Politics and Religion* 14, no. 1 (2021): 1–36.

Inboden, William. *Religion and American Foreign Policy, 1945–1960: The Soul of Containment.* Cambridge: Cambridge University Press, 2008.

Inglis, Tom. *Moral Monopoly: The Rise and Fall of the Catholic Church in Modern Ireland.* Dublin: University College Dublin Press, 1998.

Interagency Working Group on Faith-Based and Other Neighborhood Partnerships. "Report to the President: Recommendations of the Interagency Working Group on Faith-Based and Other Neighborhood Partnerships." April 2012. https://obamawhitehouse.archives.gov /sites/default/files/uploads/finalfaithbasedworkinggroupreport.pdf.

"Iraq Prelate Backs Preference for Minority Religious Fleeing Genocide." *Crux*, February 2, 2017.

Johnston, Douglas. *Faith-Based Diplomacy: Trumping Realpolitik.* New York: Oxford University Press, 2003.

Johnston, Douglas, and Cynthia Sampson. *Religion, the Missing Dimension of Statecraft.* New York: Oxford University Press, 1994.

Johnston, Lori. "Trump's Evangelical Advisory Board Violates the Law, Advocacy Group Argues in New Filing." *Washington Post*, August 30, 2018.

Jones, Robert P. *The End of White Christian America.* New York: Simon & Schuster, 201.

Joyce, Kathryn. "The Christianization of U.S. Foreign Policy." *New Republic*, September 28, 2023.

Kakkar, Jhalak. "India's New Citizenship Law and its Anti-Secular Implications." *Lawfare*, January 16, 2020. https://www.lawfareblog.com/indias-new-citizenship-law-and-its-anti-secular-implications.

Karnitschnig, Matthew. "Orbán Says Migrants Threaten 'Christian' Europe." *Politico*, September 3, 2015.

Katz, Eric. "Trump Has Slashed Jobs at Nearly Every Federal Agency; Biden Promises a Reversal." *GovExec.com.* November 19, 2020. https://www.govexec.com/workforce/2020/11/trump-has-slashed-jobs-nearly-every-federal-agency-biden-promises-reversal/170203/.

Kaufman, Robert R., and Stephan Haggard. "Democratic Decline in the United States: What Can We Learn from Middle-Income Backsliding?" *Perspectives on Politics* 17, no. 2 (2018): 1–16.

Keck, Margaret E., and Kathryn Sikkink. *Activists Beyond Borders: Advocacy Networks in International Politics.* Ithaca, NY: Cornell University Press, 1998.

Kerry, John. "Remarks at the Launch of the Office of Faith-Based Community Initiatives." Remarks. Washington, D.C., August 7, 2013. https://2009-2017.state.gov/secretary/remarks/2013/08/212781.htm.

Kertzer, Joshua D., and Ryan Brutger. "Decomposing Audience Costs: Bringing the Audience Back into Audience Cost Theory." *American Journal of Political Science* 60, no. 1 (2016): 234–49.

Kertzer, Joshua D., Kathleen E. Powers, Brian C. Rathbun, and Ravi Iyer. "Moral Support: How Moral Values Shape Foreign Policy Attitudes." *Journal of Politics* 76, no. 3 (2014): 825–40.

Kertzer, Joshua D., and Thomas Zeitzoff. "A Bottom-Up Theory of Public Opinion About Foreign Policy." *American Journal of Political Science* 61, no. 3 (2017): 543–58.

King, Kimi Lynn, and James Meernik. "The Supreme Court and the Powers of the Executive: The Adjudication of Foreign Policy." *Political Research Quarterly* 52, no. 4 (1999): 801–24.

Kohut, Andrew, Carroll Doherty, Michael Dimock, Gregory Smith, and Cary Funk. "More See 'Too Much' Religious Talk by Politicians." Washington, D.C.: Pew Research Center, 2012. https://www.pewresearch.org/religion/2012/03/21/more-see-too-much-religious-talk-by-politicians/.

Korade, Matt, Kevin Bohn, and Daniel Burke. "Controversial US Pastors Take Part in Jerusalem Embassy Opening." *CNN*, May 14, 2018.

Kosinski, Michelle, and Jennifer Hansler. "State Department Bars Press Corps from Pompeo Briefing, Won't Release List of Attendees." *CNN*, March 20, 2019.

Kostadinova, Tatiana, and Barry Levitt. "Toward a Theory of Personalist Parties: Concept Formation and Theory Building." *Politics & Policy* 42, no. 4 (2014): 490–512.

Kuru, Ahmet T. "Passive and Assertive Secularism." *World Politics* 59, no. 3 (2007): 568–94.

Lacatus, Corina. "Populism and President Trump's Approach to Foreign Policy: An Analysis of Tweets and Rally Speeches." *Politics* 41, no. 1 (2021): 31–47.

Layman, Geoffrey C., Thomas M. Carsey, and Juliana Menasce Horowitz. "Party Polarization in American Politics: Characteristics, Causes, and Consequences." *Annual Review of Political Science* 9 (2006): 83–110.

Lewis, Andrew R. *The Rights Turn in Conservative Christian Politics: How Abortion Transformed the Culture Wars*. Cambridge: Cambridge University Press, 2017.

Lewis, David E. *The Politics of Presidential Appointments: Political Control and Bureaucratic Performance*. Princeton, NJ: Princeton University Press, 2010.

Lieberman, Robert C., Suzanne Mettler, Thomas B. Pepinsky, Kenneth M. Roberts, and Richard Valelly. "The Trump Presidency and American Democracy: A Historical and Comparative Analysis." *Perspectives on Politics* 17, no. 2 (2019): 470–479.

Mandaville, Peter. "Designating Muslims: Islam in the Western Policy Imagination." *Review of Faith & International Affairs* 15, no. 3 (2017): 54–65.

——. "The Future of Religion and U.S. Foreign Policy Under Trump." Brookings Institution, March 7, 2017. https://www.brookings.edu/articles/the-future-of-religion-and-u-s-foreign -policy-under-trump/.

——. "The Geopolitics of Religious Soft Power." Berkley Center for Religion, Peace, and World Affairs. https://berkleycenter.georgetown.edu/projects/the-geopolitics-of-religious-soft -power.

——. "Right-Sizing Religion and Religious Engagement in Diplomacy and Development." *Review of Faith & International Affairs* 19, no. 1 (2021): 92–97.

Mandaville, Peter, and Shadi Hamid. "Islam as Statecraft: How Governments Use Religion in Foreign Policy." Washington, D.C.: Brookings Institution, 2018. https://www .brookings.edu/articles/islam-as-statecraft-how-governments-use-religion-in-foreign -policy/

Mandaville, Peter, and Julia Schiwal. "The U.S. Strategy for International Religious Engagement: 10 Years On." Washington, D.C., United States Institute for Peace, 2023.

Mandaville, Peter, and Chris Seiple. "Advancing Global Peace and Security Through Religious Engagement: Lessons to Improve U.S. Policy." Washington, D.C.: United States Institute of Peace, 2021. https://www.usip.org/publications/2021/11/advancing-global-peace-and -security-through-religious-engagement-lessons.

Marritz, Ilya. "Let's Recall What Exactly Paul Manafort and Rudy Giuliani Were Doing in Ukraine." *ProPublica*, June 23, 2022.

Marzouki, Nadia, and Duncan McDonnell. "Populism and Religion." In *Saving the People: How Populists Hijack Religion*, ed. Nadia Marzouki, Duncan McDonnell, and Olivier Roy, 1–12. New York: Oxford University Press, 2016.

McAlister, Melani. *The Kingdom of God Has No Borders: A Global History of American Evangelicals*. New York: Oxford University Press, 2018.

McCants, William, and Benjamin Wittes. "Should the Muslim Brotherhood be Designated a Terrorist Organization?" *Lawfare*, January 27, 2017. https://www.lawfareblog.com/should-muslim-brotherhood-be-designated-terrorist-organization.

McConnell, Michael W. "Accommodation of Religion." *Supreme Court Review* 1985 (1985): 1–59.

McDaniel, Eric L., Irfan Nooruddin, and Allyson F. Shortle. *The Everyday Crusade: Christian Nationalism in American Politics*. New York: Cambridge University Press, 2022.

McDougall, Walter A. *Promised Land, Crusader State: The American Encounter with the World Since 1776*. Boston: Houghton Mifflin, 1997.

Mead, Walter Russell. *God and Gold: Britain, America, and the Making of the Modern World*. New York: Alfred A. Knopf, 2007.

——. "The Jacksonian Revolt: American Populism and the Liberal Order." *Foreign Affairs* 96, no. 2 (2017): 2–7.

Memorandum: The Mexico City Policy. 82 Federal Register 8495. January 25, 2017.

Menchik, Jeremy. "The Constructivist Approach to Religion and World Politics." *Comparative Politics* 49, no. 4 (2017): 561–81.

——. "Soft Separation Democracy." *Politics and Religion* 11, no. 4 (2018): 863–83.

Menendez, Robert, et al. "Letter to Secretary Michael Pompeo." United States Senate, July 23, 2019. https://www.foreign.senate.gov/imo/media/doc/07-23-19%20Dems%20letter%20re%20Commission%20on%20Unalienable%20Rights.pdf.

Metropolitan Hilarion of Volokolamsk. "Presentation by the DECR Chairman Metropolitan Hilarion of Volokolamsk at the World Summit in Defense of Persecuted Christians." Remarks. Washington, D.C., May 2017. https://mospat.ru/en/news/48514/.

——. "Speech by Metropolitan Hilarion of Volokolamsk at the Forum of Representatives of the Russia-USA Forum of Christian Leaders." Remarks. November 2014. https://mospat.ru/en/news/50935/.

Michaels, Jon D. "The American Deep State Symposium: Administrative Lawmaking in the Twenty-First Century." *Notre Dame Law Review* 93, no. 4 (2017): 1653–70.

——. "Trump and the Deep State: The Government Strikes Back Essays." *Foreign Affairs* 96, no. 5 (2017): 52–56.

Mickey, Robert, Steven Levitsky, and Lucan Ahmad Way. "Is America Still Safe for Democracy: Why the United States is in Danger of Backsliding." *Foreign Affairs* 96, no. 3 (2017): 20–29.

"Mike Pompeo's Cairo Speech on Mideast Policy and Obama—U.S. News." *Haaretz*, January 10, 2019.

Miles, Rufus E. "The Origin and Meaning of Miles' Law." *Public Administration Review* 38, no. 5 (1978): 399–403.

Mitchell, Chris. "Egyptian President Meeting with US Evangelicals 'Prophetic' and 'Historic.'" *Christian Broadcasting Network*. November 3, 2017.

Mitchell, David. *Making Foreign Policy: Presidential Management of the Decision-Making Process*. Burlington, VT: Ashgate, 2005.

Moffitt, Benjamin. *The Global Rise of Populism: Performance, Political Style, and Representation*. Stanford, CA: Stanford University Press, 2016.

Moffitt, Benjamin, and Simon Tormey. "Rethinking Populism: Politics, Mediatisation and Political Style." *Political Studies* 62, no. 2 (2014): 381–97.

Moore, Art. "Trump Faith Adviser: We're in 'Heart' of Policy Conversations." *WND*, February 27, 2018.

Morello, Carol, and Steve Hendrix. "Pompeo Sets Off Debate on Boycott of Israel, Calling It an Anti-Semitic 'Cancer.'" *Washington Post*, November 19, 2020.

Mudde, Cas, and Cristóbal Rovira Kaltwasser. *Populism: A Very Short Introduction.* New York: Oxford University Press, 2017.

——. "Studying Populism in Comparative Perspective: Reflections on the Contemporary and Future Research Agenda." *Comparative Political Studies* 51, no. 13 (2018): 1667–93.

Müller, Jan-Werner. "Parsing Populism: Who Is and Who Is Not a Populist These Days?" *Juncture* 22, no. 2 (2015): 80–89.

——. *What Is Populism?* London: Penguin Books UK, 2017.

Muslim Brotherhood Terrorist Designation Act of 2017, S.B. 68, 115th Cong. (2017).

Nashrulla, Tasneem. "The White House Says It Has No Idea How the Controversial Religious Leaders Were Involved in the Jerusalem Embassy Opening." *BuzzFeed News*, May 14, 2018.

"Nigerian Church Collapses Kills at Least 160 Worshippers—Reports." Associated Press, December 10, 2016.

"Noted Peace Maker, Dr. K.A. Paul, and Indian Prime Minister Narendra Modi Will Both Face Serious Questions During President Trump's Meeting with the Indian PM Next Week in Washington, DC." *Newswire*, June 21, 2017.

Notice 10777. 84 Federal Register 25109. May 30, 2019.

Nye, Joseph S. "Soft Power." *Foreign Policy.* no. 80 (1990): 153–71.

——. *Soft Power: The Means to Success in World Politics.* New York: Public Affairs. 2004.

Office of Faith and Opportunity Initiatives. "2020 Evidence Summit on Strategic Religious Engagement." U.S. Agency For International Development. August 2020. https://www .usaid.gov/faith-and-opportunity-initiatives/2020-evidence-summit-strategic-religious -engagement.

Office of Inspector General. "Review of Allegations of Politicized and Other Improper Personnel Practices in the Bureau of International Organization Affairs." United States Department of State, 2019. https://www.stateoig.gov/report/esp-19-05.

Office of International Religious Freedom. "Declaration of Principles for the International Religious Freedom Alliance." U.S. Department of State. February 5, 2020. https://www.state.gov /declaration-of-principles-for-the-international-religious-freedom-alliance/.

——. "DRL FY20 IRF Promoting and Defending Religious Freedom Inclusive of Atheist, Humanist, Non-Practicing and Non-Affiliated Individuals." U.S. Department of State. April 21, 2021. https://www.state.gov/statements-of-interest-requests-for-proposals-and -notices-of-funding-opportunity/drl-fy20-irf-promoting-and-defending-religious -freedom-inclusive-of-atheist-humanist-non-practicing-and-non-affiliated-individuals/.

——. "Functional Bureau Strategy." U.S. Department of State. December 20, 2021. https://www .state.gov/wp-content/uploads/2022/02/IRF_FBS_FINAL_Public-Version.pdf.

——. "2019 Ministerial to Advance Religious Freedom." U.S. Department of State. December 1, 2020. https://2017-2021.state.gov/2019-ministerial-to-advance-religious-freedom/index.html.

Office of Religion and Global Affairs. "Religion and Diplomacy: A Practical Handbook," United States Department of State, 2017.

——. "U.S. Strategy on Religious Leader and Faith Community Engagement." U.S. Department of State. https://2009-2017.state.gov/s/rga/strategy/index.htm.

Olmstead, Molly. "Can the Christian Right Quit Putin?" *Slate Magazine*, March 8, 2022.

Orbán, Viktor. "Full Speech for the Beginning of his Fourth Mandate." *Visegrád Post*, May 12, 2018.

Orsi, Robert A. "Is the Study of Lived Religion Irrelevant to the World We Live In? Special Presidential Plenary Address, Society for the Scientific Study of Religion, Salt Lake City, November 2, 2002." *Journal for the Scientific Study of Religion* 42, no. 2 (2003): 169–74.

Orth, Taylor. "On Russia and Putin, Opinions of Evangelical Christians Resemble Those of Americans Overall." *YouGov*, March 15, 2022. https://today.yougov.com/topics/politics/articles-reports/2022/03/15/russia-and-putin-opinions-evangelical-christians.

Otis, John. "Hugo Chavez and the Vatican." *PRI: The World*, March 14, 2013.

"Outrage Over Right-Wing Euro-MPs' Kashmir Visit." *BBC News*, October 30, 2019.

Owen, John M. *The Clash of Ideas in World Politics: Transnational Networks, States, and Regime Change, 1510–2010*. Princeton, NJ: Princeton University Press, 2010.

Pappas, Takis S. "Populism Emergent: A Framework for Analyzing Its Contexts, Mechanics, and Outcomes." *RSCAS Working Papers* (2012).

Parke, Caleb. "Pastors Praise Trump for Skipping UN Panel on 'Imaginary' Climate Crisis." *Fox News*, September 23, 2019.

Pathi, Krutika. "India's Modi Faces No-Confidence Vote in Parliament." *Diplomat*, August 7, 2023.

Pence, Mike. "Remarks by the Vice President at the 'In Defense of Christians' Solidarity Dinner." Remarks, Washington, D.C., October 25, 2017. https://www.presidency.ucsb.edu/documents/remarks-the-vice-president-the-defense-christians-solidarity-dinner.

——. "Remarks by Vice President Pence at Ministerial to Advance Religious Freedom." Remarks, Washington, D.C., July 26, 2018. https://trumpwhitehouse.archives.gov/briefings-statements/remarks-vice-president-pence-ministerial-advance-religious-freedom/.

Pentin, Edward. "Hungary Hosts First Ever Government Conference for Persecuted Christians." *National Catholic Register*, October 14, 2017.

Pernia, Ronald A. "Human Rights in a Time of Populism: Philippines Under Rodrigo Duterte." *Asia-Pacific Social Science Review* 19, no. 3 (2019): 56–71.

Perry, Samuel L., Sarah Riccardi-Swartz, Joshua T. Davis, and Joshua B. Grubbs. "The Religious Right and Russia: Christian Nationalism and Americans' Views on Russia and Vladimir Putin Before and After the Ukrainian Invasion." *Journal for the Scientific Study of Religion* 62, no. 2 (2023): 439–50.

Peterson, Paul E. "The President's Dominance in Foreign Policy Making." *Political Science Quarterly* 109, no. 2 (1994): 215–34.

Pettula, Matias. "Prime Minister Modi in Houston." *International Christian Concern*. September 12, 2019. https://www.persecution.org/2019/09/12/prime-minister-modi-houston/.

Pew Research Group. "2019 Pew Research Center's American Trends Panel: Final Topline." February 2019. https://www.pewforum.org/wp-content/uploads/sites/7/2019/07/W44-Religious-Knowledge-TOPLINE-FOR-RELEASE-CHECK-COMPLETE.pdf.

Phillip, Abby. "Spicer: Diplomats Opposed to Immigration Ban Should 'Either Get with the Program or They Can Go.'" *Washington Post*, November 26, 2021.

Picheta, Rob, and Ivana Kottasová. "'You Don't Belong Here': In Poland's 'LGBT-free Zones,' Existing Is an Act of Defiance." *CNN*, October 2020.

Plagemann, Johannes, and Sandra Destradi. "Populism and Foreign Policy: The Case of India." *Foreign Policy Analysis* 15, no. 2 (2019): 283–301.

Pompeo, Michael. "Remarks at the Release of the 2018 Annual Report on International Religious Freedom." Remarks. Washington, D.C., June 21, 2019. https://br.usembassy.gov/secretary-of-states-remarks-at-the-release-of-the-2018-annual-report-on-international-religious-freedom/.

——. "Secretary Pompeo Addresses Values Voter Summit." Remarks. September 21, 2018. https://www.c-span.org/video/?c4750549/secretary-pompeo-addresses-values-voter-summit.

——. "Secretary Pompeo's on US India Policy June 26, 2019." Remarks. New Delhi, India, June 26, 2019. https://www.youtube.com/watch?v=TycsbmBXnoQ.

——. "Secretary of State Michael R. Pompeo Keynote Address at the Ministerial to Advance Religious Freedom." Remarks. Washington, D.C., July 18, 2019. https://2017-2021.state.gov/secretary-of-state-michael-r-pompeo-keynote-address-at-the-ministerial-to-advance-religious-freedom/.

——. "Secretary of State Michael R. Pompeo Remarks to the Press." Remarks. Washington, D.C., July 8, 2019. https://2017-2021-translations.state.gov/2019/07/08/secretary-of-state-michael-r-pompeo-remarks-to-the-press-7/.

——. "Unalienable Rights and the Securing of Freedom." Remarks. Philadelphia, PA, July 16, 2020. https://2017-2021.state.gov/unalienable-rights-and-the-securing-of-freedom/index.html.

Presidential Determination No. 2022-02. 86 Federal Register 57527. October 18, 2021.

Preston, Andrew. *Sword of the Spirit, Shield of Faith: Religion in American War and Diplomacy*. New York: Alfred A. Knopf, 2012.

Primorac, Max. "U.S. Agency for International Development Special Representative for Minority Assistance Programs in Iraq Max Primorac Interview with EWTN." Interview. Washington, D.C., November 8, 2018. https://2017-2020.usaid.gov/news-information/press-releases/nov-9-2018-special-representative-minority-assistance-iraq-interview-ewtn.

Proclamation No. 10141. 86 Federal Register 7005. January 25, 2021.

Public Region Research Institue. "More Americans, Especially White Evangelicals, Now Say Personal Immorality Not Disqualifying for Elected Officials." October 19, 2016. https://www.prri.org/research/prri-brookings-oct-19-poll-politics-election-clinton-double-digit-lead-trump/.

Putnam, Robert D. "Diplomacy and Domestic Politics: The Logic of Two-Level Games." *International Organization* 42, no. 3 (1988): 427–60.

Putnam, Robert D., and David E. Campbell. *American Grace: How Religion Divides and Unites Us*. New York: Simon & Schuster, 2010.

Rasche, Stephen. "Testimony to the Subcommittee on Africa, Global Health, Global Human Rights, and International Organizations." U.S. House of Representatives. October 3, 2017.

Rathbun, Brian C. *Partisan Interventions: European Party Politics and Peace Enforcement in the Balkans*. Ithaca, NY: Cornell University Press, 2004.

Ravid, Barak. "White House Working to Reassure Evangelicals on Middle East Peace Plan." *Axios*, March 9, 2019.

Religion and Foreign Policy Working Group. "Ensuring the Opportunity for Mutual Counsel and Collaboration." U.S. Department of State. October 16, 2012.

Rhodes-Purdy, Matthew, and Raúl L. Madrid. "The Perils of Personalism." *Democratization* 27, no. 2 (2020): 321–39.

Rogers, Melissa. "Remarks at the Launch of the Office of Faith-Based Community Initiatives." Remarks. Washington, D.C., August 7, 2013. https://2009-2017.state.gov/secretary/remarks /2013/08/212781.htm.

Rogers, Melissa, and E. J. Dionne Jr. *A Time to Heal, A Time to Build*. Washington, D.C.: Brookings Institution, October 2020. https://www.brookings.edu/wp-content/uploads /2020/10/A_Time_to_Heal_report.pdf.

Rousseau, David L., and Rocio Garcia-Retamero. "Identity, Power, and Threat Perception: A Cross-National Experimental Study." *Journal of Conflict Resolution* 51, no. 5 (2007): 744–71.

Roy, Olivier. "Beyond Populism: The Conservative Right, the Courts, the Churches, and the Concept of a Christian Europe." In *Saving the People: How Populists Hijack Religion*, ed. Nadia Marzouki, Duncan McDonnell, and Olivier Roy, 185–202. New York: Oxford University Press, 2016.

Saldinger, Adva. "What Happened with PEPFAR's Faith-Based Initiative?" *Devex*. Updated October 14, 2020. https://www.devex.com/news/what-happened-with-pepfar-s-faith-based -initiative-98295.

Sandal, Nukhet A., and Jonathan Fox. *Religion in International Relations Theory: Interactions and Possibilities*. London: Routledge, Taylor & Francis Group, 2013.

Sanders, Sarah Huckabee. "Press Briefing by Press Secretary Sarah Sanders." Remarks. White House. Washington, D.C., February 27, 2018. https://trumpwhitehouse.archives.gov /briefings-statements/press-briefing-press-secretary-sarah-sanders-022718/.

Savransky, Rebecca. "Giuliani: Trump Asked Me How to Do a Muslim Ban 'Legally.'" *The Hill*, January 29, 2017.

Schwartz, Matthias. "Acts of the Apostle." *New York Times Magazine*, November 3, 2019.

Shah, Timothy Samuel, Alfred C. Stepan, and Monica Duffy Toft. *Rethinking Religion and World Affairs*. New York: Oxford University Press, 2012.

Shimron, Yonat. "Franklin Graham Sends Disaster Response Teams to Europe; Says He Opposes War." *Religion News Service*, February 26, 2022.

Shortle, Allyson F., and Ronald Keith Gaddie. "Religious Nationalism and Perceptions of Muslims and Islam." *Politics and Religion* 8, no. 3 (2015): 435–57.

Siddiqui, Sabrina. "Meet Stephen Miller, Architect of First Travel Ban, Whose Words May Haunt Him." *The Guardian* (UK), January 7, 2021.

Silk, Mark. "Mike Pompeo Claims the Judeo-Christian Tradition for His Agenda." *Religion News Service*, August 5, 2020.

Silvestri, Sara. "Islam and Religion in the EU Political System." *West European Politics* 32, no. 6 (2009): 1212–39.

Skowronek, Stephen, John A. Dearborn, and Desmond King. *Phantoms of a Beleaguered Republic: The Deep State and the Unitary Executive*. Oxford: Oxford University Press, 2021.

Smith, Samuel. "Pompeo Faces Criticism for Giving Speech on Being a 'Christian Leader.'" *Christian Post*, October 15, 2019.

——. "US Evangelical Leaders Met, Prayed with Brazil's Conservative President Bolsonaro." *Christian Post*, March 22, 2019.

——. "Would Eliminating State Dept. Office of Religion and Global Affairs Be a Big Deal?" *Christian Post*, June 16, 2017.

Snyder, Jack L. *Religion and International Relations Theory*. New York: Columbia University Press, 2011.

Somer, Murat. "Turkey: The Slippery Slope from Reformist to Revolutionary Polarization and Democratic Breakdown." *The ANNALS of the American Academy of Political and Social Science* 681, no. 1 (2018): 42–61. https://doi.org/10.1177/0002716218818056.

Sommer, Allison Kaplan. "Trump Says Moved Israel Embassy to Jerusalem 'for the Evangelicals'—U.S. News." *Haaretz* (Israel), August 19, 2020.

Special Envoy to Monitor and Combat Anti-Semitism Act. Public Law No. 116-326. 134 Stat. 5095 (2021).

Stanley, Benjamin. "Defenders of the Cross: Populist Politics and Religion in Post-Communist Poland." In *Saving the People: How Populists Hijack Religion*, ed. Nadia Marzouki, Duncan McDonnell, and Olivier Roy, 109–28. New York: Oxford University Press, 2016.

——. "The Thin Ideology of Populism." *Journal of Political Ideologies* 13, no. 1 (2008): 95–110.

Stepan, A. "Religion, Democracy, and the 'Twin Tolerations.'" *Journal of Democracy* 11, no. 4 (2000): 37–57.

——. "Tunisia's Transition and the Twin Tolerations." *Journal of Democracy* 23, no. 2 (2012): 89–103.

"Steven Bannon Endorses Far-Right Brazilian Presidential Candidate." *Reuters*, October 26, 2018.

Stewart, Katherine. "What Was Maria Butina Doing at the National Prayer Breakfast." *New York Times*, July 18, 2018.

Stoeckl, Kristina, and Dmitry Uzlaner. *The Moralist International*. New York: Fordham University Press, 2022.

Suebsaeng, Asawin. "Inside Steve Bannon's Failed Breitbart India Scheme." *Daily Beast*, April 10, 2017.

Suleman, M. Arsalan. "Return of the Clash: Operationalizing a Tainted Worldview." *Washington Quarterly* 40, no. 4 (2017): 49–70.

Sullivan, Winnifred Fallers. *The Impossibility of Religious Freedom*. Princeton, NJ: Princeton University Press, 2005.

Sullivan, Winnifred Fallers, Elizabeth Shakman Hurd, Saba Mahmood, and Peter G. Danchin. *Politics of Religious Freedom*. Chicago: University of Chicago Press, 2015.

Tabaar, Mohammad Ayatollahi. *Religious Statecraft: The Politics of Islam in Iran*. New York: Columbia University Press, 2018.

Tamkin, Emily. "Here's What Happened to a USAID Official Who Ran Afoul of Mike Pence." *BuzzFeed News*, September 18, 2018.

Task Force on Religion and the Making of U.S. Foreign Policy. *Engaging Religious Communities Abroad: A New Imperative for U.S. Foreign Policy*. Chicago: Chicago Council on Global Affairs, 2010.

Taylor, Jessica. "Trump Calls for 'Total and Complete Shutdown of Muslims Entering' U.S." *NPR*, December 7, 2015.

Tillerson, Rex. "Letter to the Honorable Bob Corker Regarding Special Envoys and Special Representatives." Updated August 29, 2017. https://www.politico.com/f/?id=0000015e-2b43-db52-a75e-ff7b3bfa0001.

——. "Secretary of State Designate Rex Tillerson Senate Confirmation Hearing Opening Statement January 11, 2017." Remarks. Washington, D.C., January 11, 2017. https://www.foreign.senate.gov/imo/media/doc/011117_Tillerson_Opening_Statement.pdf.

Toosi, Nahal. "White House Slap at Dissenting Diplomats Sparks Fear of Reprisal." *Politico*, January 30, 2017.

Toosi, Nahal, and Gabby Orr. "White House Taps Pence Aide for Religious Freedom Role." *Politico*, February 4, 2020.

Torbati, Yeganeh. "Exclusive: Tillerson Declines to Host Ramadan Event at State Department." *Reuters*, May 29, 2017.

——. "How Mike Pence's Office Meddled in Foreign Aid to Reroute Money to Favored Christian Groups." *ProPublica*, November 6, 2019.

——. "It's Illegal for Federal Officials to Campaign at Work. A Trump Official Just Did So." *ProPublica*, March 2, 2020.

Torbati, Yeganeh, and Lesley Wroughton. "U.S. State Dept Keeps Hiring Freeze as Tillerson Looks to Downsize." *Reuters*, April 13, 2017.

Trejo, Guillermo "Religious Competition and Ethnic Mobilization in Latin America: Why the Catholic Church Promotes Indigenous Movements in Mexico." *American Political Science Review* 103, no. 3 (2009): 323–42.

Trump, Donald. "Donald Trump on Tim Kaine, Muslim Ban, Taxes, Roger Ailes." Meet the Press. *NBC News*, July 24, 2016. https://www.youtube.com/watch?v=YbvIeHC3ueU&t=452s.

——. "The Inaugural Address." Remarks. Washington, D.C., January 20, 2017. https://trumpwhitehouse.archives.gov/briefings-statements/the-inaugural-address/

——. "President Trump's Speech to the Arab Islamic American Summit." Remarks. Saudi Arabia, May 21, 2017. https://trumpwhitehouse.archives.gov/briefings-statements/president-trumps-speech-arab-islamic-american-summit/.

——. "Remarks by President Trump and Prime Minister Modi at 'Howdy, Modi: Shared Dreams, Bright Futures' Event." Remarks. Houston, TX, September 22, 2019. https://trumpwhitehouse.archives.gov/briefings-statements/remarks-president-trump-prime-minister-modi-india-howdy-modi-shared-dreams-bright-futures-event/.

——. "Remarks by President Trump at the 68th Annual National Prayer Breakfast." Remarks. Washington, D.C., February 6, 2020. https://trumpwhitehouse.archives.gov/briefings-statements/remarks-president-trump-68th-annual-national-prayer-breakfast/.

——. "Remarks by President Trump at the United Nations Event on Religious Freedom." Remarks. UN Headquarters. New York, September 23, 2019. https://trumpwhitehouse.archives.gov/briefings-statements/remarks-president-trump-united-nations-event-religious-freedom-new-york-ny/.

——. "Remarks by President Trump at Values Voter Summit." Remarks. Washington, D.C., October 12, 2019. https://trumpwhitehouse.archives.gov/briefings-statements/remarks-president-trump-values-voter-summit/.

——. "Remarks by President Trump at National Prayer Breakfast." Remarks. Washington, D.C., February 2, 2017. https://trumpwhitehouse.archives.gov/briefings-statements/remarks-president-trump-national-prayer-breakfast/.

——. "Remarks by President Trump Before White House Iftar Dinner." Remarks. Washington, D.C., June 6, 2018. https://trumpwhitehouse.archives.gov/briefings-statements/remarks-president-trump-white-house-iftar-dinner/.

——. "Remarks on Signing of an Executive Order Combating Anti-Semitism at a Hanukkah Reception." Remarks. Washington, D.C., December 11, 2019. https://www.govinfo.gov/content/pkg/DCPD-201900858/pdf/DCPD-201900858.pdf.

——. "Statement by Former President Trump on Jerusalem." Remarks. Jerusalem, Israel, December 7, 2020. https://il.usembassy.gov/statement-by-president-trump-on-jerusalem/.

"Trump Promises Tariffs on Companies That Leave U.S. to Create Jobs Overseas." *Reuters*, August 28, 2020.

"Trump Tells Pentagon 'To Top' France Military Parade." *BBC News*, February 7, 2018.

United States Agency for International Development. "ADS Chapter 303 Grants and Cooperative Agreements to Non-Governmental Organizations." December 23, 2019. https://www.usaid.gov/sites/default/agency-policy/303.pdf.

United States Department of Homeland Security. "DHS Announces New Members of Faith-Based Security Advisory Council." September 19, 2022. https://www.dhs.gov/news/2022/09/19/dhs-announces-new-members-faith-based-security-advisory-council.

United States Department of State, "Alternatives to Closing Doors in Order to Secure Our Borders." Dissent Channel. https://s3.documentcloud.org/documents/3438487/Dissent-Memo.pdf.

United States Embassy and Consulate in Poland. "Signing of Memorandum of Understanding Between USAID and the Government of Poland." U.S. Department of State. November 30, 2018. https://pl.usembassy.gov/mou_usaid/.

United States Mission Nigeria. "U.S. Consulate, Religious Leaders Launch Anti-Corruption Website." U.S. Department of State. January 31, 2022. https://ng.usembassy.gov/u-s-consulate-religious-leaders-launch-anti-corruption-website/.

Urbinati, Nadia. *Me the People: How Populism Transforms Democracy*. Cambridge, MA: Harvard University Press, 2019.

"U.S. Envoy for Religious Freedom Slams China During Hong Kong Visit." *Reuters*, March 8, 2019.

"U.S. State Department Honors Nun as Anti-Trafficking 'Hero.'" *Our Sunday Visitor*, May 18, 2022.

"US-Ghana Partnership to Tackle Child Slavery." *Anglican Communion News Service*, August 24, 2016.

Verbeek, Bertjan, and Andrej Zaslove. "Populism and Foreign Policy." In *The Oxford Handbook of Populism*, ed. Cristóbal Kaltwasser et al., 384–405. New York: Oxford University Press, 2017.

Verma, Pranshu. "Trump Appointee with History of Anti-L.G.B.T.Q. Remarks Leaves Aid Agency." *New York Times*, August 3, 2020.

Villalón, Leonardo Alfonso. "From Argument to Negotiation: Constructing Democracy in African Muslim Contexts." *Comparative Politics* 42, no. 4 (2010): 375–93.

Wadhams, Nick, and Erik Schatzker. "Kushner Is Said to Have Not Kept Tillerson Informed About Middle East Talks." *Boston Globe*, December 2, 2017.

Walker, Shaun. "Hungarian Leader Says Europe Is Now 'Under Invasion' by Migrants." *The Guardian* (UK), March 15, 2018.

Waltz, Kenneth Neal. *Theory of International Politics*. Reading, MA: Addison-Wesley, 1979.

Warner, Carolyn M., and Stephen G. Walker. "Thinking About the Role of Religion in Foreign Policy: A Framework for Analysis." *Foreign Policy Analysis* 7, no. 1 (2011): 113–35.

Weissman, Stephen R. *A Culture of Deference: Congress' Failure of Leadership in Foreign Policy*. New York: Basic Books, 1996.

"'Western Countries Stop Identifying Themselves with Christian Tradition'—Patriarch Kirill." *Interfax News*, October 29, 2015.

Weyland, Kurt. "Populism: A Political-Strategic Approach." In *The Oxford Handbook of Populism*, ed. Cristóbal Kaltwasser et al., 48–72. Oxford: Oxford University Press, 2017.

——. "Populism's Threat to Democracy: Comparative Lessons for the United States." *Perspectives on Politics* 18, no. 2 (2020): 389–406.

——. "Will Chávez Lose His Luster?" *Foreign Affairs* 80, no. 6 (2001): 73–87.

Weyland, Kurt, and Raúl L Madrid. *When Democracy Trumps Populism: European and Latin American Lessons for the United States*. Cambridge: Cambridge University Press, 2019.

White House. "Fact Sheet: Biden-Harris Administration Celebrates First Anniversary of the Reestablishment of the White House Office of Faith-Based and Neighborhood Partnerships." February 14, 2022. https://www.whitehouse.gov/briefing-room/statements-releases/2022/02/14/fact-sheet-biden-harris-administration-celebrates-first-anniversary-of-the-reestablishment-of-the-white-house-office-of-faith-based-and-neighborhood-partnerships/.

"White House Slap at Dissenting Diplomats Sparks Fear of Reprisal." *Politico*, January 30, 2017.

Whitehead, Andrew L., and Samuel L Perry. *Taking America Back for God: Christian Nationalism in the United States*. New York: Oxford University Press, 2020.

Whitehead, Andrew L., Samuel L. Perry, and Joseph O. Baker. "Make America Christian Again: Christian Nationalism and Voting for Donald Trump in the 2016 Presidential Election." *Sociology of Religion* 79, no. 2 (2018): 147–71.

Wildavsky, Aaron. "The Two Presidencies." *Society* 35, no. 2 (1998): 23–31.

Wittes, Benjamin, Susan Hennessey, and Quinta Jurecic. "Full Text of Draft Dissent Channel Memo on Trump Refugee and Visa Order." *Lawfare*. Updated January 30, 2017. https://lawfareblog.com/full-text-draft-dissent-channel-memo-trump-refugee-and-visa-order.

Wojczewski, Thorsten. "Trump, Populism, and American Foreign Policy." *Foreign Policy Analysis* 16, no. 3 (2020): 292–311.

Wroughton, Yeganeh, and Torbati Lesley. "U.S. State Dept Keeps Hiring Freeze as Tillerson Looks to Downsize." *Reuters*, April 13, 2017.

Yabanci, Bilge, and Dane Taleski. "Co-Opting Religion: How Ruling Populists in Turkey and Macedonia Sacralise the Majority." *Religion, State, and Society* 46, no. 3 (2018): 283–304.

Yang, Maya. "Trump 'Admired' Putin's Ability to 'Kill Whoever,' Says Stephanie Grisham." *The Guardian* (UK), March 9, 2022.

Yavuz, Hamza, and Mehmet Akif Okur. "Reactions of the American Jews to Trump's Jerusalem Embassy Move: Continuation of the Historical Pattern?" *Alternatives: Global, Local, Political* 43, no. 4 (2018): 207–21.

Zavadski, Katie. "Zionist Gala Toasts Donald Trump's 'Divine' Election Victory." *Daily Beast*, November 21, 2016.

Zengerle, Jason. "Rex Tillerson and the Unraveling of the State Department." *New York Times*, October 17, 2017.

Ziv, Stav. "Rex Tillerson: Anti-Semitism Could Get Worse with a State Department Special Envoy." *Newsweek*, June 15, 2017.

Zúquete, Jose Pedro. "Populism and Religion." In *The Oxford Handbook of Populism*, ed. Cristóbal Kaltwasser et al., 445–66. New York: Oxford University Press, 2017.

INDEX

Tables and figures are indicated by "*t*" and "*f*" after the page number.